AL-KINDI'S METAPHYSICS

STUDIES IN ISLAMIC PHILOSOPHY AND SCIENCE

Published under the auspices of
the Society for the Study of Islamic Philosophy and Science

AL-KINDĪ'S METAPHYSICS

A Translation of
Ya'qūb ibn Isḥāq al-Kindī's Treatise
"ON FIRST PHILOSOPHY"
(fī al-Falsafah al-Ūlā)

with Introduction and Commentary by

Alfred L. Ivry

STATE UNIVERSITY OF NEW YORK PRESS

ALBANY, 1974

Published by
State University of New York Press, Albany

Printed in the United States of America

For information, contact State University of New York Press,
www.sunypress.edu

Library of Congress Cataloging-in-Publication Data

-Kindi, d. ca. 873.
al-Kindi's Metaphysics.
"Published under the auspices of the Society for the Study of Islamic Philosophy and Science."
A revised version of the editor's doctoral dissertation, Oxford University.
Bibliography : p.
ISBN 978-0-87395-092-3 (hardcover : alk. paper) — ISBN 978-1-4384-3416-2 (pbk. : alk. paper)
1. Philosophy, Islamic. I. Ivry, Alfred L., 1935- ed. II. Society for the Study of Islamic Philosophy and Science. III. Title. IV. Title: On first philosophy.
B753.K53F3513 1974
181'.07 70-171182

10 9 8 7 6 5 4 3 2

FOR JOANN

Acknowledgments

THIS WORK is a revised version of an Oxford University doctoral dissertation. It has grown out of research begun at Oxford in 1963-65 while I was on a Fulbright Fellowship there. I am grateful to the Principal and Fellows of Linacre College for their hospitality and friendship during my stay in Oxford.

I was encouraged to work on al-Kindī by Richard Walzer, F.B.A., whose knowledge and understanding have been a constant source of inspiration. The work in its present form has also benefited from recommendations suggested by Professors S. Pines, F. Rosenthal, R. J. McCarthy, S.J., M.C. Lyons, and N. Kretzmann. The Hull Publication Memorial Fund of Cornell University has facilitated the publication of this book with a generous subvention, and the Editorial Board of the Society for the Study of Islamic Philosophy and Science has shown great interest in the publication of this work. I wish to express my sincere appreciation to all these scholars and institutions for their assistance.

Portions of this study have appeared in *Islamic Philosophy and the Classical Tradition: Essays Presented . . . to Richard Walzer* (Cassirer, 1972); *Essays on Islamic Philosophy and Science* (Albany, forthcoming). I wish to thank the editors of these publications for giving me their permission to present the material in its present form.

Cornell University
Ithaca, New York
September 1971

A.L.I.

Acknowledgments

This work is a revised version of an Oxford University doctoral dissertation. It has grown out of research begun in Oxford in 1965–66 while I was on a Fulbright fellowship there. I am grateful to the Principal and Fellows of [illegible] College for their hospitality and friendship during my stay in Oxford.

I was encouraged to work on al-Kindī by Richard Walzer, F.B.A., whose knowledge and understanding have been a constant source of inspiration. The work in its present form has also benefited from recommendations suggested by Professors [illegible] Dunne, F. Rosenthal, R. J. McCarthy, S.J., M.C. Lyons, and N. Kretzmann. The Hull Publication Memorial Fund of Cornell University has facilitated the publication of this book with a generous subvention, and the Editorial Board of the Society for the Study of Islamic Philosophy and Science has shown great interest in the publication of this work. I wish to express my sincere appreciation to all these persons and institutions for their assistance.

Portions of this study have appeared in *Islamic Philosophy and the Classical Tradition: Essays Presented* [illegible] *Richard Walzer* (Cassirer, 1972); *Essays on Islamic Philosophy and Science* (Albany, forthcoming). I wish to thank the editors of these publications for giving me their permission to present the material in its present form.

Cornell University
Ithaca, New York
September 197[illegible]

[illegible]

Contents

PART I

Introduction

CHAPTER ONE

Al-Kindī and Kindī Studies: A Résumé

THE NAME OF Abū Yūsuf Yaᶜqūb ibn Isḥāq al-Kindī, "the philosopher of the Arabs", is well known to students of Islamic culture, and recent years have seen a number of studies devoted to him. We need not, therefore, rehearse in detail the facts of al-Kindī's life and accomplishments, presented originally by Ibn al-Nadīm and others.[1] It is enough to say that al-Kindī was born probably in Kufah toward the end of the eighth Christian century or beginning of the ninth, during the tenure of his father, Isḥāq ibn al-Sabbāḥ, as governor there. The family was used to holding important positions, tracing its lineage back to the kings of the South Arabian tribe of Kindah, and counting among its ancestors a Companion of the Prophet.

Al-Kindī began his education at either Kufah or Basrah, and completed it at Baghdad, the centers of culture of his day. He became well known in the ᶜAbbāsid capital as a scholar and physician, enjoyed the patronage of the caliphs al-Ma'mūn and al-Muᶜtaṣim, and was appointed tutor of the latter's son Aḥmad. In this favorable environment he pursued his many-faceted studies,[2] becoming a famous and even legendary figure. For some reason, however (the sources are not completely satisfactory), al-Kindī fell from favor in the time of the caliph al-Mutawakkil, his large private library was confiscated and he was apparently beaten. Though the library was subsequently restored to him, al-Kindī never regained a position of official eminence, and died in Baghdad about A.D. 870.

Recent studies have served to fill out the social and cultural background of the times in which al-Kindī lived, allowing us to view him in proper perspective, and to appreciate the drama that is contained in even such a thumbnail sketch of his life as has just been given. Thus, from our knowledge of the transmission of philosophical studies from the world of late Greek thought to the major intellectual centers of the eighth and ninth centuries in Iraq (mostly through a Syriac Christian intermediary),[3] we can place al-Kindī at or near the beginning of a philosophical current that remained vital in the Islamic world for some centuries thereafter.

Al-Kindī's "audience" would have been composed of members of the caliph's family and other aristocrats, fellow scholars, students and theologians of every persuasion. That many of these, particularly the Muslims, would have had trouble following him may be inferred externally from the fact that the Arabic texts upon which he bases his views were recent—in some cases very recent—translations;[4] and internally, from the juxtaposition throughout his writing of relatively sophisticated arguments with elementary definitions and discussions. Al-Kindī was not, of course, operating in a philosophical vacuum, and Christian theologians in particular would have been familiar with many of his ideas.[5] Yet it is clear, from the dedications to many of his treatises and from the introductory comments to such treatises as *On First Philosophy* and the paraphrase of Ptolemy's *Almagest*,[6] that al-Kindī was addressing himself primarily to his fellow Muslims, for most of whom his teachings provided a philosophical initiation.

That these teachings were not necessarily well received may be deduced from the special pleading with which al-Kindī occasionally introduces his treatises (e.g., *On First Philosophy*); and we may be certain that he had to struggle against suspicious and hostile attitudes to philosophy, viewed as part of the new, secular and "foreign" culture that was anathema to more traditional circles.[7] Among these may be counted not only extreme traditionalists such as Aḥmad ibn Ḥanbal, but the more rationally oriented *Muʿtazilah* as well. Al-Kindī's relationship to this latter group—which is examined in some detail in chapter three of the introduction below—is complicated by the politicization of faith and scholarship that followed the establishment of the *Miḥnah* in A.H. 218/A.D. 833.[8] Under the sanction of that institution, and in the name of rational faith, the *Muᶜtazilah* persecuted with varying intensity, but at times great cruelty, saintly jurists as well as simple soldiers.[9]

This inquisition, in turn, ought to be seen against a background of competing social and ethnic forces,[10] among which, however, it is difficult to locate al-Kindī. It would seem that, though an Arabian aristocrat, he is to be placed with the largely non-Arab forces that introduced secular studies into Islamic society; however, there is no conclusive evidence that he identified socially or politically with any particular group or religious sect. His misfortunes under al-Mutawakkil were apparently due more to personal intrigue or to a general change of intellectual orientation at court, than to his religious beliefs.

A similar ambiguity surrounds al-Kindī's personality. Although he is often described as avaricious,[11] the newly-discovered material from al-Sijistanī's *Ṣiwān al-Ḥikmah* shows him to be virtuous as well as wise.[12] Clearly, the last word on al-Kindī the man has yet to be written, and he stands out as an interesting figure about whom we should wish to know more.

This wish has been partially granted, in the field of al-Kindī's philosophical pursuits, with the publication of an appreciable number of his treatises. To the collection of Latin translations of al-Kindī treatises edited by A. Nagy in the last century,[13] Richard Walzer has added two masterly textual analyses;[14] and M.ᶜA.H. Abū Rīdah has published a two-volume edition of twenty-five of al-Kindī's philosophical treatises, accompanied by a lengthy introductory general evaluation as well as individual introductions to each treatise.[15] From these and other sources,[16] a picture of al-Kindī the philosopher has emerged which balances somewhat the shallow, often negative judgement passed upon him by earlier philosophers and bibliographers.[17] True, his logic is not analytical and his philosophy not particularly consistent; yet there is no denying his erudition and industriousness, his attempt to comprehend and convey past philosophies as parts of an essentially unified tradition, and his desire to select from this tradition that which would make for a viable philosophy in an Islamic society.

CHAPTER TWO

On First Philosophy

TEXT AND TRANSLATION: A DESCRIPTION

THE ARABIC TEXT OF *On First Philosophy* (*FP* in later references) is found among the manuscripts of the codex Aya Sofya 4832 (no. 23, pp. 43a-53a).[1] Hellmut Ritter has described the codex as being in a format of 22 × 12 cm., on dark brown paper of 32 lines to the page, the manuscripts being written in an angular, nearly entirely unpointed *Naskhī-Kufī* hand of the 5th century A.H./11th century A.D.[2]

Since Ritter's discovery of this codex, two editions of the Arabic text of *FP* have appeared: a problematic edition by A. al-Ahwānī, and a careful, scholarly work by M. ʿA.H. Abū Rīdah.[3] No translation has hitherto appeared in any language, Western or Eastern, though a rough, preliminary edition and Italian translation was prepared by Michelangelo Guidi and Richard Walzer over thirty years ago, which Dr. Walzer kindly allowed me to consult. The translation offered herein has benefited from all these earlier readings of the manuscript.[4]

Abū Rīdah's edition (AR in later references) has been used as the primary reference for the translation, with all manuscript peculiarities which are not mentioned by Abū Rīdah, as well as all deviations from his reading of the manuscript, mentioned in the apparatus below the translation. Reference is also made there to al-Ahwānī's readings (AH), where they appear superior to AR or equally plausible.

My translation frequently differs with the determination

of sentences and paragraphs established by AR, a difference which is left unremarked in the apparatus but which the reader familiar with Arabic will immediately notice. While attempting a faithful, literal translation wherever possible, I have had at times to restructure al-Kindī's long, involved sentences, so that the English reader will find them comprehensible. The notes in the commentary should, hopefully, clarify any remaining awkwardness in the translation. The commentary itself is rather detailed, for besides elucidating al-Kindī's presentation of the argument in *FP*, it compares his remarks there with those he makes in other treatises, and relates his work wherever possible to the Greek sources which he helped introduce into Islamic thought.

While references to many of al-Kindī's other treatises abound in the commentary, detailed textual comparisons are made with such cognate texts as his treatises "On the Unity of God and the Finiteness of the Body of the World" (*UG*); "An Explanation of the Finiteness of the Body of the World" (*EF*); and "On the Essence of that which cannot be Infinite and that of which Infinity can be Predicated" (*OE*).[5] In addition, the treatise "On the Definitions and Descriptions of Things" (AR I: 165-180), offers many an important comparison with *FP*. Among the Greek works used by al-Kindī in Arabic translation, that done of the *Metaphysics* by al-Kindī's contemporary Asṭāt provides particularly intriguing textual comparisons.[6]

A brief summary of the contents of *FP* is as follows:

CHAPTER 1 (AR 97-105)

Al-Kindī begins the treatise by expressing homage to the caliph to whom the book is dedicated, al-Muʿtaṣim Billāh. He then immediately introduces his subject by extolling philosophy as the greatest and most noble human art, since it seeks to know the true nature of things. Knowledge of things is considered dependent upon knowledge of their causes, the ultimate cause of all being the "True One", knowledge of whom is "First Philosophy".

The four (Aristotelian) causes are described and related to four types of inquiry and to substance. The difficulty of obtaining all the truth evokes recognition of the joint effort required in philosophy, and gratitude for the efforts of all previous philosophers, the use of whose work al-Kindī fully (though in general terms) acknowledges. He is opposed, however, to those who do not appreciate the philosophical tradition, and who subscribe to other standards and methods of truth; impugning their motives, he calls for their ouster from positions of religious leadership within the community. The true message of faith is compatible with philosophy, he contends, claiming that one must know philosophy if only to be able to refute the necessity of knowing it. The chapter concludes with an invocation of Divine assistance in the task of establishing proof of the Divinity (i.e., existence) and unity of God.

CHAPTER 2 (AR 106-122)

Al-Kindī begins the chapter with a comparison of sensory and intellectual perception, the latter of which is deemed superior. A spatial example is chosen to illustrate the nature of a necessary intellectual perception; leading al-Kindī to assert belief in the finiteness of the universe, on the principle of the impossibility of something being infinite in actuality.

Returning to different kinds of perception, al-Kindī emphasizes the need to use the appropriate method in investigating a particular subject, not, e.g., confusing probable with demonstrative arguments in mathematics.

This leads al-Kindī to assert the principles with which he works in *FP:* they refer firstly to the concept of an eternal being, clarifying the meaning of the term logically and relating it to a unique being; and secondly, to basic ideas of corporeal equality and inequality, founded on the laws of identity, contradiction, and the excluded middle. Working with these latter principles, al-Kindī offers a number of arguments to prove that a body, and its properties of time and motion, cannot be infinite in actuality. While establishing the necessity for a finite universe, he also shows that it could not, in ordinary physical terms, either have come from nothing or have been in a state of rest before motion.

CHAPTER 3 (AR 123-143)

The chapter opens with an examination and rejection of the concepts of auto-causation, and of an essence as separate from the substance of which it is the essence. These latter terms are related to one or another of the predicables, which are defined. These predicables—the genus, species, individual (!), specific difference, property and common accident—then serve as the subjects for a detailed discussion of the ways in which "one" is predicated, al-Kindī showing that in each case the predicable is not "essentially" one.[7] The accidental unity in everything is taken as indicative of the existence of an external agent which imposes unity from without upon the predicable and related quantities, the agent possessing unity essentially.

The nature of everything in our experience is shown to require elements of both unity and multiplicity (i.e., plurality), the assumption of either existing alone in something leading to absurd conclusions, which al-Kindī works out in detail for both. The necessary association in everything of unity and multiplicity is seen as requiring a cause which cannot be similar to it in any way and must be an absolute unity.

CHAPTER 4 (AR 143-162)

Absolute unity is shown as not found in anything possessing quantity, size being relative. Nothing is absolutely large or small, not even the number 2. The possibility of 1 being a number is examined and ultimately rejected, it being viewed as the element of number, multiple in its relation to numbers. Relative sizes are applicable only to other members of the same genus, diverse examples being given.

The True One, it is reiterated, has no genus and cannot be compared with anything. It is eternal and absolutely one, and al-Kindī describes it in terms of what it is not. It is not comparable to any of the predicables and does not possess any physical properties whatsoever. The True One is likewise neither soul nor intellect, both of which are considered multiple and not essentially one. Comparison with other things is further excluded by the insistence that the True One is neither synonymous nor homonymous with anything, and its unity is one neither through number, form, genus, or analogy.

The True One is, therefore, a unique being, absolutely and essentially one, responsible through an emanative power for the unity which exists in other things accidentally, but which unity is not part of the being of the True One. The True One thus causes everything to come to be, the ultimate cause of the unity of all being; and also causes the creation of the world from nothing, being uniquely capable of initiating movement. Without unity objects would perish, the True One thus responsible also for the continuing existence of the world. Al-Kindī concludes the treatise (or, strictly speaking, the first part of it, which is the only part extant) with mention of the True One's creative, emanative and powerful nature, having shown that the unity (and thus the existence) of all else is "metaphorical".

AN ANALYSIS

ANY ATTEMPT to make philosophical sense of an al-Kindī treatise is often complicated by an abbreviated style, in which the premises of arguments may be missing,[8] important terms may be used without being defined,[9] and whole "treatises" can consist of a few pages.[10] This shortcoming is "balanced", as it were, by redundant passages and treatises,[11] and by repetitive arguments which seek to establish a universal proposition by offering the same proof in formulaic type statements for each member of a class.[12]

These stylistic characteristics indicate that al-Kindī's philosophical works ought to be read not as self-contained pieces, but in conjunction with one another. We ought, perhaps, to view each *kitāb* and *risālah* of his as part of a continuing lecture series addressed to a small and select audience, for whose philosophical inexperience or skepticism he made allowance by providing an oral commentary, as well as by referring to his other written works.[13] It is this hypothesis of a semi-private and semi-oral tradition which may best account for the unsatisfactory state of al-Kindī's written corpus, much of which was probably not only published and titled after its author's death,[14] but also collected and given its "definitive" shape then.

If one can claim a certain philosophical credibility for those Kindian treatises which are in their present form essentially fragmentary, certainly the same can be said for al-Kindī's major philosophical treatise, *fī al-Falsafah al-Ūlā*, a work which exhibits the awareness and concerns of one who was both a professing Muslim and a committed philosopher. The treatise opens with a celebration and explanation of the philosophical pursuit, which I have translated as follows.[15]

AR97.8 Indeed, the human art which is highest in degree and
most noble in rank is the art of philosophy, the definition
of which is knowledge of the true nature of things, insofar
as is possible for man. The aim of the philosopher is, as
10 regards his knowledge,/to attain the truth, and as regards
his action, to act truthfully; not that the activity is endless,
for we abstain and the activity ceases, once we have reached
the truth. We do not find the truth we are seeking without
finding a cause; the cause of the existence and continuance
of everyting is The True One, in that each thing which
has being has truth. The True One exists necessarily, and
p. 98 therefore beings exist./The noblest part of philosophy and
the highest in rank is the First Philosophy, i.e., knowledge
of the First Truth Who is the cause of all truth.

This passage makes it clear that the theoretical aim of the philosopher is to "attain the truth", which is ultimately "the First Truth Who is the cause of all truth". Such a remark may lead one to think of the Neoplatonic emphasis upon a single source of all being;[16] and looking to Plotinian models, certain obscurities in this and subsequent passages of *FP* become clear. Thus, the relation between being and truth, inadequately stated above, assumes that all beings owe their existence to the necessary existence of the True One;[17] the combination and ultimate identity of being and truth in His nature being responsible for their particular occurrences and correlations in this world.

It is significant, however, that al-Kindī does not detail this causal relationship, and that he does not develop the notion of the identity of truth and being. For the Neoplatonic doctrine of emanation posits an unbroken chain of being,[18] while its epistemology leads to a mystic unity with the One;[19] doctrines which al-Kindī eschews.[20] Indeed, the qualifications and physical limitations put upon the philosophical endeavor already in this opening paragraph seem designed to proclaim al-Kindī's awareness of the limitations—as well as possibilities—of philosophy.

It is, again, the Neoplatonic background which makes sense of al-Kindī's use of "cause" in the above quotation, since he follows this passage with another which stresses that there are just four causes, the well known Aristotelian "material", "formal", "efficient", and "final" causes;[21] and al-Kindī states clearly that every cause must be one or the other of these. This, however, apparently means every cause *except* for the "first cause" which contains all the others and is pre-eminent in everything.[22]

Granting this, however, one must also admit that al-Kindī proceeds to ignore this sense of cause for most of the treatise, and that he remains instead within the Aristotelian framework of causality. Within this framework he attempts to prove that nothing but God is essentially one. One sees an ambivalent usage of terminology, al-Kindī alluding to Neoplatonic doctrine but not really justifying it or working with it.[23]

This employment of a term in a unique, absolute sense is particularly noticeable with "the One", since al-Kindī finds against the existence of an absolute one just prior to his adoption of such a concept in relation to God.[24] Ordinarily, al-Kindī feels, there is no quantity or number that is so large that it cannot in theory be larger, nor so small that it cannot be smaller. Al-Kindī does at first make a mathematical exception to this rule, claiming that the number "two" is the lowest numerical limit, on the grounds that the term "one" is a unit of quantity and does not possess quantity itself, which "numbers" must.[25] Two is, at the same time, admitted to be double the one, and therefore not absolutely small. In admitting this, however, "one" *is* brought into a quantifiable relationship, and its exclusion from number seems ultimately arbitrary. This impression is reinforced later in the treatise,[26] when al-Kindī says that the numerically one is, through its position as the measure of *all* things, also multiple.

Al-Kindī was probably attracted to the idea of a non-numerical "one" in part because of the similarity of this concept with that of the "True One": separate from number, "one" is yet the base of all numbers; not a quantity, it is not not a quantity. It is the device whereby enumeration, quantification, in short, knowledge of this world becomes possible. So too with the First Cause, the "True One": while viewed as the source and guarantor of all being and becoming, it is explicitly divorced from them: while certainly not unrelated to the world, neither is the "True One" related in any demonstrable sense. Nothing is to be predicated of the "True One" whatsoever, not even, as we have seen, numerical oneness. It is at most a homonym, though al-Kindī does not admit even this much.[27]

Yet, despite its philosophical ambiguity, al-Kindī refers —albeit seldom—to the "True One", as he does to "The First" and "The Eternal" (which is said to have "being" and to be "self-subsistent").[28] His use of these terms is certainly not careless nor could he be using them merely as homonyms. The thrust of his entire conceptual system depends upon the positing of an essentially unified, independent source of all reality; even as his logic undermines credibility in such an entity as rationally defensible.[29]

Similarly, al-Kindī establishes at one point in *FP* that the motion of the universe could neither have begun from nothing —since, assuming the impossibility of *creatio ex nihilo*, an external prior body would have to be posited as the source of motion, and this would lead to an inadmissible infinite regression—nor could the motion have begun from a prior state of rest, since there would be no reason for a change to motion.[30] This indicates that al-Kindī was certain that there is no strictly philosophical explanation, at least not along Aristotelian lines, for the origin of motion and matter, in which he believed.

It is the equivocal use of terms that enables al-Kindī to resolve physical problems with non-physical concepts; which, however, he couches in physical terminology. Yet however few the epithets used to describe God in physical relation with the world, they are too many in terms of al-Kindī's own argument. The *via negativa* can lead only to a *Deus Negativus* or *Absconditus;* a Creator—the one non-philosophical term al-Kindī uses—about whom, however, we *know* nothing.[31]

This problem is sensed by al-Kindī, though he was certainly not aware how ultimately self-defeating his negative approach is. It is the emanationist structure—barely mentioned in this treatise—which is intended, as we have seen, to bridge this cognitive and ontological gap. It is therefore suprising to find that al-Kindī borrows so little explicit doctrine from the major work of Neoplatonism, Plotinus' *Enneads;* the paraphrase of which he is credited with having "corrected" —*aṣlaḥahu*—for al-Muᶜtaṣim Billāh.[32]

Indeed, after some initial resemblance between the two works,[33] textual parallels with the *Theology* suggest themselves only towards the end of *FP*, when background knowledge of the former work can clarify al-Kindī's position.

Thus his description of the relation of the "True One" to "caused" or "accidental" unity, i.e., the relation of God to the world, revolves around the words "unity", "being", and "emanation", *waḥdah*, *huwīyah*, and *fayḍ*. It is, al-Kindī contends, by some (unexplored) emanative process that qualifiedly "unified" things "come to be" from the absolutely unified Being.[34]

Now the *Theology of Aristotle* is primarily a detailed examination of this very structure of emanation, describing the various universal hypostases of intellect, soul and nature, and analysing their relation to each other and to the One. The fact that al-Kindī virtually ignores this world of intelligible entities probably reflects his unresolved relationship to the Neoplatonic metaphysic. He is, however, congenial to the *idea* of emanation if not to the details, and receptive to the terminological shell of Neoplatonism, while altering its inner meaning. Thus he apparently treats the *process* of "coming to be" (as distinct from the act of the Divine agent) as equivalent to physical generation, since he views practically all "being" as multiple, hence divisible, and perishable. However, in the equivalent *Theology* passage, which treats of the relation between "the first cause and the things which originate from it", *huwīyah* is considered as the first emanation which "gushes forth"—*inbajasa*—from The One; and from it the universal intellect and subsequent entities are formed.[35] In other words, *huwīyah* is treated in the *Theology* as a creative principle emanating from the One, though the One is, as such, above it. Al-Kindī, I suggest, may well be reacting against this idea, even as he uses the terms, claiming that the True One's Unity is His Being, which Being is never in any way shared by the rest of creation, though it owes *its* being, *somehow*, to the Being of the One.

Thus al-Kindī's use of the *Theology* and—possibly—related writings is very circumspect; apparently he rejects Neoplatonic ontology but is drawn to its view of the transcendent One Who is, nevertheless, the Creator.[36]

We ought, therefore, to locate al-Kindī's philosophy within a more narrowly Aristotelian framework, particularly as it is clear that he is modeling his *First Philosophy* to a large extent after parts of the *Metaphysics*. Indeed, al-Kindī's opening remarks read like a paraphrase of certain chapters in *Alpha Elatton*. We know, moreover, that al-Kindī was keenly interested in the *Metaphysics*, and that a certain Asṭāt (or Eusṭāt) translated it for him.[37] Moreover, al-Kindī openly states his admiration for Aristotle, and the Stagirite clearly is a primary moral as well as intellectual influence upon him.[38] Nevertheless, certain extra, even anti-Aristotelian conclusions are meant to be drawn from the *First Philosophy*, though al-Kindī does not spell them out in great detail.

There is an indication of this ambivalent attitude to Aristotelian teachings already in the opening remarks of "First Philosophy", even, one may say, in the very choice of such a title. For al-Kindī prefers, in *First Philosophy* as in his other writings, to discuss that aspect of Metaphysics which Aristotle called σοφία, *viz.*, the general principles of all being, τὸ ὂν ᾗ ὄν.[39] He thereby in effect ignores the existence of separate and unmovable substances, i.e., the area of "Theology" as defined and developed by Aristotle in the *Metaphysics* also.[40] Thus, though he calls his treatise *al-Falsafah al-Ūlā*, using Aristotle's third designation of Metaphysics, al-Kindī treats "First Philosophy", unlike Aristotle, as σοφία removed from θεολογική.[41] This is apparent in spite of the above quoted remarks regarding "First Philosophy" as "knowledge of the First Truth Who is the cause of all truth"; and other introductory comments in the same vein, such as his statement that, "Knowledge of the first cause has truthfully been called 'First Philosophy', since all the rest of philosophy is contained in its knowledge. The first cause is, therefore, the first in nobility, the first in genus, the first in rank with respect to that the knowledge of which is most certain; and the first in time, since it is the cause of time."[42]

By hailing knowledge of the "First Truth" and the "First Cause" as "First Philosophy", al-Kindī, it could be thought, is within the Aristotelian θεολογική tradition, even if the formulation has a Neoplatonic ring. Yet these statements are not followed up by any examination of the "first cause" or "first truth" *per se* whatsoever, or by an analysis of any separate and unmovable substance; instead we are given a work devoted to general principles of causation and "truth", i.e., being.

Al-Kindī may thus be telling us that all we *can* know about the first Truth, i.e., God, is that our knowledge of all else is not applicable to Him; or, more positively put, He is what the world is not. Of course the possibility exists that al-Kindī discussed "First Philosophy" as θεολογική in the lost second part of the book;[43] yet the absence in his other writings of a philosophical analysis of this topic along either Aristotelian or Neoplatonic lines, makes this unlikely. Most probably al-Kindī felt that his arguments concerning the finite and contingent nature of the universe forced one to certain conclusions about the existence and nature of the Creator; and that this indirect approach was the only method philosophically feasible for a "First Philosophy".

Philosophical "feasibility" or validity is indeed a primary criterion for al-Kindī, and Aristotelian texts and commentaries provide the authority for the instruction in methodology, definition of terms, and logical rules which we find in *First Philosophy*. Al-Kindī in fact accepts most of Aristotle's arguments for contingent substances as found in the *Metaphysics* (and *Physics*), viz., that form and matter, actuality and potentiality, are primarily attributes of a substance;[44] that time and movement also exist only in relation to substance, as functions of a body;[45] and that, while a causal sequence must be invoked to explain physical relations, an infinite causal regression is impossible.[46]

Aristotle exempts time and motion from this last generalization, as he considers them, by the definition of their natures, to be eternal; entailing, thereby, the positing of an eternal body which, while spatially finite, is eternally in motion. This in turn allows Aristotle to posit the existence of an eternal first cause, the unmoved mover.[47] Al-Kindī, however, rejects this basic exception of the nature of time and motion.[48] He rather views them, like everything else, as possessing infinity in potentiality in the sense, apparently, of a fanciful, hypothetical possibility only; and he emphasizes that *in actuality* nothing is and nothing could be infinite. Everything is subject, al-Kindī argues, to quantification and hence limitation. Far from dragging body with them into eternity, time and motion are always confined by an actual body to finite, measurable dimensions. In effect one cannot speak of time, motion or body in isolation from each other, al-Kindī insists, in actuality they are mutually dependent concepts which refer to finite corporeal and therefore perishable being.

Al-Kindī proceeds to belabor this doctrine of "conceptual reciprocity" in chapters 3 and 4 of *First Philosophy*, partly using a method and discussing a problem along lines enunciated by Plato in his *Parmenides*, and which may have reached al-Kindī from some Neoplatonic or possibly Middle Platonic source, as some scholars have suggested.[49] Thus we find al-Kindī arguing for the necessary existence of unity and plurality in all things and in all concepts. Nothing is itself by itself, i.e., essentially one, and the world is characterized by an apparently accidental combination, in themselves and together, of subjects and predicates.

Now in arguing against Aristotle's idea of an eternal world, al-Kindī offers an actual finite world which requires a first, non-finite cause; one, however, which he is unable to present within the confines of Aristotelian philosophy, since he rejects Aristotle's move in the direction of separate, unmovable forms which yet serve as the cause of eternal motion. In his discussion of the one and the many, al-Kindī again refutes the possibility of separate and independent, hence eternal existents. Yet the very "accidental" existence of substances legitimizes for him the affirmation of a prior "essential" existent, i.e., a being which is completely "one"; even though the nature of such an existent is beyond the competence of philosophical discourse. Hence al-Kindī's argument concludes with a metaphorical use of descriptive terms, borrowing, at least partially, from the Neoplatonic vision of the One, which, while the source for all becoming, is beyond Aristotelian distinctions and analysis. Al-Kindī, however, is not willing—or able—to detail the relation of this One to the world; it is enough, he feels, to have "proved" that the world needed the Creator Who is the True One.[50]

Al-Kindī's Aristotelianism, then, like his Neoplatonism, is tempered with other intellectual currents, some of which are discussed in Chapter 3 of the introduction below. The most significant of his deviations from Aristotle and the Peripatetic tradition are his rejection of an eternal universe, achieved in part by a highly qualified attitude to the concept of potentiality;[51] and, relatedly, his assertion of what amounts to a fifth kind of causality, that produced by God and most evident in the act of creation from nothing.[52] This in turn leads to regarding all other causes and actions, and the unity of all substances, as "metaphorical", a perspective on this world which, if not representative of al-Kindī's total view, is yet foreign to Aristotelian thought.

It is the Neoplatonic tradition in philosophy, as well as Christian and Islamic theological perspectives, which here make their contribution to al-Kindī's thought. Other influences are at work as well, those inspired by Hellenistic philosophical commentaries and late Greek mathematical works. Indeed, in discussing the one and the many and in defining number in *First Philosophy*, al-Kindī blends dialectical philosophy and mathematics, an approach that is not uncommon for the Neoplatonic tradition.[53] His specific treatment of number, moreover,[54] shows him as familiar with arithmetical theory, and raises the possibility of his having used an arithmetical source here; which possibility is rendered more plausible by our knowledge of his other work.[55] Moreover, his pupil, Abū Sulaymān Rabī' ibn Yaḥyā, wrote a paraphrase to Nichomachus of Gerasa's *Introduction to Arithmetic*,[56] in which he often acknowledges his teacher's views.

Nevertheless, a comparison of our text and Nichomachus' yields little by way of specific comparisons. Even the particularly arithmetical passages of *FP* seem to be derived from secondary sources, probably from some such discussion as is found in the introduction to the *Isagoge* commentaries, a source al-Kindī uses elsewhere in this work.[57] Certain remarks concerning both books would seem to be in order, however, for al-Kindī may be reacting to Nichomachus' text indirectly; and, as we shall see, may be following some outline of the work which is later reflected in the *Rasā'il Ikhwān al-Ṣafā'*.

While al-Kindī would have been in sympathy generally with Nichomachus' description of philosophy as concerned with the knowledge of eternal beings,[58] he would not have agreed with Nichomachus' positing of the elements of number, the monad and dyad, as such beings, or with his equally Neo-Pythagorean assumption of the existence of universal, eternal numerical patterns by which the world is ordered.[59] It is only with Nichomachus' identification of the monad and dyad with the same and the other, the one and the many, viewing number as equivalent to form,[60] that al-Kindī would have been more sympathetic (though he would not have granted an independent existence to such principles); for al-Kindī too proclaims the necessity of positing both unity and multiplicity, the one and the many together in all things, and, like Nichomachus, he considers the one as more basic than the many.[61]

However, as Nichomachus himself points out, the concept of the same and the other, the divisible and indivisible, are pre-Socratic and are found in Plato,[62] so that al-Kindī's familiarity with these themes cannot be traced specifically to Nichomachus' *Introduction*. Moreover, the emphasis upon the one as the original element and cause of all is, as we have seen, a tenet of Neoplatonism.

There is, nevertheless, an additional point that is worth mentioning in considering the possible relation between Nichomachus and al-Kindī. In his *Theologomena Arithmeticae*, Nichomachus explicitly compares the monad to God; as He is seminally in all things, so the monad is in all numerical forms (i.e., in all things).[63] Now, while al-Kindī's views on the relation of the numerical one to number may evoke in the reader an analogy with God's relation to the world,[64] al-Kindī is quite emphatic in denying any real comparison between the two, his True One being considered as completely unique and having nothing in common with the rest of creation. In making this point, and in being concerned with the entire question of the nature of number, al-Kindī may be reflecting an awareness of Nichomachus' position, and a reaction to it.

It is interesting to note that the encyclopedia composed by the *Ikhwān al-Ṣafā'* roughly 100 years after al-Kindī's death, compares the Creator's relation to all beings to that of the number one's relation to other numbers;[65] and that in general the first chapter of the work, "On Numbers", is frequently indebted to Nichomachus' *Introduction to Arithmetic*.[66] The authors of the *Rasā'il* state explicitly, however, that numbers do not have an independent existence, indeed that complete knowledge of their various subdivisions leads to the realization that all are accidents whose being and existence is to be located only in the soul. Thus one is led, in the pursuit of knowledge, from number to the soul.[67]

Al-Kindī, of course, has a similar view as that of the *Ikhwān* regarding the accidental nature of numbers; and, more than they profess, of the accidental nature of soul too.[68] It may not be merely coincidental that he proceeds, shortly after a discussion of the numerical one, to a discussion of the soul, soon continuing from there to the highest subject of all theoretical science, the nature of God. In so doing, he may well be following a method prescribed by a source common to the *Ikhwān* and himself,[69] which source had possibly already incorporated some of the basic views as well as arithmetical propositions of Nichomachus.

CHAPTER THREE

Al-Kindi and the *Muʿtazilah*: A Reevaluation

IT HAS OFTEN been asserted that al-Kindī had an affinity for certain viewpoints of that group of rationalizing theologians known as the *Mu'tazilah*, and that he gave a philosophical formulation to some of their basic tenets.[1] Support for this assertion has been collected mostly by Walzer and Abū Rīdah. The former, in his article "New Studies on Al-Kindī",[2] presents both "external" and "internal" evidence to buttress the claim, made in an earlier study,[3] that al-Kindī is "the philosopher of the Mu'tazilite theology". The external evidence relies upon the dedications of some of al-Kindī's treaties to the caliphs who supported the *Mu'tazilah*, as well as a number of dedications to the caliph al-Muʿtaṣim's son Aḥmad, al-Kindī's pupil.[4]

This type of evidence at most indicates, as Walzer himself declares, that "al-Kindī cannot be completely at variance with the official Muʿtazilite interpretation of Islam which was followed by the caliphs al-Maʾmūn and al-Muʿtaṣim".[5] It would indeed have ill become al-Kindī, living in the shadow of the court, to be "completely at variance" with the officially endorsed religious doctrine of the state. It would, moreover, have been gratuitously poor taste for him not to dedicate at least some treatises to his patrons. That he was not an opponent of the caliphs may indeed be deduced from these dedications and from all we know of al-Kindī's life; yet that he espoused *Muʿtazilah* doctrine in any significant way is an unwarranted inference from this particular source. Walzer does not, it should be mentioned, so infer, acknowledging that "it would be rash to build too much on information of this kind unless it is supported by internal evidence";[6] and it is therefore to this kind of evidence that we must next turn.

The information here is more varied and impressive. Walzer quotes an intriguing passage from al-Kindī's treatise "On the Number (literally 'Quantity') of the Books of Aristotle" which mentions that the "Divine Science" (Walzer, "knowledge", العلم الالهي), i.e., knowledge of theological matters, is acquired effortlessly, without preparation and instantly, being as such superior to "human sciences" (العلوم الانسانية), i.e., philosophy broadly conceived.[7] The prophets (literally, the "apostles" الرسل) are viewed as the recipients of this unique knowledge, granted them by God's will, which distinguishes their nature from that of other men.

Al-Kindī follows these remarks with an assertion, referring to *surah* 36, verses 78-82, of the inimitable supremacy of the rhetorical argumentation of the *Qur'ān* over any possible philosophical reasoning, the issues being such basic articles of faith as creation of the world from nothing and resurrection. Verse 82 reads, "His command, when He desires a thing, is to say to it 'Be' and it is"[8] (إنما أمره اذا أراد شيئاً ان يقول له كن فيكون). Al-Kindī interprets the statement, that God utters the word "be", in a non-literal, metaphorical way, referring to the analogy of poetic metaphor as practised by pre-Islamic poets.[9] Walzer then identifies these remarks of al-Kindī with views held by the *Muᶜtazilah* concerning the supremacy of revealed truth, and the inimitability of Sacred Scripture (*iᶜjāz al-Qur'ān*), beliefs the *Muᶜtazilah* often based on philological and rhetorical criteria; and specifically with the denial of creative speech attributed to Bishr ibn al-Muᶜtamir (d. A.D. 825-6) and his pupil, Abū Mūsā ᶜIsā b. Ṣabīḥ al-Murdār.[10]

The *Muᶜtazilah*, of course, were not at all unique among the believers in subscribing to the belief in *iᶜjāz al-Qur'ān*, or in the supremacy of revelation—God's word—to any other kind of knowledge;[11] though their approach, as characterized by the affirmation of a created *Qur'ān* and by their exegetical methods, was to qualify the dogmatic nature of religious beliefs by interpreting them in a more rational way.[12] Thus al-Kindī may indeed be identified with the *Muᶜtazilah* in his use of philological and poetic criteria to achieve a non-literal understanding of God's Word; though this type of understanding is what one would expect from a rationally oriented person, one who considers himself to be a philosopher.

In fact, the arguments al-Kindī brings in defense of this Koranic passage, the truth of which he first affirms dogmatically, are philosophically rooted. They rest on the principle of the generation of contraries from contraries, which general principle is then applied to the creation of being (أيس) from its contrary, non-being (ليس).[13] It is this belief in *creatio ex nihilo*, held by al-Kindī alone among Islamic philosophers, together with his use of rational principles introduced by philological and rhetorical methods of *tafsīr* in explanation of Islamic dogma which Walzer feels links al-Kindī quite securely to the *Mu^{c}tazilah*, and would indeed seem to indicate a strong affinity between them.

Abū Rīdah, for his part, writing on the relation between al-Kindī and the *Mu^{c}tazilah* in the introduction to his edition of al-Kindī,[14] mentions the titles of some treatises ascribed to him by the bibliographers; which treatises apparently dealt with such particularly Mu^{c}tazilite themes as God's "unity" and "justice".[15] Abū Rīdah then refers to titles of treatises ascribed to al-Kindī in the fields of polemics, prophecy and physics, subjects common to all the *Mutakallimūn*. Unfortunately, the only treatises which are brought in support of this "external" evidence are *On First Philosophy* and the above-discussed treatise "On the Number of the Books of Aristotle".

Abū Rīdah turns next to expressions and themes common to al-Kindī and all the *Kalām* writers of his day and later, particularly concerning the necessary finiteness of all things and their createdness. As he mentions, however, the theologians were not unanimous in their views concerning the ultimate termination of the world; and despite his general claims, Abū Rīdah has no parallel for al-Kindī's views on this subject. There is, however, no denying that al-Kindī shared common concerns with the *Mu^{c}tazilah*, as with all the *Mutakallimūn*, and this is often expressed in a similar vocabulary and form of expression.[16]

Additional parallels between al-Kindī and the *Muʿtazilah* writings emerge from H. Davidson's recent study of medieval arguments for creation.[17] Davidson has shown that both al-Kindī and the *Muʿtazilah*, as well as many other writers, used similar and often the same arguments, mostly derived from John Philoponus, to establish the doctrine of creation of the universe.[18]

Thus, in an adaptation of one of Philoponus' proofs of the generation of the universe based on the impossibility of eternal motion, al-Kindī as well as al-Iskāfī (d. A.D. 854) and al-Naẓẓām (d. A.D. 845) are shown to have argued that the present moment could never have been reached if it were preceded by infinite time, on the principle that an infinite time (or series of events) cannot be traversed;[19] while al-Kindī, Abū al-Hudhayl (d. ca. A.D. 841) and al-Naẓẓam have variations, in temporal and spatial terms, of an offshoot of Philoponus' contention of the impossibility of infinity, contending that what is finite in one direction must be finite in the other (or others) as well.[20] Still other Philoponus-based arguments which al-Kindī uses appear in the later *Mutakkallimūn*, and may well have been used in al-Kindī's time as well. Thus al-Kindī's argument against infinity which shows the absurd conclusions reached in adding to and subtracting from an infinite magnitude is used, in a slightly different way, already by al-Naẓẓam;[21] while al-Kindī's statement that body, being necessarily associated with certain "concomitants", i.e., accidents (particularly, for al-Kindī, motion and time), does not precede them and is therefore as finite as they are, is apparently an early formulation of an argument, reportedly used by Abū al-Hudhayl as well, which became, in Davidson's words, "the standard *Kalām* proof for creation."[22]

It ought to be borne in mind that these similarities of al-Kindī's with the views of John Philoponus do not obviate the important differences which exist in the philosophies of the two men. True, both men insist upon the finitude of time and motion, the corporeality and hence perishable nature of all body, and creation from nothing by the will of God.[23] Yet though al-Kindī argues, in the *First Philosophy* and elsewhere, for the finitude and hence corruptibility of all body,[24] in still other treatises, some subsequent to *On First Philosophy*, he apparently accepts the Aristotelian description of the fifth element as a simple, ceaselessly moving substance; and agrees with Aristotle's description of the supra-lunar spheres as not having generation and corruption, being perfectly circular and concentric.[25] This means, apparently, that al-Kindī accepts in principle John Philoponus' contention that celestial and terrestrial phenomena have identical natures, and proves to his own satisfaction, and following Philoponus both directly and indirectly, that all the universe is subject to the same laws of finite time and space; but that he rejects much of the Alexandrian's specific arguments, as well as his astronomical and empirical refutations of Aristotle.[26] Al-Kindī seems to be saying that the world, though not eternal, is in other respects as Aristotle said it was; except it *need* not be so and *would* not be so, were it not for God's will.[27] Put another way, it appears that al-Kindī is satisfied that he can prove theoretically that the world is ultimately finite; and, this being understood, he feels that Aristotelian physics, including celestial physics, can explain the phenomena of daily existence.[28]

This example of al-Kindī's complicated relation to John Philoponus may help us understand his equally qualified position vis-à-vis the *Muᶜtazilah*. He has, as they do, the notion of the finiteness of the world and its dependance on a Creator who brings it into being from nothing, proving this by similar arguments which emphasize the accidental nature of all existence and, as most of the *Muᶜtazilah*, the impossibility of any sort of infinity. In addition, both al-Kindī and the *Muᶜtazilah* are concerned with the Unique Oneness of God, and try to limit the extent to which attributes may be predicated of Him.[29]

None of this, however, is particularly unique to the *Muᶜtazilah*, since in the intellectual climate of ninth and tenth century Baghdad these themes and arguments were apparently the common stock of most rationally inclined people. Thus, for example, we find the Christian encyclopaedist Job of Edessa (born ca. A.D. 760) referring, before al-Kindī, to a number of philosophical points and arguments which also occur in al-Kindī; while the Jewish philosopher Saadya Gaon (A.D. 882-942) shortly after al-Kindī, has many of the very same arguments which are found in *On First Philosophy* and other al-Kindī treatises. While Davidson has shown in detail the striking similarities between al-Kindī and Saadya,[30] it is worth noting the parallels with Job's few but important philosophical remarks. Thus Job contrasts the "true unity" of God, due to His unique infinite nature, which admits of no increase or decrease, with the "relative unity" of everything else, which is finite. This finiteness is proven by the combination of elements—which combination circumscribes their external dimensions—in forming a body, the argument being explicity that whatever has an end (or limit in one direction) has also a beginning (i.e., a limit in the other [or other] direction[s]). This beginning, moreover, is depicted as a creation from nothing by the will of God, with Job quite insistent that there is no physical relation between God and His creation, and thus no emanative process of being.[31] It is God also who is seen as the one agent capable of combining contrary elements which by themselves are mutually antagonistic, an argument al-Kindī doesn't use but which is found among Christian, Jewish and Islamic theologians alike, and can be traced to John of Damascus and the fourth century Athanasius.[32] Job also has the distinction between essence and accident which is crucial to al-Kindī in chapter three of First Philosophy, though unlike al-Kindī he distinguishes between elements which may be viewed as essences when considered by themselves, and as accidents when considered in relation to other elements, forming bodies by their relationship.[33]

On the one hand, then, similarities with al-Kindī's thought are not limited to the *Muᶜtazilah*, while on the other, his differences with the *Muᶜtazilah*, philosophical and otherwise, are real and significant. Thus, referring only to the theologians already mentioned, al-Iskāfī follows his assertion of a necessary beginning of the world with a statement, quite foreign to al-Kindī, that the world, having come into being from an unchanging source, may be kept in existence eternally, and that this notion of an infinity *a parte post* (لا إلى آخر) does not contradict the notion of an "agent" preceding its "activity"

(الفاعل، الفعل) as does the view of an infinity *a parte ante* (لا إلى اول).[34] Al-Naẓẓām, on the other hand, follows his proofs of finiteness with the apparently contradictory assertion that all bodies, and the space which they traverse, are infinitely divisible.[35] This latter notion is of course related to al-Naẓẓām's well known denial of the existence of atoms,[36] which existence Abū al-Hudhayl, for example, is known to have affirmed.[37] Abū al-Hudhayl and al-Naẓẓam, moreover, are both shown to be engaged in typical *Muʿtazilah* disputations on the question of the survival of the blessed and dammed in the next world.[38]

Now al-Kindī has no sympathy with an atomistic physics, and apparently no taste for rationalizing theological dogma beyond the most basic beliefs, the ones most amenable to philosophical inquiry.[39] Where he does touch on a typical theological issue, such as the subject of Divine attributes, he does so in the most general of terms, avoiding the *Kalām*-type discussion of the corporeal attributes found in the *Qur'ān*. It would seem that al-Kindī's point of reference, his total perspective, is essentially different from that of the *Muʿtazilah.* While they take their point of departure from the *Qur'ān* and tradition and use whatever philosophical tools they feel are appropriate to explain and support their faith,[40] al-Kindī, it appears, begins from a philosophical body of literature and tradition, accommodating it to religious doctrine wherever he can and asserting religious dogma wherever he must, but essentially aiming for a coherent, philosophical affirmation of the truth.

It is worth reexamining, in this perspective, the passage from al-Kindī's treatise *On the Number of the Books of Aristotle* described above.[41] We note firstly that the entire passage stands in strong contrast to the rest of the treatise, which is a description of the sciences knowledge of which man—i.e., the average man—must have for attaining the truth; and of the Aristotelian *corpus* of writings. As though interrupting himself, al-Kindī assures his reader that this entire scientific tradition cannot compare with sacred Scripture, the philosopher cannot equal the prophet. Having said this, and given a few examples in support of the claim, al-Kindī then resumes introducing his reader (or listener) to the scientific tradition, the acquisition of which he himself has mastered and which he clearly values most highly for all but the messengers of God.

The impression thus received is that al-Kindī believes that for the likes of himself, i.e., under normal circumstances for all men, philosophy is the only approach to the truth and the philosopher the actual ideal figure.

This impression is strengthened by careful scrutiny of al-Kindī's assertion, in this passage, of prophetic superiority and Koranic truth; for this assertion is made from within a philosophical perspective and applying philosophical criteria. Firstly, prophetic knowledge is portrayed as superior to the philosophical only in degree, not in kind, the prophet becoming thereby a sort of extraordinarily gifted philosopher. Then, the revelation granted him is reformulated along philosophical lines (and cf. below, *FP* 104.10 and n. there), which reformulation is then accepted as "proof" of the Koranic truth.

The reformulation of the Koranic assertion of the creation of the world is particularly interesting. Creation is viewed, as has been mentioned, as an instance of the general principle of the generation of contraries from contraries: as fire is from non-fire, warmth from non-warmth, so in general that which is (هو) comes from that which is not (لا هو), bodies from non-bodies and being (أيس) from non-being (ليس).[42] Now, inasmuch as God is viewed as responsible for the unique, a-temporal act of creation of matter from nothing, so one could think He is also responsible, in al-Kindī's estimation, for the creation of each and every contrary which also comes to be, in one sense at least, from its state of non-being. This would bring al-Kindī close to the *Muᶜtazilah* and general *Kalām* view of continuous Divine creation from nothing, and Walzer rightly notes the absence of any allusion to potentiality which would ruin this association.[43]

However, that this is not al-Kindī's full view may be inferred from a comparison of this passage with a remark in the *First Philosophy* to the effect that it is only the form (literally "predicate", المحمول) of a thing which changes and not its primary substratum, which is called "being" (الأيس) and which is said to be eternal.[44] As we must understand this use of "eternal" (الأزلي) for the primary substratum, i.e., first matter, there in the sense of enduring only so long as God wills, so we should understand the contraries here as contraries of a common substratum. God is responsible ultimately, al-Kindī would say, for the creation of the entire world, including the creation of contrary states of being for every thing; but He is not really involved in the generation and destruction of each thing at every moment. True, al-Kindī does not wish to expand upon potential existence, with which concept he is generally not happy;[45] but he would not wish the reader for whom the treatise is intended to assume continuous Divine intervention in nature either, particularly since this would go against the basic physical world view of Aristotle with which al-Kindī is eager to acquaint him.[46]

We may assume that al-Kindī's approach in the (as yet) lost "Treatise on Unity by Exegesis" (literally "commentaries", رسالة التوحيد بتفسيرات) was similar to that which we find in this passage and in the work called *An Explanation of the worship of the Uttermost Body and its Obedience to God*.[47] There as here religious statements are put into a non-literal, philosophical framework, in keeping with a physics that establishes God as the ultimate source of all being and yet allows His creation an independent daily functioning. This acceptance of a quasi-independent physical universe moves al-Kindī generally to the left of a *Muᶜtazilah* tradition which sees God as continuously involved with the world and intimately responsible for the physical survival of each of its parts; in Aristotelian terms, the efficient as well as final cause of the universe.

That al-Kindī distinguishes between these two roles is evident, further, from his treatise *On the True, First, Perfect Agent and the Deficient Agent which is (an Agent) Metaphorically*.[48] However much he wishes to qualify the nature of agents other than God, al-Kindī clearly ascribes to created beings the immediate responsibility for acting upon other beings, God being the remote (i.e., final) cause of all but the first created being. In his treatise *On the Explanation of the Active Proximate Cause of Generation and Corruption*,[49] al-Kindī singles out the sun and moon as the immediate proximate causes of generation and corruption in the sub-lunar world; their creation, in turn, being due to God.

Al-Kindī's attitude to the physical world view of the *Muʿtazilah* may be further inferred from an important passage in *On First Philosophy*, in which he establishes that everything one can think of in the world is only accidentally and not essentially one, and that its unity, i.e., its identity and being, comes from an outside agent. As everything is equally seen as "accidental", al-Kindī is led, on the principle that an essential existent is a prerequisite for the existence of an accidental one of the same genus (and assuming the impossibility of an infinite regress of accidental existents), to the assertion of an essential One (i.e., God), the external agent of all being.[50]

In making this statement, al-Kindī could not have been unaware of the similarity of his remarks to those of the *Muʿtazilah*, who also claimed no essential existence to anything, and considered all as created from an external agent, viz., God.[51] Most of the *Muʿtazilah* however, divided all being into atoms and accidents, and though both were considered as created, the atoms were understood to be indivisible. Al-Kindī would appear to be rejecting this view, insisting that nothing can be thought of as one in itself, that the very concept is absurd.[52] All, then, would be accidental in al-Kindī's thought, it appears, and as such completely without set characteristics.

It is clear, however, that al-Kindī did not conceive of "accidents" in this way, viewing them rather as permanent categories of real existence. "Accidental" is for him significant as opposed to "essential" only as regards the question of "unity", accepting as he does all the individual beings which comprise the Aristotelian world as units of substance, if only "accidental" units. Moreover, having made his point regarding essential unity, al-Kindī proceeds in *FP* to show that unity, together with multiplicity, is an essential ingredient in the composition of all being. It is form and matter which al-Kindī accepts, with the proviso that they, together with everything else, are not independent existents. Having said this, he is content to allow them to function as if they were independent.

Thus al-Kindī is both refuting the *Muʿtazilah* doctrine of the division of the world into atoms and accidents; and, while affirming the contingent, accidental nature of all being (which would return him to the *Muʿtazilah* camp), clearly works with creation as though it were independent. The accidental theory of being is for him a theoretical truth that is significant for the ultimate question of creation and God's existence; for knowledge of the world as it is "otherwise", it is irrelevant.

That al-Kindī's concern is with the world as it is, in all its variety, and with man's various scientific accomplishments, is clear from the long list of his writings.[53] He has, judging from this source, apparently little inclination for insisting upon the particulars of religious or political creeds. The one extant record of his style when engaged in a religious polemic shows him as taking the high road of philosophical disputation.[54] Apparently he is not interested either in the advancement of particularist, ethnic claims, which we can also infer from the fact that though of pure aristocratic Arabian stock, he is dedicated to a field of learning identified with foreign ideas and pursued mostly by non-Arab *mawālī*.[55]

It would, therefore, be a reasonable assumption to see al-Kindī largely as his own man, a person of considerable learning, with a dispassionate concern for the truth within limits acceptable to the society at large and, no doubt, to his own religious beliefs; with which, however, he felt scientific knowledge was compatible. The real al-Kindī may well have been like the sage historical figure about whom stories were told and in whose name proverbs were recounted.[56] Such a figure would probably not have been happy with the *Muʿtazilah* supported *miḥnah* initiated by al-Maʾmūn and followed by a number of his successors, which furthered the polarization of society and intimidation of intellectual inquiry.[57] One could imagine al-Kindī using his position at court to express his resentment of Muʿtazilite practices, both theoretical and political; and, indeed, we find him speaking out in the introductory chapter of *First Philosophy* in such a way that, in the context of his remarks and in the terminology which he chooses, the passage is best understood as a thinly veiled indictment of the *Mu^c^tazilah*.

The lines in question follow a paraphrase of part of chapter one of *Metaphysics alpha elatton*, in which al-Kindī praises Aristotle by name and seconds his remarks concerning gratitude to all who have gone before in the search for truth. Al-Kindī states that his method is to present his predecessors' views fully, and to supplement them wherever necessary, "while being wary of the bad interpretation of many of those who are in our day acclaimed for speculation, (but) who are strangers to the truth, even if they are enthroned undeservedly with the crowns of truth." Such people, he says, understand neither the "methods of truth" nor the proper usage of "opinion" and "judgement". They are consumed by envy, and, to preserve their "spurious thrones," regard virtuous people as their enemy. These men, he declares, traffic in religion, though actually devoid of faith, which is also shown by their opposition to the philosophical pursuit of knowledge (with which religion is compatible), calling it "unbelief."[58]

In referring to the "usages" (الأنفاع) of "speculation" (نظر), "opinion" (رأى) and "judgement" (اجتهاد), al-Kindī is specifying methods of reasoning with which the *Mu^c^tazilah* were identified, and which to al-Kindī cannot compare with the "methods of truth" (أساليب الحق), i.e., syllogistic proofs. That it is the *Mu^c^tazilah* particularly whom al-Kindī is attacking may be deduced further from the fact that, at the time of the composition of this treatise, they alone enjoyed positions of authority and official sanction, using political office to impose their religious beliefs by threats and accusations of unbelief, to all of which the passage alludes.

Thus, as a man who is prepared to call for the ouster of the *Mu^c^tazilah* from government and official favor, al-Kindī should not be overly identified with them. On the other hand, one should not take this passage as the last word on al-Kindī's relationship with the *Mu^c^tazilah* either, since he does have, as we have seen, many points of contact with them; and he avoided, as far as we know, real political activity of any sort. This relatively neutral stance did not help him with al-Mutawakkil; but from the fact that his library was eventually restored, we may gather that he was not considered a serious political or religious threat.[59] Al-Kindī's life, as much as we are able to reconstruct it, thus exemplifies the personal difficulties and conflicting forces with which Muslim philosophers had to cope.

NOTES

CHAPTER ONE

1. Cf. Ibn al-Nadīm, *Kitāb al-Fihrist*, ed. by Gustave Flügel (Leipzig, 1871), I: 255 ff., II: 118 f.; Ibn Abī Uṣaybiʿa, *Kitābʿ Uyūn al-Anbā' fī Ṭabaqāt al-Aṭibbāʾ*, ed. by A. Müller (Königsberg, 1884), I:206 ff.; Ibn al-Qifṭī, *Taʾrīkh al-Ḥukamāʾ*, ed. by J. Lippert (Leipzig, 1903), pp. 35 ff., 366 ff. Flügel has repeated Ibn al-Nadīm's list of al-Kindī's written work, with comparative notes taken from al-Qifṭī and Ibn Abī Uṣaybiʿa, summarizing the facts of al-Kindī's life as presented mostly by these sources; cf. Gustave Flügel, "Al-Kindī, genannt 'der Philosoph der Araber' ", *Abhandlungen für die Kunde des Morgenlandes*, vol. I, no. 2 (Leipzig, 1857) : 1-54. Among other bio-bibliographers who have written on al-Kindī we should mention Ibn Juljul al-Andalusī, *Kitāb Ṭabaqāt al-Aṭibbā' wa-l-Ḥukamā'*, ed. by F. Sayyid (Cairo, 1955), p. 73; and Ṣāʾid al-Andalusī, *Kitāb Ṭabaqāt al-Umam*, ed. by Louis Cheikho (Beirut, 1912), pp. 50 ff. (French translation by Regis Blachère [Paris, 1935], pp. 104 ff.). H. Malter, availing himself of all these sources (as collected mainly by Flügel and Moritz Steinschneider), has reviewed both the facts of al-Kindī's life and the knowledge and opinions held of him by later writers; cf. H. Malter, "Al-Kindī: 'The Philosopher of the Arabs' ", *Hebrew Union College Annual*, 1904, pp. 55-71.

A fair number of the treatises mentioned in the early sources have happily turned up in manuscript, particularly in the codex Aya Sofya 4832 discovered by Hellmut Ritter; cf. Hellmut Ritter and Martin Plessner, "Schriften Jaʿqūb Ibn Isḥāq Al-Kindī In Stambuler Bibliotheken", *Archiv Orientální* 4 (1932) : 363-372. On the basis of this and other discoveries—and cf. particularly, in the field of science and philosophy, the manuscripts turned up and discussed by Franz Rosenthal, "Al-Kindī and Ptolemy", *Studi Orientalistici In Onore Di Giorgio Levi Della Vida* (Rome, 1956), II: 436-456; "From Arabic Books and Manuscripts VI: Istanbul Materials on al-Kindī and as-Saraḫsī", *Journal of the American Oriental Society*, 76 (1956) : 27-31—there is now a sizable amount of primary and secondary source material on al-Kindī's life and work. Thus Richard J. McCarthy has been able to assemble a revised list of works attributed to al-Kindī, *Al-Taṣānīf al-Mansūba ilā Faylasūf al-ʿArab* (Baghdad, 1962), pp. 1-122; and Nicholas Rescher has edited *Al-Kindī: An Annotated Bibliography* (Pittsburgh, 1964), pp. 13-155.

For recent general histories and evaluations of al-Kindī's life and writings, cf. W. Montgomery Watt, *Islamic Philosophy and Theology* (Edinburgh, 1962), pp. 45-47; A. el-Ehwany, *A History of Muslim Philosophy*, ed. by M.M. Sharif (Wiesbaden, 1963), I: 421-434; and Henry Corbin, *Histoire de la Philosophie Islamique* (Paris, 1964), pp. 217-221. Mention should be made also of George N. Atiyeh's book, *Al-Kindī: The Philosopher of the Arabs* (Rawalpindi, 1966), pp. 1-147, in which the author passes in review the details of al-Kindī's life and the various genres of his philosophical writings. Appendices to the book include an English translation of the *Fihrist* list of al-Kindī writings, with current information on the published state of various treatises (pp. 148-210) ; an English translation of al-Kindī's *Treatise On the Intellect* (pp. 211-215) ; and, most importantly, the abridged text and translation of Abū Sulaymān al-Sijistanī's *Ṣiwān al-Ḥikmah*, containing many additional sayings and remarks attributed to al-Kindī. (Cf. Atiyeh's edition of this material, pp. 216-238, with English translation by A.S. Bazmee Ansari, pp. 239-257). See also n.14 below.

2. To name just the major areas of his writings as given by the early bibliographers mentioned in the preceding note, al-Kindī published in the fields of arithmetic, geometry, music and astronomy, pharmacology, meteorology, chemistry, medicine, astrology, divination, and polemics; as well as in most of the various divisions of philosophy, viz., logic, physics, (including "celestial" or "spherical" physics), metaphysics, psychology and ethics.

3. Cf. the recent studies mentioned in note one above, and see particularly Max Meyerhof, "Von Alexandrien nach Bagdad", *Sitzungsberichte der Preussischen Akademie der Wissenschaften*, phil.-hist. Klasse, Vol. 33 (1930), pp. 389-429, pp. 402-405 in particular for the cultural milieu of al-Kindī's Baghdad; and also Francis E. Peters, *Aristotle and the Arabs: The Aristotelian Tradition in Islam* (New York—London, 1968), pp. 7-55.

4. Cf., for studies summarizing our current knowledge of Arabic philosophical translations, and of the translators themselves, Richard Walzer, "New Light on the Arabic Translations of Aristotle", *Greek into Arabic* (Oxford, 1962), pp. 65-70; Francis E. Peters, *Aristoteles Arabus: The Oriental Translation History of the Aristotelian Corpus* (Leiden, 1968), pp. 1-75; ibid., *Aristotle and the Arabs*, pp. 57-67. Much of the philosophical and scientific information which reached al-Kindī did so not by way of direct translation of the original texts, but rather through translations and oral knowledge of such varied types of literature as paraphrases and commentaries, encyclopedias and doxographies (Cf. Peters, *Aristotle and the Arabs*, pp. 96-129). Al-Kindī's *Treatise On the Soul Abridged from the Books of Aristotle and Plato*, edited by M. ʿA.H. Abū Rīdah, *Rasāʾil al-Kindī al-Falsafīyah* (Cairo, 1950-53), I: 272-280, is an example of a doxog-

raphical work, while *On First Philosophy*, for example, has much material best attributed to such secondary sources as commentaries and epitomes. The nature of such sources often makes it difficult to know whether al-Kindī is indeed the one responsible for a variation upon or disagreement with the ultimate original source.

5. Cf. n. 3 above, and see too Louis Gardet and M. Anawati, *Introduction à la Théologie Musulmane* (Paris, 1948), pp. 192 ff.

6. Cf. Franz Rosenthal, "Al-Kindī and Ptolemy", p. 444 f.

7. An echo of the struggle al-Kindī waged, and which had to be waged in every generation of philosophers, is heard in a disputation reported by Yāqūt on the authority of Abū Ḥayyān al-Tawḥīdī, and edited by D.S. Margoliouth, "Abū Bishr Mattā and Abū Saʿid al-Sīrāfī on the Merits of Logic and Grammar", *Journal of the Royal Asiatic Society*, 1905, 79-129. Al-Kindī is depicted as in attendance at the debate (though it was held in A.H. 320, i.e., at least two generations after his death), and al-Sīrāfī mimics his style (rather well), considering him as pursuing absurd questions. Abū Bishr Mattā, for his part, defends logic, and thus the philosophical tradition built upon it, with arguments portraying its universal validity and utility. Besides indirectly testifying to one type of opposition al-Kindī encountered, this disputation indicates al-Kindī's stature in the century following his death, and his influence upon both critics and sympathizers alike.

8. The man most responsible for the initiation of the *Miḥnah*, which lasted until A.H. 234/A.D. 848, was the chief Qāḍī, Aḥmad b. Abī Duʾād, a gifted as well as zealous Muʿtazilite spokesman. Al-Muʿtaṣim appears to have been a less eager proponent of the Muʿtazilite creed than his predecessor al-Maʾmūn; and was persuaded for political rather than religious reasons to continue the persecution of Ibn Ḥanbal. Cf. Patton, *Aḥmed ibn Ḥanbal and the Miḥna* (Leiden, 1897), pp. 52 ff., 101 ff., 120 ff.

9. Cf. the preceding note and see too the sources gathered by Ignác Goldziher, *Vorlesungen über den Islam* (Heidelberg, 1925), pp. 96-116. The *Muʿtazilah*, as Goldziher rightly says (p. 114), were rationalists but not liberals.

10. Cf. Hamilton A.R. Gibb, "The Social Significance of the Shuʿūbīya", *Studia Orientalia J. Pederson Dicata* (Copenhagen, 1953), pp. 105-114, reprinted in Gibb's *Studies on the Civilization of Islam* (Boston, 1962), pp. 62-73; and see also W. Montgomery Watt, "Political Attitudes of the Muʿtazila", *JRAS*, 1963, pp. 38-57.

11. Cf., for example, the influential opinion of al-Jāḥiẓ, *Kitāb al-Bukhalāʾ* (Beirut, 1963), pp. 116-132; trans. by C. Pellat, *Le Livre Des Avares* (Paris, 1951), pp. 115-134. However, after depicting al-Kindī as a bad host and landlord, al-Jāḥiẓ presents al-Kindī's side of the argument, in which a credible rebuttal is made of these charges.

12. Cf. the *Muntakhab Ṣiwān al-Ḥikmah* in Atiyeh, *Al-Kindī*, particularly nos. 39, 42, 45, 46, 71-73, for remarks which indicate that al-Kindī was (at least ostensibly) against avarice and similar mean practices. In

his judicious description of al-Kindī's position and person, Franz Rosenthal has cautioned against uncritical acceptance of the oral tradition regarding al-Kindī; cf. Franz Rosenthal, "Al-Kindī als Literat", *Orientalia*, n.s. 11 (1942) : 262-288, particularly pp. 268 ff. As regards the *Munthakhab Ṣiwān al-Ḥikmah*, it would appear on internal grounds that al-Kindī is indeed the author of the philosophical views attributed to him, and possibly of the gnomic utterances as well; though both genres and their contents are clearly indebted to ultimately Greek sources. Attributing these moralistic remarks to al-Kindī, of course, does not necessarily mean that he practised what he preached, though there is no necessity to believe he did not, either.

13. Cf. A. Nagy, "Die Philosophischen Abhandlungen der Jaʿqūb ben Isḥāq Al-Kindī", *Beiträge zur Geschichte der Philosophie des Mittelalters*, vol. 2, no. 5 (1897) : 1-64.

14. Cf. Richard Walzer, "Studi su al-Kindī I: Uno scritto introduttivo allo studio di Aristotele" (with Michelangelo Guidi), and "Studi su al-Kindī II: Uno scritto morale inedito di al-Kindī" (with Hellmut Ritter), *Memorie della Reale Accademia Nazionale dei Lincei* (Classe di Scienze Morali, Storiche e Filologiche), ser. VI, vol. 6 (1937-40), pp. 375-419, and ser. VI, vol. 8, fasc. 1 (1938), pp. 5-63, respectively. Walzer has, in addition, written a number of general evaluations of al-Kindī's thought; cf. in particular "New Studies on Al-Kindī", *Oriens* X (1957) : 203 ff., reprinted in Richard Walzer, *Greek into Arabic* , pp. 175-205.

15. Cf. Abū Rīdah, *Rasāʾil al-Kindī Al-Falsafīyah,* I: 1-80 introduction, 81-374; II: 5-133.

16. Cf. particularly the observations on al-Kindī's philosophy which A. Altmann and S.M. Stern have made apropos of their study of another philosopher, one very influenced by al-Kindī. See A. Altmann and S.M. Stern, *Isaac Israeli* (Oxford, 1958), p. 220 (index); cf. also S.M. Stern, "Notes on Al-Kindī's Treatise On Definitions", *JRAS,* 1959, pp. 32-43.

17. Assembled by Malter, "Al-Kindī: 'The Philosopher of the Arabs' ", pp. 66-67.

CHAPTER TWO

1. Cf. Ritter and Plessner, "Schriften Jaʿqūb Ibn Isḥāq Al-Kindī", p. 368.

2. Ibid., p. 363.

3. Cf. *Kitāb al-Kindī fī al-Falsafah al-Ūlā*, ed. by Aḥmad Fuʾad al-Ahwānī (Cairo, 1948), pp. 77-143; Abū Rīdah, *Rasāʾil Al-Kindī Al-Falsafīyah,* I: 97-162.

4. The manuscript itself was studied through two sets of photographs,

generously loaned by Drs. Richard Walzer and Richard J. McCarthy, S.J.

5. Cf. *FP* 114.12 ff., and see n. to 114.11.

6. Asṭāt's translation is preserved in Averroes' Grand Commentary of the Metaphysics, *Tafsīr Mā Baᶜd Aṭ-Ṭabīᶜat*, ed. by Maurice Bouyges (Beirut, 1938-52).

7. This and the following chapter are summarized in greater detail by Michael Marmura and John M. Rist, "Al-Kindī's Discussion of Divine Existence and Oneness", *Mediaeval Studies* 25 (1963): 339-346.

8. Cf., e.g., the *FP* extract quoted below and ensuing discussion.

9. As al-Kindī's use of *annīyah* in the extract below (and cf. *FP* 97.13 and n. there); or his use of infinity (*FP*, p. 109), of which the assertion is made—but not explained there—that it cannot be in actuality; and of a number of logical terms (*FP* , p. 132).

10. Cf., e.g., his article on "The True First, Complete Agent and the Deficient Agent which is (Spoken of) Metaphorically", Abū Rīdah I: 182-184; or his abridged "Treatise On the Soul", I: 281-282. Short treatises of this sort, mostly "epistles" (*rasā'il*), are apparently a stylistic innovation of al-Kindī's, as the author of the *Muntakhab Ṣiwān al-Ḥikmah* claims (cf. Atiyeh, *Al-Kindī*, p. 217, and see D.M. Dunlop, "Biographical Material from the *Ṣiwān al-Ḥikmah*", *JRAS*, 1957-58, pp. 88, 89.

11. Thus, e.g., *creatio ex nihilo* and the finitness of the world are similarly treated, in addition to *FP*, pp. 114-122, in three other treatises (Abū Rīdah, *Rasā'il Al-Kindī Al-Falsafīyah*, I: 186-192, 194-198, 201-207), as well as elsewhere.

12. Cf. *FP*, p. 114, where al-Kindī lists as a "true first premise" that the finite cannot be infinite; which categorical proposition is then followed by repeated individual "confirmations", based on circular reasoning. Cf. also *FP*, pp. 127 ff. and 152 ff. for separate though essentially similar "proofs" of the composition of predicables by a combination of (accidental) unity and multiplicity, and the examination of these latter terms in various relationships; though the definition of unity at p. 132 and multiplicity at p. 134 should have precluded such extensive illustration. This particular approach may be at least partially due to al-Kindī's use of the conditional type of argument, the disjunctive syllogism with its appeal to fact and simplification of alternatives. Al-Kindī apparently feels obliged to present many such individual "proofs", in order to proceed (illegitimately) to a kind of universal statement.

13. Cf. the cross-references in al-Kindī's writings, assembled by Franz Rosenthal, "Al-Kindī and Ptolemy", *Studi Orientalistici in Onore di Giorgio Levi Della Vida* (1956) II: 440-443.

14. Following Rosenthal's suggestion, ibid.

15. Cf. *FP* 97.8-98.2 below with nn.

16. Cf. second n. to *FP* 97.13 in the commentary below. The Plotinian corpus in Arabic (the prevalence of which in Islam has been studied by Paul Kraus, "Plotin chez les Arabes", *Bulletin de l'Institut d'Égypte* 23

[1941]: 266-279), has been assembled in English translation by G. Lewis in Vol. II of *Plotini Opera*, ed. by P. Henry and H.R. Schwyzer (Paris-Brussels, 1959). Much of this material is now found in ᶜAbd al-Raḥmān Badawī's Arabic edition, *Aflūṭīn ᶜinda al-ᶜArab* (Cairo, 1955). Badawī has also edited much of the Arabic Proclus extant (cf. his *Neoplatonici apud Arabes* [Cairo, 1955]), including the Arabic paraphrase (formerly edited by Bardenhewer) of that classic of Neoplatonism, *The Elements of Theology*. While the Latin version of this paraphrase, the *Liber de Causis*, made a great impact upon the Scholastic West (cf. E.R. Dodds, *Proclus: The Elements of Theology* [Oxford, 1963], p. xxvii), the Arabic version, *Kitāb al-Īḍāḥ fī al-Khayr al-Maḥḍ*, was barely read in the Muslim world (cf. Peters, *Aristoteles Arabus*, p. 57), even though it was attributed to Aristotle. While this work was probably translated well after al-Kindī's death, some, at least, of the *Elements of Theology* itself was translated, by Abū ᶜUthmān al-Dimashqī (*fl. ca.* A.D. 914), only a generation or so after al-Kindī (cf. the fragment of propositions 15-17 [Dodds], published in ᶜAbd al-Raḥmān Badawī, *Arisṭū ᶜinda al-ᶜarab* [Cairo, 1947], pp. 291-292, and discussed by both B. Lewin, *Orientalia Suecana* IV [1955] : 101-108, and Shlomo Pines, *Oriens* VIII [1955]: 195-203) ; so that the work, in some form or another, was probably circulating in his time, and al-Kindī may well have had indirect knowledge of its contents from his Greek reading informants.

Moreover, a much earlier adaptation of the *Elements*, the sixth century *Mystical Theology* of Pseudo-Dionysius , had already spread Proclus' conception of a transcendent, unknowable and indescribable God throughout Christianity (cf. the English translation of this work in A.B. Sharpe, *Mysticism: Its True Nature and Value* [London, 1910], pp. 207-229); and in the person and writings of John of Damascus (died c. 750) the Muslim intellectual world would have become acquainted with an essentially Proclean formulation of these ideas.

One may thus assume some familiarity with Proclus' ideas on al-Kindī's part, though he might not, in some cases, have known Proclus to be their author. While he would not have agreed with Proclus' notions of the eternity of the world and its dialectically designed, hierarchically related substances of Being, Intelligence, Life and Soul, not to mention Proclus' henads, al-Kindī would have been responsive to Proclus' views on the "Pure True One", who is above all epithets and yet the "cause" and "creator" of all (cf. e.g., ᶜAbd al-Raḥmān Badawī, ed., *Kitāb al-Khayr al-Maḥḍ*, pp. 7, 12, 22, and elsewhere). As it is unlikely, however, that al-Kindī read any Proclus himself, while he *was* directly familiar with Plotinian-based material, the following notes will draw comparisons only between the Arabic Plotinus and al-Kindī.

17. Cf. *FP* 97.13[a]; and see further in Plotinus, *Opera*, pp. 207 Lewis ("Theology") /51 Badawī; 291 Lewis (ibid.) /134 Badawī (cf. *Enn.* V. 2. 1, 1); 353 f. Lewis (*"Epistola De Scientia Divina"*) /181 f. Badawī (cf. *Enn.* V. 5. 9, 33 ff.); 474 Lewis (*"Dicta Sapientis Graeci"* I) /186 Badawī (cf. *Enn.* VI. 9.6, 7).

18. Besides the references in the preceding n., cf. further, ibid., pp. 263 Lewis ("*Theology*") /108 Badawī, and 487 Lewis (ibid.) /6 Badawī.

19. Ibid., 375 Lewis /56 Badawī (*Enn.* V. 8. 1, 1), 403 Lewis /116 Badawī; expressed in a more qualified way as a unification with the intelligible world of eternal substances (which is derived from and "reverts" in its own way to the One), in, e.g., pp. 225 Lewis/22 Badawī (*Enn.* IV. 8. 1, 1), 251 Lewis /91 Badawī (*Enn.* IV. 8. 8, 22).

20. Al-Kindī does assume (cf. his treatise "On the Number of the Books of Aristotle", Abū Ridah I: 372, edited earlier, with an Italian translation, by Guidi and Walzer, op. cit., pp. 395, 409) that the prophetic soul undergoes "purification" and "illumination" by God, the prophet receiving "inspiration" from Him; terms which have been seen as deriving ultimately from Proclus' "upward way" towards unity with the One (cf. Altmann and Stern, *Isaac Israeli*, p. 185 f., and see Walzer, "New Studies on Al-Kindī", pp. 178 ff.). "Inspiration" (*ilhām*), however, is not ordinarily used for "union" (*ittiḥād*), as Altmann mentions; and there is no reason to assume al-Kindī is so alluding, both from the context of the passage and because nowhere in his writings does he even discuss this favorite mystic topic. What is said of the prophet, here and elsewhere (cf. particularly *FP*, p. 104), does not compel us to conclude that the content of prophetic knowledge is different in kind from that of the philosopher; but only that it differs in degree, style, and method of acquisition. Indeed, it would seem that the explanation of Qur'ānic material which follows in the "Number" treatise assumes that the "mystery" of Qur'ānic truth *is* explicable; and the explanation is invariably framed, despite rhetorical statements to the contrary, along philosophical lines. The prophet should be regarded as a master philosopher, thanks to Divine assistance; but he does not therefore become one with God.

21. Cf. *FP* below, p. 101.3, and see n. there.

22. Cf. the "first cause" sense of cause in the *Theology*, pp. 205 f. Lewis /50 f. Badawī; 231 Lewis /26 Badawī; 263 Lewis /108 Badawī.

23. Cf. *Theology*, e.g., pp. 271 f. Lewis/112 Badawī (*Enn.* V. 1. 5, 3 ff.) ; 291 f. Lewis/134 f. Badawī (*Enn.* V. 2. 1, 1 ff.) ; and the "*Dicta Sapientis Graeci*" I, 474-476 Lewis/186-189 Badawī. As contrasted with these places, al-Kindī does not follow his logical argument for the existence of an essential unity (i.e., God) with any scheme which would show how this One relates to the world. Cf. *FP*, p. 132.

24. Cf. *FP*, pp. 140-143.

25. *Ibid.*, p. 151; this whole discussion being in *FP* pp. 143 ff. Cf. Plotinus' discussion of number, *Theology*, pp. 271 Lewis /113 Badawī (*Enn.* V. 1. 5, 6), and "*Epistola De Scientia Divina*", pp. 345 Lewis /180 Badawī (*Enn.* V. 5. 4, 12) ; and see Aristotle's *Met.* XIV. 1 1087b 33 ff. This Aristotelian doctrine (which may be of Pythagorean origin; cf. T. Heath, *A History of Greek Mathematics* [Oxford, 1921] I: 69) of the one as not itself a number because a measure is not the things measured, appears in Nichomachus of Gerasa's *Introductionis Arithmeticae*, ed. by R. Hoche

(Leipzig, 1866), ii 6.3, 7.3; translated by Martin L. D'Ooge (New York, 1926), pp. 237 and 239. Al-Kindī was familiar with this latter work, and its influence may be appearing here as well as in other writings; see further below, p. 20.

26. Cf. *FP* p. 158.

27. Ibid., p. 155 f.

28. Ibid., pp. 113 and 162.

29. I.e., nothing exists in reality of which essential unity can be predicated. The "essentially one" is a logical construct derived from the existence of the "accidentally one"; but any attempt to comprehend this concept is precluded by al-Kindī's demonstration of its philosophical meaninglessness.

30. Ibid., p. 118.

31. Cf. the *Theology*, pp. 291 Lewis/134 Badawī (*Enn.* V. 2.1,1); "*Epistola De Scientia Divina*", 321 f. Lewis/174 f. Badawī (*Enn.* V.3.12, 43); "*Dicta Sapientis Graeci*" II 281 Lewis/185 Badawī; "*Dicta*" IX 481 Lewis/196 Badawī (*Enn.* VI. 7. 32, 6). As the above places indicate, Plotinus moves very easily from negative to positive assertions regarding the nature and actions of the One; even if such positive statements are not meant, ostensibly, to be taken literally. Al-Kindī, however, makes very few such positive assertions, and those only of a general sort. He seems to wish to remain within that sphere of philosophy which "is concerned only with that of which inquiry can be made... universal delimited things the true nature of which knowledge can comprehend perfectly" (*FP* pp. 124, 125).

32. Cf. *Theology*, pp. 486 Lewis/ 3 Badawī. Al-Kindī's role as a reviser-stylist of this and another translation is mentioned by Ibn al-Nadīm in his *Kitāb al-Fihrist*, ed. by Gustave Flügel, pp. 252, 268. That al-Kindī was not himself a translator, though he received such a reputation, has been recently shown by M. Moosa, "Al-Kindī's Role in the Transmission of Greek Knowledge to the Arabs", *Journal of the Pakistan Historical Society*, vol. 15, no. 1 (1967): 3-14.

33. Compare *FP* 97.13, 101.3 below. This resemblance is probably due to a common Aristotelian source (*Met. alpha elatton*) in the introduction of both works. They both commence by distinguishing between the theoretical pursuit of truth and truthful action; and proceed to an enumeration of the four Aristotelian causes (presented mostly as substantives and not adjectives): "matter" is given as *al-hayūlā* (*Theology*) and *ᶜunṣur* (*FP*), "form" as *al-ṣūrah*, "active (efficient) cause" as *al-ᶜillah al-fāᶜilah*, and "perfection" (or "completion", i.e., final cause) as *tamām* (*Theology*), *mutammimah* and *tamamīyah* (*FP*). Other identical terminology appears, in, e.g., the use of *al-ḥaqq*, *ᶜamal*, *fiᶜl* and *sarmad*.

34. Cf. *FP* p. 161 f.

35. Cf. *Theology*, p. 291 Lewis/134 Badawī (*Enn.* V. 2. 1, 5). Lewis translates *huwīyah* (*to on*) as "identity" rather than "being", probably reflecting the Latin *ipseity* (used as such by Stern, op. cit., p. 19), which in this context appears misleading.

36. Al-Kindī may have been helped to this emphasis upon the One, sacrificing the creative roles of the other universal substances, by the Arabic Plotinus corpus, in which such a tendency—reflecting a Christian source—has been discerned (cf. Kraus, op. cit., pp. 292, 293.).

37. Cf. the *Fihrist*, ed. Flügel, p. 251, and see Bouyges' bio-bibliographical discussion of this translator and his relations to al-Kindī (op. cit., p. cxviii f.). As Bouyges remarks, little is known of Asṭāt (or Asṭāth) whose name in the sources—اسطاب—could as well be pronounced Eusṭāt/Eusṭāth; and is therefore found, e.g., in Peters, loc. cit., as Eustathius.

38. Cf., e.g., *FP* p. 103.

39. Cf. *Met.* I. 2. 982a 4 ff., 982b 9; and see *Met.* IV. 1. 1003a 21 f.

40. Particularly in *Met.* XII 7. 1072a 19-1073b 3; but defined in *Met.* VI. 1. 1026a 10-19 (and cf. Ross' notes there) and XI. 1064a 33-b 3.

41. Cf. *Met* VI. 1. 1026a 29-32: "if there is an immovable substance, the science of this must be prior and must be first philosophy, and universal in this way, because it is first. And it will belong to this to consider being *qua* being—both what it is and the attributes which belong to it *qua* being" (in Ross' translation). At *Met.* XI. 4. 1061b 19 (and see 26), "first philosophy" is used solely in the sense of being *qua* being, which is closer to al-Kindī's actual usage, though not to his stated intention.

42. Cf. *FP* p. 101.15.

43. If indeed there was a second part; cf. Franz Rosenthal, op. cit., p. 437, concerning a similar "incomplete" Kindian treatise.

44. And not substances themselves; i.e., understanding substance as a sensible individual thing (cf. *Met.* VII, VIII and IX), and not as the unchanging substances of *Met.* XII. 6.-10.

45. I.e., a magnitude; cf., for example, Physics IV. 11., 14, VI. 1.-4; ignoring, however, Aristotle's conclusions (Physics VIII) regarding an eternal first mover and motion.

46. Cf., e.g., *Met.* II. 2. 994a 1 ff., XII. 8. 1074a 29.

47. Cf. *Physics* III. 7. 207b 23; VI. 2. 232a 23 ff., and *Physics* VIII. in particular. See too *Met.* XII. 6. 1071b 3 ff.

48. Cf. *FP* p. 116.5 ff.

49. Cf. Marmura and Rist, op. cit., p. 347; and see Walzer, "New Studies on Al-Kindī", pp. 201, 202. The difference between al-Kindī's treatment of the relation between the one and the many and that of his predecessors, from Plato to Proclus, is, generally speaking, that the latter argue from a necessary co-dependancy of the one and the many to a one which is inside the scheme and yet transcendent; while al-Kindī reasons to a one who is completely outside the scheme and yet somehow immanent.

50. The ontological gap in al-Kindī's universe is also evident in his discussion of intellection and the intellect, in which the implications of the relationship between an individual intellect and the universal intellect are not explored. Cf. *FP* 155. 1 ff., and see particularly the note to 155.9.

51. Cf. *FP* 116. 13 ff. and notes there.

52. Cf. *FP* 162.7 and note there.

53. Cf. S. Breton, *Philosophie et Mathematique chez Proclus* (Paris, 1969), p. 13.

54. Cf. *FP* 146.15-151.5.

55. That al-Kindī wrote many treatises on mathematics is known from the bibliographers; cf. e.g., Ibn al-Nadīm, op. cit., pp. 256, 257; in Flügel's extract, op. cit., pp. 22-23, 25-27 German, 38-39, 41-43 Arabic; translated into English by Atiyeh, op. cit., pp. 165-166, 175-179. Included among these we find an "Introduction to Arithmetic", "An Explanation of the Numbers Which Plato Mentions in His Book *The Republic*" (السياسة), and "An Epistle on Unity by Way of Number"; from any of which (unfortunately lost) treatises al-Kindī may be borrowing in our work. F. Rosenthal, "Al-Kindī and Ptolemy", op. cit., pp. 440, 441, has established possible cross-references to some of these treatises by al-Kindī in his *Almagest* paraphrase.

56. Nichomachus' work was translated into Arabic by Thābit ibn Qurra (d. A.D. 901), and has been edited by W. Kutsch, *Ṯabit b. Qurra's Arabische Übersetzung der* 'Αριθμητικὴ 'Εισαγωγή *des Nikomachus von Gerasa* (Beirut, 1959). Rabīc ibn Yaḥyā's paraphrase is preserved in manuscript (cf. Moritz Steinschneider's *Die Hebraeischen Übersetzungen des Mittelalters* [Berlin, 1893], pp. 517-519), and Steinschneider has edited extracts of Kalonymos b. Kalonymos' Hebrew translation in "Miscellena 26", *MGWJ*, 1893, pp. 68-77. Stern mentons Rabīc ibn Yaḥyā's paraphrase, and contends that al-Kindī was "intimately acquainted" with Nichomachus' work (cf. *Isaac Israeli*, pp. 28, nn. 1 and 35).

57. Cf. *FP*, the note to 146.15, and see too *FP* 124.17 ff., as well as 101.5 ff. and 105.2 ff.

58. Cf. Nichomachus' work, edited by R. Hoche, op. cit. I: i, 2; English translation, op. cit. p. 181; quoted in Rabīc ibn Yaḥyā's paraphrase as well (cf. Steinschneider, "Miscellena 26", op. cit., p. 70, translated by Stern, op. cit., p. 35).

59. Ibid., ed. Hoche, I: iv., 2; I: vi, 1-4; D'Ooge translation, pp. 187, 189, 190.

60. Ibid., ed. Hoche, II: xviii, 1, 4; D'Ooge translation, pp. 257-259, and see Frank E. Robbins' remarks in Pt. I of the English edition, pp. 97-100 and 188. This view is expressed also in Nichomachus' *Theologomena Arithmeticae*, ed. F. Ast (Leipzig, 1817), pp. 3-12, 58 (and cf., for Nichomachus' authorship of this work, Robbins' study, op. cit., Pt. I, pp. 82-87).

61. Regarding Nichomachus' paradoxical position, in which both the one and the many are considered necessary principles of all existence and yet the one is often regarded as more fundamental, cf. Robbins, op. cit., p. 115.

62. Cf. Nichomachus' *Introduction*, ed. Hoche II: xviii, 1, 4; pp. 257-259 in the English translation of D'Ooge, and see, for example, *Timaeus* 35a.

63. Cf. Ast., op. cit., pp. 4, 5, and see Robbins' remarks in Pt. I of the *Introduction,* op. cit., pp. 95, 96.

64. Cf. above, p. 14.

65. Cf. *Rasā'il Ikhwān al-Ṣafā'* (Beirut, 1957), I: 53. 2 is then compared to the Intellect, 3 to the Soul, and 4 to Matter.

66. Nichomachus is singled out with Pythagoras by the *Ikhwān* as sources for the knowledge of arithmetic (ibid., p. 49), even as Euclid is regarded as the source for geometry and Ptolemy for astronomy. Cf. B. Goldstein's translation of this entire first chapter of the *Rasā'il* (op. cit., pp. 48-77) in his article, "A Treatise On Number Theory from a Tenth Century Arabic Source" *Centaurus* 10 (1964): 135-160; and see his comparison of the Ikhwān's views with those of Nichomachus, ibid., pp. 129-131.

67. The nature of the soul being regarded as the first of the "metaphysical sciences" (العلوم الالهية), which lead to knowledge of God. Cf. *Rasā'il,* op. cit., pp. 75, 76; in Goldstein's translation, op. cit., pp. 157, 158.

68. Cf. *FP,* 155.15.

69. This notion of a common source, rather than of an influence exerted by al-Kindī upon the *Ikhwān* (which Stern considers and rejects, "Notes on Al-Kindī's Treatise on Definitions", op. cit., p. 37), may also explain the apperance of a number of eschatologically-oriented definitions in the British Museum manuscript of *On Definitions* which do not appear in the manuscript used by Abū Rīdah but which do recur in the *Rasā'il Ikhwān al-Ṣafā'* (cf. Stern, ibid., pp. 34-37). As Stern remarks, the evidence that these definitions belong to al-Kindī's text is rather slight, as they occur nowhere else in his writings, and, one may add, express the concept of one universal soul, concerning which al-Kindī is nowhere else so explicit. Yet there is nothing at all in al-Kindī's other extant writings on the soul which preclude his having believed in a universal soul from which and to which particular souls come and go (cf. *FP* n. 155.9 below); and he could as well have included among his definitions, particularly on religiously sensitive matters, views which he copied from his source but which he did not necessarily subscribe to fully without qualification.

CHAPTER THREE

1. Cf. Louis Gardet, "Le Problème de la 'Philosophie Musulmane'", *Mélanges offerts à Étienne Gilson* (Toronto-Paris, 1959), p. 269; Henri Laoust, *Les Schismes Dans l'Islam* (Paris, 1965), p. 106; and see W. Montgomery Watt, *Islamic Philosophy and Theology* (Edinburgh, 1962), pp. 45-47. For the *Mu'tazilah* school (or schools) of theology in general, of

which we still know all too little, cf. as yet *The Encyclopaedia of Islam*, 3:787-793.

2. *Oriens* 10 (1957): 203 ff., reprinted in *Greek into Arabic* (from which future citations will be drawn), pp. 175-205.

3. "The Rise of Islamic Philosophy", *Oriens* 3 (1950): 9.

4. Cf. "New Studies", op. cit., pp. 176, 177, and see nn. to *FP* 97.3 and 97.5 below.

5. Cf. "New Studies", op. cit., p. 176.

6. Ibid., p. 177.

7. Cf. the edition of this treatise prepared by Walzer and Michelangelo Guidi, "Studi su al-Kindī I", op. cit., 395, 396 of the Arabic text, 409, 410 of the Italian translation; and see too Abū Ridah's *Rasā'il*, I: 372, 373. Al-Kindī employs the term العلم الالهي in *FP* to denote metaphysics, considered as within the philosophical syllabus and as such, it may be inferred, a "human science" (see below, 112.15 and n. 112.15[1]). We may therefore assume that it is not العلم الالهي as such which is superior to لعلوم الانسانية, but only that العلم الالهي which is received through revelation, in which case it is not metaphysics as commonly understood but a supposedly unique kind of knowledge. However, as we shall see, al-Kindī proceeds to convert this "divine knowledge" into what we commonly recognize as metaphysics.

8. Following Arthur J. Arberry, *The Koran Interpreted* (New York, 1955), p. 149.

9. A method employed by al-Kindī elsewhere as well. Cf. Walzer, "New Studies", op. cit., pp. 183, 198. Walzer's analysis (ibid., pp. 196-199) of al-Kindī's interpretation of *surah* 55 verse 5 in this treatise, "An Explanation of the Worship of the Uttermost Body and Its Obedience to God" (الابانة عن سجود الجرم الاقصى وطاعته لله عز وجل, AR I: 244-247), provides additional proof of al-Kindī's use of philological criteria to further philosophical understanding of the *Qur'ān*.

10. Cf. "New Studies", op. cit., p. 183 and see al-Ashʿarī's *Maqālāt al-Islāmīyīn*, ed. Hellmut Ritter, *Die dogmatischen Lehren der Anhanger des Islam* (Wiesbaden, 1963), p. 510. Al-Ashʿarī also presents the argument against this view which denied the literal meaning of this passage. Cf. his *Kitāb al-Luma'* ed. by R. McCarthy, *The Theology of al-Ash'arī* (Beirut, 1952), pp. 15 ff. Arabic, 21 ff. English.

11. Cf. Walzer's parallels from late Greek and Christian thought, from Philo on, for this latter belief, in "New Studies", op. cit., pp. 179, 180.

12. Cf. Ignác Goldziher, *Die Richtungen der Islamischen Koranauslegung* (Leiden, 1920), pp. 130 ff., and see Walzer, ibid., pp. 197, 198.

13. Cf. Walzer, ibid., pp. 184-187.

14. Cf. AR I: 28-31. At p. 31 mention is made of the Qur'ān exegesis discussed above.

15. Ibid., p. 28, and see Ibn al-Nadīm's *Fihrist*, op. cit., p. 259; Flügel's

Al-Kindī, op. cit., pp. 46 Arabic, 30 German translation; Atiyeh, op. cit., pp. 191-193; and Walzer, "New Studies", op. cit., p. 183.

16. While Aristotelian syllogisms and systematic, rigorous definitions were not adopted until the eleventh century at the earliest, the *Muᶜtazilah* of the preceding centuries used a kind of dialectic in which analogies are drawn upon the basis of either externally obvious similarities and differences, or relationships suggested by the *Qurʾān*; and they employed (unexamined) concepts of necessity, possibility and impossibility of a sort which we find spelled out by al-Kindī. All this without his sense of a causal relationship between events, or of independent natural or logical "laws"; the absence of which, however, strengthened their impression of a finite universe with clearly delimited possibilities, knowledge of which may be considered certain because revealed by God. Cf., for remarks concerning this earliest period of *Kalām* logic, Josef Van Ess, *Die Erkenntnislehre des ᶜAḍudaddīn Al-Īcī* (Wiesbaden, 1966), pp. 17 ff., 114, 358 ff., 373, 385 ff.; Shlomo Pines, *Beiträge zur islamischen Atomenlehre* (Berlin, 1936), pp. 26 ff.; Louis Gardet and M.M. Anawati, *Introduction à la Théologie Musulmane* (Paris, 1948), pp. 357 ff. See also al-Baghdadī's eleventh century summation of this logic, in the first chapter of his *Kitāb Uṣūl al-Dīn*, translated by W. Montgomery Watt, "The Logical Basis of Early Kalam", *The Islamic Quarterly* 6 (1962): 3-10 and 7 (1963): 31-39.

17. Cf. Davidson, "John Philoponus as a Source of Medieval Islamic and Jewish Proofs of Creation", *JAOS* 89 (1969): 357-391.

18. See also, regarding Philoponus' influence, H. Wolfson, "The Kalām Arguments for Creation in Saadia, Averroes, Maimonides, and St. Thomas", *Saadia Anniversary Volume* (New York, 1943), pp. 201-203; and Walzer, "New Studies", op. cit., pp. 190-196. For later, critical reaction to Philoponus, see Muhsin Mahdi, "Alfarabi Against Philoponus", *Near Eastern Studies* 26 (1967): 233-260.

19. Cf. Davidson, op. cit., pp. 371-373, 375, and see *FP* below, 121.5 ff. and the n. to 121.15-122.1.

20. Cf. Davidson, op. cit., pp. 378, 379. He does not mention the occurence of this argument in al-Kindī; see, however, *FP* below, 122.13-15 and n. there.

21. Cf. Davidson, op. cit., pp. 376, 379 and 390, and see *FP* below, 115.1-116.4, and the n. to 114.18.

22. Discussed also by the *mutakallimūn* usually in terms of accidents and body, not atoms. Cf. Davidson, op. cit., pp. 382-388, and see *FP* below, pp. 117-120. Al-Kindī has two arguments for the inter-dependence of body and the accidents of time and motion, the second of which (p. 120), discussing the composition of body, is clearly traceable to a similar proof of the generation of the universe from the finiteness of the power contained within it used by Philoponus; the latter's argument running, that what is composite is not self-sufficient, and what is not self-sufficient does not have infinite power (cf. Davidson, ibid., pp. 362-363, 371-372).

23. John Philoponus' ideas have been summarized by S. Sambursky, *The Physical World of Late Antiquity* (New York, 1962), pp. 157 ff.

24. Cf. the fourth through sixth treatises in AR I: 186-207. B. Lewin, referring to one of these treatises in his article, "La Notion de Muḥdaṯ dans le Kalām et dans la Philosophie", *Orientalia Suecana* 3, fasc. 2/4 (1954): 86, also traces the theme of the finitude of all body to Philoponus.

25. Cf. AR I: 219, 220, 246; II: 10, 12 (Abū Rīdah's Arabic translation of the Latin *Liber de quinque essentiis*, ed. Nagy, op. cit., pp. 29, 30); 44ff. (the treatise being titled "An Explanation That the Nature of the Heavenly Spheres Differs from the Nature of the Four Elements"); 48 ff. (treatise translated by Haig Khatchadourian and Nicholas Rescher, "That the Elements and the Outermost Body Are Spherical in Form", *Isis* 56 [1965]: 190-195, reprinted in the latter's *Studies in Arabic Philosophy* [Pittsburgh, 1967], pp. 9-14).

26. For which cf. Sambursky, loc. cit. Many of John Philoponus' technical arguments, as well as fundamental positions, find no echo in al-Kindī; e.g., Philoponus' concept of time, privation, and denial of the existence of the aether, of perfect circular motion, and unchanging uniform celestial phenomena.

27. Cf., e.g., al-Kindī's statement in "On . . . the Cause of Generation and Corruption" (AR I: 220), that the heavens and the four elements undergo neither generation nor corruption, remaining for as long as God has appointed them to be.

28. In this perspective, the fact that John Philoponus also apparently acknowledges God's will as a possible factor in deferring the otherwise necessary destruction of the heavens (Cf. Simplicius' commentary to Aristotle's *Physics*, *CAG X* [Berlin, 1895]: 1331, 11. 23-25, and see Davidson, op. cit., p. 362, n. 46), does not affect the quite basic difference between his unified, universal physics and the more complicated, dual physics of al-Kindī.

29. Cf., for the early *Kalām* views of God's unity and His attributes of will, action, creation (both original and continuous creation, of the world and of each of its atoms) and infinity, al-Ashᶜarī's *Maqālāt*, op. cit., pp. 136 f., 163 ff., 177, 232, 312, 377, 393, 407, 418, 480, 484, 551; and see too al-Khayyāṭ's *Kitāb al-Intiṣār*, edited and translated into French by Albert Nader (Beyrouth, 1957), pp. 80 ff.,; and for the various "accidents" of initiation (*ibtidā'*) and duration of being, its motion and cessation or extinction (*fanā'*), cf. *Maqālāt*, pp. 137, 319 ff., 355 ff., 363, 570, and *Kitāb al-Intiṣār*, pp. 52 ff.

30. Op. cit., pp. 362-373.

31. Cf. Job's *Book of Treasures*, ed. A. Mingana (Cambridge, 1935), pp. 16 f. English translation, 305 f. Syriac text, and see too Mingana's introduction, pp. xxvii-xxix. While Job was acquainted with Muᶜtazilite ideas and had met some of their early leading figures (cf. Shlomo Pines, "Études sur Awḥad al-Zaman Abu'l Barakāt al-Baghdādī", *REJ*, n.s. 3 [1938]: 45, n. 168), he clearly did not receive all his philosophical knowl-

edge from their circles, differing with them on many issues. Cf. the *Book of Treasures,* pp. 153, 154 English, 388, 389 Syriac.

32. Cf. Davidson, op. cit., pp. 373-375, and see the *Book of Treasures,* pp. 15 English, 304 Syriac. This argument occurs as well in the Christian polemical work *The Book of the Demonstration* by the tenth century Eutychius of Alexandria, who also briefly mentions the argument for the impossibility of an infinite regression and the doctrine of negative attributes. Cf. Pierre Cachia's edition of the Arabic text and W. Montgomery Watt's separate English translation (both published in Louvain, 1960 and 1961), pp. 3, 4, 16, 17 Arabic, 2, 3, 13, 14 English.

33. Cf. the *Book of Treasures,* pp. 11 English, 302 Syriac.

34. Cf. al-Khayyāṭ, op. cit., pp. 19 Arabic, 12 French (which, however, mistranslates the latter argument). Cf. also, for the lack of a distinction in infinity, *FP* below, n. 113.5.

35. Cf. al-Khayyāt, op. cit., pp. 33 Arabic, 32 French.

36. Ibid., pp. 32 Arabic, 30 French. Al-Naẓẓām says, in terminology like that of al-Kindī, that all parts of bodies can be divided in the mind into two (by the *wahm*); which al-Naẓẓām feels is sufficient reason to discredit the *actual* existence of atoms.

37. Cf. al-Ashᶜarī, op. cit., pp. 302, 307, 311, 314, 315, 319.

38. Ibid., pp. 358, 359, and see al-Khayyāṭ, op. cit., pp. 16-18, 21-22 Arabic, 9-11, 15-16 French.

39. While for their part, the Muᶜtazilah rejected not only the notions of causality and of substance as composed of "form" and "matter", but the notions of universal being and essence as well, the terms for which concepts are missing entirely from the vocabulary of Abū al-Hudhayl, for example. Other terms, such as those for generation and corruption, are used differently than when employed by the philosophers. Cf. Richard Frank, *The Metaphysics of Created Being According to Abū l-Hudhayl al-ᶜAllāf* (Istanbul, 1966), pp. 8, 16.

40. Cf. Frank, ibid., pp. 5-7, for a recent evaluation of the priority of faith to reason as valued in the *Kalām.* See also H. Nyberg's characterization of the Muᶜtazilah as heavily oriented towards apologetics and polemics, as well as Koranic inspired speculation (*The Encyclopaedia of Islam,* 3: 790).

41. See p. 23 above, and n. 7 there.

42. Cf. AR I: 375, and see Walzer, "New Studies", op. cit., p. 186.

43. Cf. "New Studies", op. cit., p. 185.

44. Cf. below, FP 113.11, and see n. there.

45. See above, pp. 18,19.

46. Al-Kindī elsewhere clearly accepts Aristotle's *hylē.* At FP 111.1,2 matter (*al-hayūlā*) is said to be a "substratum for affection" (موضوعة للانفعال, similarly defined in *On Definitions,* AR I: 166); and "nature" is there viewed as "the primary cause of everything which moves and rests" (and see below, notes to 111.1,2). Cf. also al-Kindī's description of matter

in relation to substance, genus and form, in the *Liber de quinque essentiis*, ed. Nagy, op. cit., pp. 30-33, AR II: 12-18.

47. Cf. AR I: 244-47. The "Treatise on Unity by Exegesis" is apparently referred to by al-Yāqūt in Ibn ᶜAbd Rabbihi's *Kitāb al-ᶜIqd al-Farīd*, ed. A. Amin *et al.* (Cairo, 1940) II: 382, 383 (a reference for which I am indebted to Professor Franz Rosenthal). Al-Kindī is there reported to have expressed himself, in the ninth chapter *(fann)* of the "*Tawḥīd*", in a manner which makes him appear as a typical Muᶜtazilite. Thus he is said to have written that God rules the world by that combination of transcendence and immanence known as *qaḍā*ᵓ and *qadar*, each thing being given its due, produced—*maᶜlūl*—by the most perfect (*al-tamām*) means. Objects are created *(khalaqa, abdaᶜa)* and do not diverge from their Divinely appointed states. Not everything, however, is necessary in this creation, for part of God's will is to bless certain of His creatures with freedom of choice and action.

Without minimizing the similarity of this view to that held by many Muᶜtazilites, it may be pointed out that al-Kindī could have fairly easily translated these remarks, particularly those concerning necessary and free actions, into Aristotelian terms; though proper evaluation of this passage must await the discovery of the entire treatise, or at least a considerable portion of it.

48. رسالة الكندي في الفاعل الحق الأول التام والفاعل الناقص الذي هو بالمجاز ; cf. AR I: 182-184.

49. كتاب الكندي في الابانة عن العلة الفاعلة القريبة للكون والفساد , AR I: 219, 226-237.

50. Cf. FP below, 132.3 ff., and see n. to 132.8 there.

51. Cf. Davidson, op. cit., pp. 370, 385; and see also his article, "Arguments from the Concept of Particularization in Arabic Philosophy", *Philosophy East and West XVII* (1968): 300-302.

52. Al-Kindī we know wrote a specific refutation of the atomistic view (cf. *Fihrist*, ed. Flügel, p. 259, and see Pines, op. cit., p. 94, and Walzer, op. cit., p. 184). Not all the Muᶜtazilah, of course, held to an atomistic physics, though alternative views were similarly based on a discrete structure of being. Cf. al-Ashᶜarī's *Maqālāt*, op. cit., pp. 281, 303 ff., 321, 395. While al-Kindī's minimization of the significance of potential existence leads him to an attitude towards actual beings which similarly emphasizes their ultimately discrete, and not continuous, nature, there is nothing in al-Kindī even remotely resembling the *Muᶜtazilah* denial of causality and substitution of "habitual" occurrences with their "entailment" *(tawallud)* of action and thought. Cf. ibid., pp. 408, and al-Khayyāṭ, op. cit., p. 122; and see, for a discussion of the various *Muᶜtazilah* formulations of physical and quasi-physical principles, Majid Fakhry, *Islamic Occasionalism* (London, 1958), pp. 26 ff.; Pines, op. cit., pp. 3 ff., 27 ff.; Van Ess, op. cit., pp. 211 ff., 289 ff.; Frank, op. cit., pp. 13 ff., 39 ff.; and H. Wolfson, "Muᶜammar's Theory of Maᶜna", *Arabic and Islamic Studies in Honor of H.A.R. Gibb* (Leiden, 1965), pp. 682-683.

53. Cf. above, chapter one of the introduction, n. 2. It is worth noting that most of al-Kindī's "polemical" writings are separated by the bibliographers from his other, more strictly scientific and philosophical treatises (cf. the *Fihrist*, op. cit., I: 259; Flügel, *Al-Kindī*, pp. 30 German, 46, 47 Arabic; Atiyeh, op. cit., pp. 191-193), probably following in this al-Kindī's own distinction. The term translated "polemical", *jadalī*, has also been called "dialectical", and it is a term with which the *Kalām* type of reasoning has been identified; cf. Gardet and Anawati, op. cit., p. 358. Judging by the titles of the treatises listed as كتبه الجدلية, al-Kindī did indeed discuss under this heading both *Muʿtazilah*-type religious and physical themes; except that in the latter category he clearly attacks notions held by many of the *Muʿtazilah* concerning the discontinuous motion of bodies and the existence of atoms.

54. Cf. Yaḥyā ben ʿAdī's excerpts from al-Kindī's "Refutation of the Christians" (مقالة في الرد على النصارى), in Yaḥyā's rebuttal, edited and translated into French by A.Périer as "Un Traité de Yaḥyā Ben ʿAdī : Défense du Dogme de la Trinité Contre les Objections d'Al-Kindī", *Revue de l'Orient Chrétien*, 3d ser. II (1920), 3-21 (French translation reprinted in Périer's *Petits Traités Apologétiques de Yaḥyā ben ʿAdī* [Paris, 1920], pp. 118-128). It appears that in his treatise al-Kindī argued, in a manner similar to his technique in chapter three of *FP*, that the concept of an eternal Trinity of one substance, though of three persons, is incompatible with each of the predicables outlined in the *Isagoge*. Instead, however, of drawing the conclusion that the Trinity, like the True One of *FP*, is a unique kind of unity, al-Kindī believes the argument shows the logical meaninglessness of the concept. He buttressed the argument, moreover, with an inquiry into the mathematical as well as logical senses of the term "one" (for which compare chap. 4 of *FP*), from which he deduces that the Trinity fits no acknowledged sense of the term. These contentions, however fallacious Yaḥyā may find them, have the merit of addressing the issue philosophically. Compare this, for example, with Jāḥiẓ's slanderous attack on Christians and Christianity in his contemporary polemic, الرد على النصارى, edited by J. Finkel, *Three Essays of Abū Othmān ʿAmr Ibn Baḥr al-Jāḥiẓ* (Cairo, 1926), pp. 10-38; discussed by Finkel and partially translated into English as "A Risāla of al-Jāḥiẓ", *JAOS* 47 (1927) : 311-334.

55. Cf. above, p. 5, n. 10. Al-Kindī's leading followers, al-Sarakhsī and Isaac Israeli, are also highly versatile learned types who cannot be identified readily, through their own writings at least, with any particular sectarian interest in their communities (cf. Franz Rosenthal, *Aḥmad B. Aṭ-Ṭayyib As-Saraḫsī* [New Haven, 1943], p. 35; Altmann and Stern, *Isaac Israeli*, pp. xi-xxiii).

56. Cf. above, p. 5, and see n. 12 there.

57. Cf. above, p. 5 f., and n. 9 there.

58. Cf. below, *FP* 103.1-104.7 and see nn. there.

59. Al-Kindī's punishment in the time of al-Mutawakkil, as that of the eminent Christian translator Ḥunayn ibn Isḥāq (for whom cf. Max

Meyerhof, "New Light on Ḥunain ibn Isḥāq and His Period", *Isis* VIII [1926] : 689), is apparently due more to personal court intrigue and a general animus to philosophical and scientific inquiry, than to any particular identification with the *Muᶜtazilah.* Al-Kindī's disciple al-Sarakhsī was even more the victim of internecine factionalism in ᶜAbbāsid society: falling out of favor with the caliph al-Muᶜtaḍid, al-Sarakhsī was removed from his high position at court, imprisoned and beaten, succumbing apparently to this treatment in A.D. 899. While opinions differ, al-Sarakhsī was ostensibly persecuted by the anti-Muᶜtazilite regime for his unorthodox opinions; though he receives no sympathy either from Ibn al-Munajjim, an allegedly Muᶜtazilite poet (cf. Rosenthal, op. cit., pp. 25 ff., and see p. 37 there, n. 117).

PART II

Text and Commentary

p. 97 *IN THE NAME OF GOD THE MERCIFUL*
THE COMPASSIONATE
MY SUCCESS IS IN GOD ALONE

Al-Kindī's Book, for al-Mu'taṣim Billāh

On First Philosophy

/May God grant you long life, O son[1] of the highest of princes and of the (strongest) bonds of bliss; of those who, whoever holds fast to their guidance is happy in the abode of this life and the abode of eternity; and may He adorn you with all the accoutrements of virtue and cleanse you from all the dirtiness of vice.

Indeed, the human art which is highest in degree and most noble in rank is the art of philosophy, the definition of which is knowledge of the true nature of things, insofar as is possible for man. The aim of the philosopher is, as regards his knowledge, /to attain the truth, and as regards his action, to act truthfully; not that the activity is endless, for we abstain and the activity ceases, once we have reached[2] the truth.

We do not find the truth we are seeking without finding a cause; the cause of the existence and continuance of everything is the True One, in that each thing which has being has truth. The True One exists necessarily, and therefore[3] beings exist.

---

[1]Ms. يابن , as AH. AR يا ابن .
[2]AR انتهينا . Ms. بلغنا انتهينا with a line through بلغنا .
[3]Ms. اذا . AR إذن .

p. 98 /The noblest part of philosophy and the highest in rank is the First Philosophy, i.e., knowledge of the First Truth Who is the cause of all truth. Therefore it is necessary that the perfect and most noble philosopher will be the man who fully
p. 101 understands* /this most noble knowledge; for the knowledge of the cause is more noble than knowledge of the effect, since we have complete knowledge of every knowable only when we have obtained full knowledge of its cause.

Every cause will be either matter or form or agent, i.e., that from which motion begins; or final, i.e., that for the sake of which the thing is. /Scientific inquiries are four, as we have determined elsewhere in our philosophical treatises; either "whether", "what", "which", or "why". "Whether" is an investigation only of the existence (of something); "what" investigates the genus of every existent which has a genus; "which" investigates its specific difference; /"what" and "which" together investigate its species; and "why" its final cause, since it is an investigation of the absolute cause. It is evident that when we obtain full knowledge of its matter we thereby obtain full knowledge of its genus; and when we obtain full knowledge of its form we thereby obtain full knowledge of its species, knowledge of the specific difference being subsumed within knowledge of the species. When, therefore, we obtain full knowledge of its matter, form and final cause, we thereby obtain full knowledge of its definition, and the real nature of every defined object is in its definition.

/Knowledge of the first cause has truthfully been called "First Philosophy", since all the rest of philosophy is contained in its knowledge. The first cause is, therefore,[1] the first in nobility, the first in genus, the first in rank with respect to that the knowledge of which is most certain;[2] and the first in time, since it is the cause of time.

---

*The rest of pp. 98-100 in AR is devoted to editorial comment, which is not part of the text.

[1]Reading وإذا هي with the ms. AR وإذ هي.

[2]Reading الشيء الأيقن علميه . AR علمية. Cross in ms. above word suggests dissatisfaction with it.

p. 102 /The truth requires that we do not reproach anyone who is even one of the causes of even small and meagre benefits to us; how then shall we treat those who are (responsible for) many causes,[1] of large, real and serious benefits to us? Though deficient in some of the truth, they have been our kindred and associates in that they benefited us by the fruits of their thought, which have become our approaches and instruments, leading to much knowledge of that the real nature of which they fell short of obtaining. (We should be grateful) /particularly since it has been clear to us and to the distinguished philosophers before us who are not our co-linguists, that no man by the diligence of his quest has attained the truth, i.e., that which the truth deserves, nor have the (philosophers as a) whole comprehended it. Rather, each of them either has not attained any truth or has attained something small in relation to what the truth deserves. When, though, the little which each one of them who has acquired the truth is collected, something of great worth is assembled from this.

/It is proper that our gratitude be great to those who have contributed even a little of the truth, let alone to those who have contributed much truth, since they have shared with us the fruits of their thought and facilitated for us the true (yet) hidden inquiries, in that they benefited us by those premises which facilitated our approaches to the truth. If they had not lived, these true principles with which we have been educated towards the conclusions of our hidden inquiries would not have been assembled for us, even with intense research throughout our time. But indeed this has been assembled only in preceding past /ages, age after age, until this our time, accompanied by intensive research, necessary perseverance and love of toil in that. In the time of one man—even if his life span is extended, his research intensive, his speculation subtle and he is fond of perseverance—it is not possible to assemble as much as has been assembled, by similar efforts,—of intense research, subtle speculation and fondness for perseverance—over a period of time many times as long.

---

[1]Reading أكثر أسباب with AH. AR أكبر.

p. 103 /Aristotle, the most distinguished of the Greeks in philosophy, said: "We ought to be grateful to the fathers of those who have contributed any truth, since they were the cause of their existence; let alone (being grateful) to the sons; for the fathers are their cause, while they are the cause of our attaining the truth." How beautiful is that which he said in this matter! We ought not to be ashamed of appreciating the truth and of acquiring it wherever it comes from, /even if it comes from races distant and nations different from us. For the seeker of truth nothing takes precedence over the truth, and there is no disparagement of the truth, nor belittling either of him who speaks it or of him who conveys it. (The status of) no one is diminished by the truth; rather does the truth ennoble all.

It is well for us—being zealous for the perfection of our species, since the truth is to be found in this—to adhere in this book of ours to our practice in all our compositions of presenting the ancients' /complete statement on this subject according to the most direct approach and facile manner of the disciples of this approach; and completing that which they did not state completely, following the custom of the language and contemporary usage, and insofar as is possible for us. (This) in spite of the disadvantage affecting us in this of being restrained from (going into) an extended discussion (necessary) to solve difficult, ambiguous problems; (and) while being wary of the bad interpretation of many of those who are in our day acclaimed for speculation, (but) who are strangers to the truth even if they are enthroned undeservedly with the crowns of truth, because of their narrow understanding of /the methods of truth and their scant knowledge of what befits the august (scholar) as regards opinion and
p. 104 judgement in those /common usages which are all pervasive. (They are strangers to the truth) also due to the dirty envy which controls their animal souls and which, by darkening its veils, obscures their thought's perception from the light of truth; and due to their considering those with human virtue—in attainment of which they are deficient, being on its remote fringes—as audacious, harmful opponents; thereby defending their spurious thrones which they installed /unde-

servedly for the purpose of gaining leadership and traffic in religion, though they are devoid of religion. For one who trades in something sells it, and he who sells something does not have it. Thus one who trades in religion does not have religion, and it is right that one who resists the acquisition of knowledge of the real nature of things and calls it unbelief be divested of (the offices of) religion.

The knowledge of the true nature of things includes knowledge of Divinity, unity and virtue, and a complete knowledge of everything useful, and of the way to it; and a distance from anything harmful, with precautions against it. It is the acquisition of /all this which the true messengers brought from God, great be His praise. For the true messengers, may God's blessings be upon them, brought but an affirmation of the Divinity of God alone, and an adherence to virtues, which are pleasing to Him; and the relinquishment of vices, which are contrary to virtues both in themselves and in their effects.[1]

p. 105 /Devotion to this precious possession is, therefore, required for possessors of the truth, and we must exert ourselves to the utmost in its pursuit, in view of that which we have said previously and that which we shall say now, namely, acquisition of this is required necessarily (even) according to the tongues of its adversaries; for they must say that acquisition of this is either necessary or not necessary. /If they say that it is necessary, then its pursuit is necessary for them. If, on the other hand, they say that it is not necessary, it is necessary for them to bring a cause of this, and to give a demonstration of this; and the presentation of cause and demonstration are part of the possession of knowledge of the real nature of things. Pursuit of this acquisition is, therefore, required by their own tongues, and devotion to it is necessary for them.

/We ask Him Who examines our inner thoughts and who knows our diligence in establishing the proof of His Divinity and the explanation of His Unity, and in defending (Him) against His opponents who disbelieve in that in Him by proofs

---

[1] وآثارها. Ms. as AR, وايثارها.

which subdue their disbelief and rip the veils[1] of their shameful actions that show the deficiencies of their vicious[2] creeds; (ask) that He encompass us, and anyone who follows our approach, within the fortress of His everlasting might, and that He clothe us with the garments of His protective armor and bestow upon us the assistance of the penetrating edge of His sword and the support of the /conquering might of His strength. (We ask this) so that He bring us to our ultimate intention of assisting the truth and supporting veracity; and so that he bring us to the level of those whose intentions He likes and whose actions He accepts and to whom He grants success and victory over His opponents who deny His grace and who deviate[3] from the truthful approach which is pleasing to Him.

Let us now complete this section, with the support of the Patron of virtues and Recipient of good works.

---

[1]Reading الهاتكة بسجوف with the ms. AR لسجوف .

[2]Reading مردئة . AR مردية .

[3]Reading والعاندين with the ms. AR والحائدين .

p. 106 *CHAPTER TWO OF THE FIRST PART OF*

On First Philosophy

Inasmuch as that which ought to precede has been given priority in the beginning of this book, let us follow this with what follows naturally, and say: /there are two kinds of human perceptions, one of which is nearer to us and further from nature. This is the perception of the senses which belong to us from the beginning of our development, and belong to the genus common to us and to many others, i.e. life, which is common to all animals. Our perceiving with the senses, through the contact of the sense with its sensible object, takes neither time nor effort, and it is unstable, due to the motion and fluctuation of that which we contact, its change in every case being through one of the kinds of /motion. Its quantity is differentiated by "more" or "less", "equal" and "unequal", while its quality is contrasted by "similar" and "dissimilar", "stronger" and "weaker". Thus it always occurs in continuous motion and uninterrupted change.

It (sc. sensory perception) is that the forms of which are established in the imagination, which conveys them to the memory; and it (sc. the sensible object) is represented and portrayed[1] in the soul of the living being. Though it has no stability in nature, being far from nature and therefore hidden, it is very near to the perceiver, in that his perception is due to the sense, with the /contact of the sense with it (sc. the
p. 107 sensible). /All sensibles, moreover, are always material, and the sensible is always body and in a body.

The other (perception) is nearer to nature and further from

---

[1]Reading فهو متمثّل ومتصوَّر . AR متمثّل ومتصوَّر .

us, being the perception of the intellect. It is right that there should be two kinds of perception, sensory perception and intellectual perception, since things are universal and particular. I mean by "universal" the genera of species and the species /of individuals; while I mean by "particular" the individuals of species. Particular, material individuals fall under the (perception of the) senses, whereas genera and species do not fall under the senses nor are they perceptible by sensory perception; they fall, rather, under (the perception of) one of the faculties of the perfect, i.e., human soul, that which is termed the human intellect.

As the senses perceive the individual objects, every sensible object represented in the soul /belongs to the faculty which employs the senses. Every specific concept and that which is above the species, however, is not represented by the soul, for all representation is sensible. Rather, the concepts are verified in the soul, validated and rendered certain through the veracity of the intellectual principles which are known necessarily, as that "it is" and "it is not" cannot both be true
p. 108 of the same thing without /its changing. This is a perception of the soul which is not sensory, is necessary, (and) does not require an intermediary; and an image will not be represented for it in the soul, since it has no image, having neither color, sound, taste, odor or anything palpable; it is, rather, a non-representational apprehension.

Everything which is material is representational, (and) the common sense will represent it in the soul, /while everything which is immaterial may exist with the material, as shape which is perceived through color; since it is the limit of the color, it happens that the shape is perceived by the visual sense, as it is the limit of that which is perceived by the visual sense.

It is sometimes believed that it (sc. the immaterial) is represented in the soul through the common sense's acquiring of it, and that the attachment which attaches to the colored image—as the attachment which attaches to color, which is the limit of that which is colored (sc., shape)—is represented in the human soul. (However) /the perception of the limit, which is the shape, is an intellectual perception which occurs

through sensation but is not really sensible. Therefore everything which has no matter and exists with matter is sometimes believed to be represented in the soul, but is it only thought of, not represented, with the sensible;[1] whereas whatever has no matter and is not joined to matter is not represented in the soul at all, and we do not think that it is a representation. We
109 acknowledge it only because /it is a necessity to affirm it, as when we say that outside the body of the universe there is neither void nor plenum i.e., neither emptiness nor body. This statement is not represented in the soul, for "neither void nor plenum" is something which the sense has not apprehended, and (it) is not attached to a sense so that it could have an image in the soul, or be believed to have an image. It is something which only the intellect necessarily perceives, in accordance with the premises /which will be set forth.

For we say, in the investigation of this, that the meaning of "void" is a place without any spatial object in it. Now "place" and "a spatial object" are in that type of relation where one does not precede the other, so that if there is place there is, necessarily, a spatial object, and if there is a spatial object there is, necessarily, place. It is therefore not possible for place to exist without a spatial object; whereas by "void" a place without a spatial object is meant. /It is not possible, therefore, for an absolute void to exist.

We then say: if the plenum is a body, then either the body of the universe is quantitatively infinite or quantitatively finite. It is impossible that there is a thing which is infinite in actuality, as we shall explain shortly, /and thus it is impossible for the body of the universe to be quantitatively infinite, and therefore there is no plenum beyond the body of the universe. For if there were a plenum beyond it, this plenum would
p. 110 be a body; and if, beyond this plenum, /there were a plenum, and beyond every plenum a plenum, there would be an infinite plenum, and this would necessitate (the existence of) a quantitatively infinite body, and would necessitate (the exis-

[1]Reading تعقل مع المحسوس لا تتمثل. AR تعقل من المحسوس لا بتمثل.

tence of) an actual infinity, whereas it is impossible for there to be an actual infinity.

Therefore[1] there is no plenum beyond the body of the universe, in that there is neither a body nor a void beyond it, as we have explained. /This (statement) is absolutely necessary, and it has no form in the soul, it being solely a necessary intellectual perception. Whoever examines things which are beyond nature, i.e., those which have no matter and are not joined to matter, will not find for them a representation in the soul, but will perceive them by means of intellectual inquiries.

Preserve—may God preserve you (with) all virtues and defend you from all vices—this /preface, that it may be your guide, leading to like truths; and a star, removing the darkness of ignorance and cloudiness of perplexity from the eye of your intellect.

By these two ways is the truth on the one hand easy and on the other hand difficult:[2] for one who seeks a representation of the intelligible in order to perceive it thereby, despite its clarity in the intellect, will be blind[3] to it as the eye of the bat is blind to acquiring (perception of) the individual objects which are distinct and clear to us in the rays of the sun.

For this reason many of the inquirers into things which are beyond nature have been confused, since they, as children (do), have used in the investigation of them their representation in the soul, corresponding to their customary practices for the sense. Instruction is easy only in customary things, the proof of this being the speed of those who learn from sermons and epistles, or from poetry or stories—that is, whatever is a narrative—as they are used to the narrative and legends from the beginning of their development.

(Many of the inquirers have been confused) also in physical

---

[1]Ms. فاذا . AR فاذن .

[2]Ms. عسرا . AR عسيرا .

[3]Reading عشى , as AH. AR عمى .

p. 111 things, whenever[1] they have used /mathematical investigation, for this is suitable only in what has no matter; for matter is a substratum for affection, and it moves, and nature is the primary cause of everything which moves and rests. Therefore every physical thing is material and hence it is not possible for mathematical investigation to be used in the perception of physical things, since it is the property of that which has no matter. Since, then, mathematics is such that /its investigation[2] concerns the non-physical, whoever uses it in the investigation of physical objects has left[3] and is devoid of the truth.

Therefore it is incumbent upon everyone inquiring into any science to inquire firstly what is the cause of what falls under that science. If we inquire what is the cause of the natural dispositions, which are the cause of physical things, we find, as we have said in "The Principles of Physics", that it is the cause of all motion. Therefore the physical is everything which moves, /and hence the science of physical objects is the science of everything which moves. Thus that which is beyond the physical objects does not move. For it is not possible that something should be the cause of its own generation, as we shall explain shortly. Thus[4] the cause of motion is not motion nor the cause of that which moves something moving, and therefore what is beyond physical objects is not one of the moving objects; hence it has been explained that the knowledge of what is beyond physical objects is knowledge of what does not move.

We ought not to seek[5] an apodictical perception in the apprehension of every pursuit. For not every /intellectual pursuit is found through demonstration, since not everything

---

[1]Reading إذا with the ms., against AR's emendation to إذ .

[2]Ms. فالفحص بها . AR في الفحص به .

[3]Reading حاد with the ms., rejecting AR's emendation حار . AR 2, 3, 4, and 5 of p. 111 correspond, in the Notes section, to nn. 3, 4, 5, and 2.

[4]Ms. فاذا . AR فاذن .

[5]Reading نطلب , as AH. AR يطلب .

p. 112 has a demonstration, demonstration /being of some things (only); nor does a demonstration have a demonstration, for this would be without end. If there would be a demonstration for every demonstration, then there would never be perception of anything; for that which does not end in knowledge of its principles is not knowable; and it would not be knowledge at all. Thus, if we desired to know what is man, he being that which is living, speaking and mortal, and we did not know what is "living", "speaking" and "mortal," then we would not /know what is man.

Similarly, we should not[1] seek probable arguments in mathematical sciences, but rather demonstrative; for should we use probability in the science of mathematics, our comprehension of it would be conjectural and not scientific. Similarly, every distinctive inquiry has a particular perception different from the perception of another. Therefore many of those inquiring into distinctive things err—some proceeding /in accord with a pursuit of probability, some proceeding in accord with parables, some proceeding in accord with historical witness, some proceeding in accord with sensation, and some proceeding in accord with demonstration—when they are unable to distinguish between the pursuits.

There are some, moreover, who want the use of (all of) this in finding their pursuit, either due to failing to know the methods of the pursuits or due to a passion for increasing the methods of truth. We ought, however, to aim at what is required for each pursuit, and not pursue /probability in the science of mathematics, nor sensation or exemplification in the science of the metaphysical; nor conceptual generalizations in the principles of the science of the physical; nor demonstration in rhetoric, nor demonstration in the principles of demonstration. Surely if we observe these conditions, the pursuits which are intended will become easy for us; but if we disobey this, we will miss the objectives of our pursuits, and the perception of our intended objects will become difficult.

Inasmuch as these admonitions have now preceded, we

[1] ينبغي أن لا, following AR in emending the ms. to include لا.

ought to set forth beforehand the canons[1] the employment of which we require /in this craft, and we accordingly say:
p. 113 /The eternal is that which must never have been a non-existent being, the eternal having no existential "before" to its being; the eternal's subsistence is not due to another; the eternal has no cause; the eternal has neither subject nor predicate, nor agent nor reason, i.e., that for the sake of which it is—for there are no causes other than the ones which have been previously stated. /The eternal has no genus, for if it has a genus, then it is species, a species being composed of its genus, which is common to it and to others, and of a specific difference which does not exist in others. It (sc. species), moreover, has a subject, viz., the genus which receives its form and the form of others; and a predicate, viz., the form particular to it and not to others. It (sc. the eternal) therefore has a subject and predicate. It has, however, already been explained that the eternal has neither subject nor predicate, and this (contradiction) is an impossible absurdity; the eternal then, /has no genus.

The eternal does not perish, perishing being but the changing of the predicate, not of the primary substratum; as for the primary substratum, which is being, it does not change, for the perishing of a perishable object does not involve the being of its being. Now every change is into its nearest contrary only, i.e., that which is with it in one genus, as heat which changes with cold—for we don't consider opposition like that of heat with aridity, or with /sweetness or with length, or anything like that—and related contraries comprise one genus.
p. 114 /A perishable object therefore has a genus, and if the eternal is corruptible, it has a genus. However, it has no genus, this is an impossible contradiction, and therefore it is impossible for the eternal to perish.

Motion is change, and the eternal does not move, for it neither changes nor removes from deficiency to perfection. Locomotion is a kind of motion, and the eternal does not

[1]Reading القوانين, as AH. AR الفوايد (for الفوائد ?).

remove[1] to perfection, since it does not move. /Now the perfect object is that which has[2] a fixed state, whereby it excels; while the deficient object is that which has no fixed state, whereby it may excel. The eternal cannot be deficient, for it cannot remove to a state whereby it may excel, since it cannot ever move to (a state) more excellent, nor to (a state) more deficient, than it; the eternal is, therefore, of necessity perfect.

Now, inasmuch as a body has genus and species, while the eternal has no genus, a body is not[3] eternal; /and let us now say that it is not possible, either for an eternal body or for other objects which have quantity or quality, to be infinite in actuality, infinity being only in potentiality.

I say, moreover, that among the true first premises which are thought with no mediation are: all bodies of which one is not greater than the other are equal; equal bodies are those where the dimensions between their limits are equal in actuality and potentiality; that which is finite is not infinite; /when a body is added to one of equal bodies it becomes the greatest of them, and greater than what it had been before that body was added to it; whenever two bodies of finite magnitude are joined, the body which comes to be from both of them is of finite magnitude, this being necessary in (the case of) every magnitude as well as in (the case of) every object which possesses magnitude; the smaller of every two generically related things is inferior to the larger, or inferior to a portion of it.
p. 115 /Now, if there is an infinite body, then whenever a body of finite magnitude is separated from it, that which remains of it will either be a finite magnitude or an infinite magnitude.

If that which remains of it is a finite magnitude, then whenever that finite magnitude which is separated from it is added to it, the body which comes to be from them both together is a finite magnitude; though that which comes to be from them both is /that which was infinite before something

[1] لا ينتقل, following AR in emending the manuscript's ينتقص . The error may have occurred by a scribal omission, as لا ينتق[ل من النق]ص .

[2] الذي له , following AR and AH in striking ليست .

[3] ليس or ليس هو , as AR, in lacuna of ms.

was separated from it. It is thus finite and infinite, and this is an impossible contradiction.

If the remainder is an infinite magnitude, then whenever that which was taken from it is added to it, it will either be greater than or equal to what it was before the addition.

If it is greater than it was, then that which has infinity will be greater than that which has infinity,[1] /the smaller of two things being inferior to the greater, or inferior to a portion of it, and therefore the smaller of two bodies which have infinity being inferior to the greater of them or inferior to a portion of it—if the smaller body is inferior to the greater, then it most certainly is inferior to a portion of it—and thus the smaller of the two is equal to a portion of the greater. Now two equal things are those whose similarity is that the dimensions between their limits are the same, and therefore the two things /possess limits—for "equal" bodies which are not similar are those (in) which one part[2] is numbered the same, though (as a whole) they differ in abundance or quality or both, they (too) being finite—and thus the smaller infinite object is finite, and this is an impossible contradiction, and one of them is not greater than the other.

p. 116 /If it is not greater than that which it was[3] before it was added to, a body having been added to a body and not having increased anything, and the whole of this is equal to it alone—it alone being a part of it—and to its (own) part, which two (parts) join, then the part is like the all, (and) this is an impossible contradiction.

/It has now been explained that it is impossible for a body to have infinity, and in this manner it has been explained that any quantitative thing cannot have infinity in actuality. Now time is quantitative, and it is impossible that time have infinity in actuality, time having a finite beginning.

---

[1] مما لا نهاية له, following AR in adding له, on the basis of its repeated usage (cf. this same sentence and 115.1 above); compare also UG, 202.22.

[2] جزء, as at AR I: 203.3. Ms. as AR جرم.

[3] مما كان, following AR in adding كان. Cf. above, 115.9, and compare UG 203.6.

Things predicated of a finite object are also, of necessity, finite. /Every predicate of a body, whether quantity, place, motion or time—that which is segmented through motion—and the sum of everything which is predicated of a body in actuality, is also finite, since the body is finite. Therefore, the body of the universe is finite, and so is everything inferior predicated of it.

As it is possible through the imagination for something to be continually added to the body of the universe, if we imagine something greater than it, then continually something greater than that—there being no limit to addition as a /possibility—the body of the universe is potentially infinite, since potentiality is nothing other than the possibility that the thing said to be in potentiality will occur. Everything, moreover, within that which has infinity in potentiality also potentially has infinity, including motion and time. That which has[1] infinity exists only in potentiality, whereas in actuality it is impossible for something to have infinity, for (reasons)
p. 117 which we have given previously, /and this is necessary.[2]

It has thus been shown that it is impossible for time in actuality to have infinity. Time is the time, i.e., duration, of the body of the universe. If time is finite, then the being[3] of (this) body is finite, since time is not an (independent) existent. /Nor is there any body without time, as time is but the number of motion, i.e., it is a duration counted by motion. If there is motion, there is time; and if there were not motion, there would not be time.

Motion is the motion of a body only:

If there is a body, there is motion, and otherwise there would not be motion. Motion is some change: the change of place, (either) of the parts of a body and its center, or of all the parts of the body only, is local motion; the change of place, to which the body is brought by its /limits, either in

[1]Reading فان الذي as UG 203.19, instead of the ms. فاذ الذي .

[2]Reading و إن ذلك as UG 204.1, and as there concluding the paragraph. AR begins the next paragraph (117.1) with these words, reading with the ms. و إذ ذلك.

[3]أنية . AR إنية .

nearness to or farness from its center, is increase and decrease; the change only of its predicate qualities is alteration; and the change of its substance is generation and corruption. Every change is a counting of the number of the duration of the body, all change belonging to that which is temporal.

If, therefore, there is motion, there is of necessity a body, while if there is a body, then there must of necessity either be motion or not be motion.

/If there is a body and there was no motion, then either there would be no motion at all, or it would not be, though it would be possible for it to be. If there were no motion at all, then motion would not be an existent. However, since body exists, motion is an existent,[1] and this is an impossible
p. 118 contradiction /and it is not possible for there to be no motion at all, if a body exists. If furthermore, when there is an existing body,[2] it is possible that there is existing motion, then motion necessarily exists in some bodies, for that which is possible is that which exists in some possessors of its substance; as the (art of) writing which may be affirmed[3] as a possibility for Muḥammad, though it is not /in him in actuality, since it does exist in some human substance, i.e., in another man. Motion, therefore, necessarily exists in some bodies, and exists in the simple body, existing necessarily in the simple body; accordingly body exists and motion exists.

Now it has been said that there may not be motion when a body exists. Accordingly, /there will be motion when body exists, and there will not be motion when body[4] exists, and this is an absurdity and an impossible contradiction, and it is not possible for there to be body and not motion; thus, when there is a body there is motion necessarily.

It is sometimes assumed that it is possible for the body of the universe to have been at rest originally, having the possi-

---

[1] إذ الجرم موجودة وهي موجودة ; emending the ms. و إذ الجرم موجود هي موجودة .

[2] Ms. جرما موجودا . AR, as AH, جرم موجودا .

[3] Reading موجبة as the ms., rejecting AR's emendation of موجودة .

[4] الجرم . Printer's error in AR, الجرم الجرم .

bility /to move, and then to have moved. This opinion, however, is false of necessity: for if the body of the universe was at rest originally and then moved, then (either) the body of the universe would have to be a generation from nothing or eternal.

If it is a generation from nothing, the coming to be of being from nothing being generation, then its becoming is motion in accordance with our previous classification[1] of motion,
p. 119 (viz.) that generation is one of the species of motion. /If, then, body is not prior (to motion, motion) is (of) its essence[2] and therefore the generation of a body can never precede motion. It was said, however, to have been originally without motion: Thus it was, and no motion existed, and it was not, and no motion existed, and this is an impossible contradiction and it is impossible, if a body is a generation from nothing, /for it to be prior to motion.

If, on the other hand, the body (of the universe) is eternal, having rested and then moved, it having had the possibility to move, then the body of the universe, which is eternal, will have moved from actual rest to actual movement, whereas that which is eternal does not move, as we have explained previously. The body of the universe is then moving and not moving, and this is an impossible contradiction and it is not possible for the /body of the universe to be eternal, resting in actuality, and then to have moved into movement in actuality.

Motion, therefore, exists in the body of the universe, which, accordingly, is never prior to motion. Thus if there is motion there is, necessarily, a body, while if there is a body there is, necessarily, motion.

It has been explained previously that time is not prior to motion; nor, of necessity, is time prior to body, /since there is no time other than through motion, and since there is no body unless there is motion and no motion unless there is

---

[1]Reading صنفنا with the ms., rejecting AR's emendation of وصفنا.

[2]Emending the ms. to read وإذا لم يسبق الجرم الحركة كانت الحركة من ذاته. AR's emendation فاذا لم يسبق الجرم الكون كان الكون ذاته. In its corrupt state the ms. has فاذا لم يسبق الجرم كان ذاته.

body. Nor does body exist without duration, since duration is that in which its being is, i.e., that in which there is that which it is; and there is no duration of body unless there is motion, since body always occurs with motion, as has been explained. The duration of the body, which is always a concomitant of the body, is counted by the motion of the body, which is (also) always a concomitant of the body. Body, therefore, is never prior to time; /and thus body, motion and time are never prior to one another.

p. 120 It has, in accordance with this,[1] already been explained that it is impossible for time to have infinity, since it is impossible for quantity or something which has quantity to have infinity in actuality. All time is therefore finite in actuality, and since body is not prior to time, it is not possible for the body of the universe, due to its being, to have infinity. The being of the body of the universe is thus necessarily finite, and it is impossible for the body of the universe /to be eternal.

We shall, moreover, show this by means of another account —after it has been explained by what we have said— which shall add to the skill of the investigators of this approach in their penetration (of it). We therefore say:

Composition and combination are part of change, for they are a joining and organizing of things. A body is a long, wide, deep substance, i.e., it possesses three dimensions. It is composed of the substance which is its genus, and of the long, wide and deep which is its specific difference; and it is that which is composed of /matter and form. Composition is the change of a state which itself is not a composition; composition is motion, and if there was no motion, there would not be composition. Body is, therefore, composite, and if there was not motion there would not be body, and body and motion thus are not prior to one another.

/Through motion there is time, since motion is change; change is the number of the duration of that which changes, and motion is a counting of the duration of that which changes. Time is a duration counted by motion, and every body

[1]Reading فاذا , as the ms. (for فاذ إن ?). AR فاذن .

has duration, as we said previously, viz., that in which there is being, i.e., that in which there is that which it is. Body is not prior to motion, as we have explained. Nor is body prior to duration, which is counted by motion. /Body, motion and time are therefore not prior to one another in being, and they occur simultaneously in being. Thus if time is finite in actuality, then, necessarily, the being of a body is finite in actuality,
p. 121 if /composition and harmonious arrangement are a kind of change, though if composition and harmonious arrangement were not a kind of change,[1] this conclusion would not be necessary.

Let us now explain in another way that it is not possible for time to have infinity in actuality, either in the past or future. We say:

/Before every temporal segment there is (another) segment, until we reach a temporal segment before which there is no segment, i.e., a segmented duration before which there is no segmented duration. It cannot be otherwise—if it were possible, and after every segment of time there was a segment, infinitely, then we would never reach a given time—for the duration from past infinity /to this given time would be equal to the duration from this given time regressing in times to infinity; and if (the duration) from infinity to a definite time was known, then (the duration) from this known time to temporal infinity would be known, and then the infinite is finite, and this is an impossible contradiction.

/Furthermore, if a definite time cannot be reached until a time before it is reached, nor that before it until a time before it is reached, and so to infinity; and the infinite can neither be traversed nor brought to an end; then the temporally infinite
p. 122 can never be traversed so as to /reach a definite time. However its termination at a definite time exists, and time is not an infinite segment, but rather is finite necessarily, and therefore the duration of body is not infinite, and it is not possible for body to be without duration. Thus the being of a body does

[1]Reading تبدلا ما with the ms. AR omits ما .

not have infinity; the being of a body is, rather, finite, and it is impossible for body to be eternal.

/It is (also) not possible for future time to have infinity in actuality: for if it is impossible for (the duration from) past time to a definite time to have infinity, as we have said previously; and times are consecutive, one time after another time, then whenever a time is added to a finite, definite time, the sum of the definite time and its addition is definite. If, however, the sum was not definite, then something quantitatively definite would have been added to something (else) quantitatively definite, with something quantitatively infinite assembled by them.

/Time is a continuous quantity, i.e., it has a division common to its past and future. Its common division is the present, which is the last limit of past time and the first limit of future time. Every definite time has two limits: a first limit and last limit. If two definite times are continuous through one limit common to them both, then the remaining limit of each one of them is definite and /knowable. It has, however, been said that the sum of the two times will be indefinite;[1] it will then be both not limited by any termini and limited by termini, and this is an impossible contradiction. It is thus impossible, if a definite time is added to a definite time, for the sum to be indefinite; and whenever a definite time is added to a definite time, all of it is definitely limited, to its last (segment). It is, therefore, impossible for future time to have /infinity in actuality, and let us now complete this second section.

[1] لا محدودة, emending the ms. المحدودة, which AR alters to محدودة.

p. 123 *THE THIRD CHAPTER OF THE FIRST PART*

An investigation whether it is or is not possible for a thing to be the cause of the generation of its essence, shall now follow the previous (discussion). We say that it is not possible for a thing to be the cause of the generation of its essence. /I mean by "the generation of its essence" its becoming a being, either from something or from nothing—generation usually being predicated, in other places, of that which comes to be particularly from something—for it is necessary that (a thing) will be either an existent and its essence non-existent; or it will be a non-existent and its essence existent; or it will be a non-existent and its essence non-existent; or it will be an existent and its essence existent.

If (a thing) were a non-existent, and its essence were non-existent, then it would be nothing, and its essence would be nothing; and nothing is neither a cause /nor an effect, for both cause and effect are predicated only of something which has existence of some sort. Therefore[1] it is not the cause of the generation of its essence, since it is no cause whatsoever. However, it has been said that it is the cause of the generation of its essence, and this is an impossible contradiction. Thus it is not possible for a thing to be the cause of the generation of its essence, if it is a non-existent and its essence is non-existent.

A similar thing would occur if a thing were a non-existent and its essence were existent. For, again, since it is a non-existent, it would be nothing, /and nothing is neither cause nor effect, as we stated previously. Therefore it would not be the cause of the generation of its essence, As, however, it has been said previously that it is the cause of the generation of

---

[1]Ms. إذا . AR إذن .

its essence, this is an impossible contradiction, and it is not possible for a thing to be the cause of the generation of its essence if it is a non-existent and its essence is existent.

It would appear from this discussion also that the essence of a thing is different from the thing, because things which are different from each other are those of which it is possible
p. 124 /for something to occur to one and not to the other. If, therefore, it occurred to a thing to be non-existent, and to its essence to be existent, then its essence would not be it, though the essence of every thing is that thing. Thus a thing would not be itself and it would be itself, and this is also an impossible contradiction.

A similar thing would occur if a thing were an existent and its essence were non-existent; I mean that its essence would be different from it, since that /which occurs to it would be different from that which occurs to its essence. It follows necessarily from this, as we stated previously, that a thing would be itself, and it would not be itself, this also being an impossible contradiction. It is not therefore possible for a thing to be an existent and its essence not existent.

A similar thing would occur if a thing were an existent and its essence were an existent, and it were the cause of the generation of its essence. For if it were the cause of its essence which it generates, then its essence would be its effect, and the cause is different from the effect. It therefore would /occur that it would be the cause of its essence, while its essence would be its effect. Its essence would then not be it, though the essence of every thing is that thing. Thus it follows necessarily from this kind (of argument) that it would not be itself, and that it would be itself, and this is an impossible contradiction; and it is not possible, assuming a thing were the cause of the generation of its essence, for it to be an existent and its essence an existent.

Similarly, if it were a non-existent and its essence were non-existent, and it were the cause of its essence, /and its essence were also the effect; it would occur that a thing would be itself and it would not be itself. It is not, therefore, possible for a thing to be the cause of the generation of its essence, and this is what we wanted to clarify.

Inasmuch as this has been explained, we now say that every utterance must be either meaningful or not meaningful. That which has no meaning has nothing of which inquiry can be made; philosophy is concerned only with that of which inquiry can be made, and it is not in the nature of philosophy to employ that of which no inquiry can be made.

/That which has meaning must be either a universal or particular thing. Philosophy does not inquire into particular things, for particular things are not limited, and that which
p. 125 cannot be limited, knowledge cannot comprehend. /Philosophy is a knowing of things, its knowledge being of their true natures. It therefore inquires only into universal, delimited things the true natures of which knowledge can comprehend perfectly.

Universal general things must be either essential or non-essential. I mean by "essential" that which establishes the essence of a thing, namely, that by the existence of which the being of a thing is sustained /and maintained, and by the absence of which the destruction and corruption of a thing occurs: as "life", by which the sustenance and maintenance of a living being occurs, and by the absence of which the corruption and destruction of a living being occurs. Life is essential in a living being, and the essential is that which is called substantial, for in it the substance of a thing is sustained.

The substantial must be either a collective or distinct thing. The collective refers to many things, each one receiving its definition and name from it, and it /thereby combines them. That which refers to many things, in that each one receives its name and definition from it, can refer either to individuals —as "man", which refers to each one of the units of man, i.e., every human individual, and this is what is called "species", since it is one species referring to every one of these individuals—/or it can refer to many species, as "animal", which refers to every species of animal, such as man and horse; and this is called "genus", since with one genus it refers to every one of these species.

As for the substantially distinct entity, it is that which distinguishes between the definitions of things; as the "rational", which differentiates some living beings from others.

This is called a "specific difference", due to its differentiating some things from others.

/As for that which is not essential, it is contrary to that
p. 126 just described, and it is that the sustaining /and maintaining of which is due to something which is its substrate; while its absence is due to the absence of that thing which is its substrate. Therefore that which is non-essential is in a substance which is its substrate and is not substantial. On the contrary, it is an accident of the substance and is therefore called *accidens*.

That which is in a substance must be either in one thing, peculiar to it and proper to it alone, as laughter in /man and the braying in a donkey, this being called a "property", as it is proper to one thing; or it will be in many things, common to them all, as the whiteness in paper and cotton. This is called a "common accident" as it is, in that it happens to many things.

Thus, every utterance has a meaning which will be either a genus, species, individual, specific difference, property or /common accident. Together two things are comprised by these, substance and *accidens*. The genus, species, individual and specific difference are substantial; while the property and common accident belong to *accidens;* and every utterance will be either universal or particular, and either collective or separate.

Let us now, since the foregoing has been discussed, speak of the number of ways "one" is predicated. We say that "one" is predicated of /every continuum, and also of that which does not receive multiplicity. It is thus predicated of diverse kinds, including the genus, species, individual, specific difference, property and common accident, and of all which has already been discussed previously.

The individual will be either natural, as an animal or
p. 127 plant, and what is similar to them; /or artificial, as a house and what is similar to it. A house is continuous by nature, though its composition is continuous by accident, viz., through the (builder's) technique. It is one by nature and its composition one by technique in that the composition can become one

only through an accidental unity, while the house itself is one through a natural unity.

"One" is predicated also of "all" and "part", "whole" and /"some". Now it may be thought that there is no difference between "all" and "whole", in that "all" is predicated of things having both similar and dissimilar parts; as in our remark "all the water", water being one of the things having similar parts; and "all the body", body being composed of bone, flesh and what follows these of (those organs) having different parts; and "all the tribe", /these being different individuals. However (there is a difference between "all" and "whole"): "whole" is not predicated of things having similar parts—one does not say, "the whole water"—for "whole" is predicated equally of an aggregate heterogeneous by accident or in some sense unified though each diverse element is sustained by its own nature without the other, the name "totality" referring to it.

"All", however, is predicated of every unified thing in whatever way the unity comes about. Therefore one does not say "the whole water", since water is not made of /heterogeneous things each of which is sustained by its own nature. One says, rather, "all the water", since it is a unified thing.

In a similar way there is a distinction between "part" and
p. 128 "some". /"Part" is predicated of that which enumerates and divides the "all" into equal amounts; while "some" is predicated of that which does not enumerate the all (uniformly) but divides and apportions it into unequal amounts; there is no equality among its "somes" (i.e., the portions which comprise the all), for then it would be a "part" of it.

"One" is, then, predicated of each one of the predicables, and that which derives from the predicables, whether /genus, species, individual, specific difference, property, common accident, all or part, whole or some. As for the genus, it is in each one of its species, since it is predicated of each one of its species univocally, while the species is in each one of its individuals, since it is predicated of each one of /its individuals univocally. The individual is one only by convention, in that every individual is divisible and therefore not one by essence. The individual unity is separable from individuals, and is not essentially one; the unity which is in it, by convention, is not in it essentially. It therefore does not have true unity. /That which is not essential in the true nature of a thing is in it in an accidental manner, and that which occurs accidentally to a thing does so in virtue of something other than itself. That which occurs accidentally is an effect in that in which the accident occurs. An effect is a relative term, the effect coming from an agent. Thus unity in the individual is, necessarily, an effect of an agent.

The species is that which is predicated of a multiplicity of individually different things. It is multiple, inasmuch as it has many individuals; and also as a composite of things, inasmuch as it is composed of genus and specific difference;
p. 129 /as the human species, which is composed of living, reasoning and mortal (elements). That which is a species through its essence is multiple, by way of its individuals and its being composite. The unity it has is by convention only, in a non-essential sense, and therefore its unity is not true unity. Unity is thus in the species in an accidental manner, and that which occurs accidentally to a thing does so in virtue of something other than itself. The accident is an effect in that in which the accident occurs. An effect is /a relative term, the effect coming from an agent, and unity in the species is also, necessarily, an effect coming from an agent.

The genus, which is that which is predicated of many things different in species, indicates the essence of a thing. The genus is multiple, inasmuch as it has many species, each one of its species being both an independent substance and many individuals; and each one of its individuals being also an independent substance. The genus is multiple in this way, and its unity is also not true unity. Unity is therefore in it in an /accidental manner, and that which occurs accidentally to a thing does so in virtue of something other than itself. The accident is an effect in that in which the accident occurs. An effect is a relative term, an effect coming from an agent, and unity in the genus also is, necessarily, an effect coming from an agent.

The specific difference, which is that which is predicated of a multiplicity of things different in species, indicates the

quality of a thing. It is predicated of each one of the individuals of those species of which a specific difference, which indicates a quality, is predicated. It is multiple by way of the species and the individuals of which the /species are predicated. Its unity is also not true unity, and it is therefore in it in an accidental manner, and that which occurs acciden-
p. 130 tally /to a thing does so in virtue of something other than itself. The accident is an effect in that in which the accident occurs. An effect is a relative term, an effect coming from an agent, and unity in the specific difference is also an effect coming from an agent.

The property, which is that which is predicated of one species and of each one of its individuals, indicates the existence of a thing. It is not an (essential) part (of a thing), in that it is indicative of its existence. It is multiple, because it exists /in many individuals and because it has motion and motion is divisible. Its unity is also not true unity, and it exists therefore in an accidental manner, and that which occurs accidentally to a thing does so in virtue of something other than itself. The accident is an effect in that in which the accident occurs. An effect is a relative term, an effect coming from an agent, and unity in the property is also an effect coming from an agent.

The common accident is also predicated of many individuals. It is multiple since it exists in /many individuals. It will be either a quantity, and be subject to augmentation and diminution, being divisible; or it will be a quality, and be subject to the similar and dissimilar and the stronger and weaker. (The common accident thus) is subject to divergent things and is multiple, and its unity is also not true unity. It is therefore in it in an accidental manner, and that which occurs accidentally, as we stated previously, is an effect coming from an agent. Thus the unity in a common accident is also an effect coming from an agent.

The all which is predicated of the predicables has portions, in that every one of the predicables is /a portion of it. The all which is predicated of one predicable also has portions, in that every predicable is a genus, and every genus has many species, and every species has individuals. The all is thus multiple, in that it has many divisions. Its unity is also not true unity. It is therefore in it in an accidental manner, and it therefore comes from an agent, as we said previously, concerning that which occurs in an accidental manner.

Similarly, the whole is also multiple, in that it is predicated
p. 131 of a multiplicity of combined things. /Its unity also is not true unity, and it is in it in an accidental manner. It is therefore in it as an effect coming from an agent, as we said previously.

A part will be either substantial or accidental, and a substantial part will have either similar or dissimilar parts. /That which has similar parts is like water,[1] the part of which is completely water. All water is subject to division into parts, and a part of water, as it is completely water, is multiple. That which does not have similar parts, i.e., that which has different parts, is like the living body which is (made) of flesh, skin, nerves, arteries, veins, ligaments, peritoneum, diaphragms, bone, brain, blood, bile, phlegm, and everything, which[2] does not have similar (parts), from which the living body is composed; /and every one (of the parts) of the living body we have mentioned is subject to division into parts and is also multiple.

The accidental part inheres within the substantial part; as, for example, length, breadth and depth in the flesh, bone and other parts of a living body; and color, taste and other accidents, each of which is divisible through the divisions of the substantial (parts). The accidental part has, therefore,[3] parts, and is also multiple, and the unity in the part is also not true unity.

/Both the naturally and accidentally continuous thing have parts: as a house, whose natural continuity is its shape, having sides; and whose accidental continuity, i.e., the artificial, is achieved through combination of its component parts, like its stone and mortar and (other) parts of its structure. It is also multiple, and its unity is not true unity.

---

[1]Ms. فكلما . AR كالماء .

[2]Ms. والّتي . AR الّتي .

[3]Ms. إذا . AR إذن .

The one may also be predicated in relation to other things, among some of the things which we have previously mentioned; /as the mile, for one says, "one mile", since it is an "all" of (many) stadia as well as a part of a parasang, and in that it is continuous and combined, because its stadia are continuous and combined, and it is the whole of its stadia; and in that it
p. 132 is separate from /other miles, i.e., those whose totality is a parasang. The unity in this is also not true unity, but rather it is an accident.

The unity in everything which we have defined is not true unity. Rather it is in each one of them in that they are not divided as they are found. The unity in them is in an accidental manner, and that which occurs accidentally to something /is not part of its essence. That which occurs accidentally to a thing comes from something else, and therefore an accident in something which receives an accident is an acquisition from something else, and is an acquisition from a donating agent. It is an effect in that which receives the accident. An effect comes from an agent, in that the effect and the agent are in a relation where one does not precede the other.

Furthermore, everything which is an accident in one thing is essential in another thing, in that everything which exists in one thing by accident is in another thing by essence. /Since we have explained that the unity in all these things is by accident, no part being by essence but rather by accident, the unity which occurs in a thing by accident is acquired from that in which it occurs by essence.

Thus here is a one, true, of necessity uncaused unity, and let us explain this by more (evidence) than what has preceded. We say:

/The nature of every predicate, in that which takes a predicate, i.e., everything which the sense perceives and the essence of which the intellect comprehends, must be either one or multiple, or one and multiple together, or some of these
p. 133 things one and not multiple at all, /while others[1] are multiple and not one at all.

---

[1]Reading وبعضها with the ms., rejecting AR's emendation of أو بعضها.

If the nature of every predicate were multiplicity only, then participation in one state or one concept would not occur. This occurrence exists, however, i.e., the participation in one state or one concept, /and therefore unity exists with multiplicity. We had, however, postulated that unity is not an existent; (therefore) unity is an existent non-existent, and this is an impossible contradiction.

If, furthermore, every predicate were multiplicity only, then there would be nothing contrary to multiplicity, in that the contrary of multiplicity is unity, and there would be no contrary. If there were no contrary to predicates, they would both /occur and not occur, in that participation in one state or one concept does occur. This however, is an impossible contradiction, and it is not possible unless there is unity.

If, furthermore, there were multiplicity only without unity, then it would be dissimilar, in that similarity has one thing which is common to all its members, with which they are similar to one another, and there is no "one" with multiplicity, as we have postulated. Thus there would be no one thing common to all its members, and they would be both dissimilar *and* similar, through the absence of unity. They would thus be a similar dissimilarity /together, and this is an impossible contradiction, and it is not possible for there to be multiplicity unless there is unity.

If, moreover, there were multiplicity only without unity, they would be moving, in that if there were no unity, there would not be a state which remains one, and if there were not a state which remains one, there would be no resting, as the quiescent is that which occurs in a state which remains one, unchanging and non-transferable. If there were no resting, there would be no quiescent state; and if there were no quiescent state, it would be moving.

/If there were multiplicity only, they would also be non-moving, in that motion is alteration, either in place, quantity, quality or substance. Every alteration is to something else,
p. 134 /and that which is other than multiplicity is unity. If there were no unity, there would be no alteration of multiplicity. We had postulated that unity does not exist, and thus an alteration of multiplicity would not exist, and motion would

not exist. Thus, if there were multiplicity only without unity, they would be without both motion and rest, as we stated previously. This is an impossible contradiction, and it is not possible (for there to be multiplicity) unless there is unity. /If, also, there were multiplicity only, then it would have to be (composed) either of individual members or not of individual members at all. If it were (composed) of individual members, then either the individual multiple entities would be units or would not be units. If they were not units, and the multiplicity were not reduced to units at all, then the multiplicity would be infinite.

/If a section were separated from the infinite, all of that which is divisible being greater than that section which is separated from it, then the separate part would be either finite in multiplicity or infinite in multiplicity. If the section were finite in multiplicity, an infinity of multiplicity already having been postulated, then it would be both finite in multiplicity and infinite in multiplicity, and this is an impossible contradiction.

/If the section were infinite in multiplicity, it being smaller than that which is divisible, then infinity[1] would be greater than infinity, and this is an impossible contradiction, as we stated previously.

There would thus be individual multiple entities being units necessarily, and unity would exist, in that every individual is one; and then there would be multiplicity only and non-multiplicity /only, in that unity would exist with it, and this is an impossible contradiction.

If, furthermore, multiplicity were not (composed) of individual members, and there were no multiplicity at all, in that the concept of multiplicity is a combination of individuals, it would then be non-multiple and multiple together, and this is an impossible contradiction, and it is not possible (for there to be multiplicity) unless there is unity.

p. 135 /If, also, there were multiplicity only without unity, then each one of the individual multiple entities would be unlim-

[1]Ms. ولا متناه . AR فلا متناه .

ited, in that the limit is a "one" which falls under the concept of "one", and if there were no one in multiplicity, there would be nothing limited. If there were nothing limited, then there would be no limit. However, the individual multiple entities are limited, and they would thus be limited and non-limited, and this is an impossible contradiction, and it is not possible for unity not to /occur.

If, also there were multiplicity only without unity, then multiplicity would not be subject to number, in that the principles of number are units, as number is a multiplicity composed of units, and the disparity between multiple entities is due to the units. If there were no units there would be no number, and if there were multiplicity without units, it would not be /numbered. Now multiplicity is numbered, and units occur with multiplicity. However, we had postulated that units do not occur with it, and this is an impossible contradiction, and it is not possible for units[1] not to occur.

If, also, there were multiplicity only without "one", there would be no knowledge, in that knowledge impresses /the description[2] of that which is known into the soul of the knower as one state, for if it were not impressed as one state in which the soul of the knower and the description of that which is known are united, there would be no knowledge. Knowledge does exist, however, and the one state does exist, and unity exists. We had, however, postulated that unity does not exist; this is therefore an impossible contradiction, and it is not possible for unity not to occur.

If, also, there were multiplicity only without "one", and every[3] predicate either will be a thing /or will not be a thing, and if it is a thing it is one, then unity would exist with multiplicity. We had, however, postulated that it is multiplicity only. It would then be multiplicity only without unity and multiplicity and unity, and this is an impossible contradiction.

---

[1] آحاد, though ms., followed by AR (and cf. his n. 3) has آحاداً.

[2] Reading ترسم رسم المعروف (المعرفة). AR .... برسم ، رسم .. .

[3] Ms. وكل as AH. AR فكل.

p. 136 /If the predicate were not a thing, then multiplicity would not be composed from it, nor, moroever, would it be multiplicity. It had, however, been postulated that it is multiplicity, and it would then be multiplicity non-multiplicity; this is an impossible contradiction, and it is not possible for unity not to occur.

It shall now be clear that it is not possible for some things to be multiplicity only, in that it is /not possible for any thing to be multiplicity only, since it will either be a thing or it will not be a thing, and if it is a thing it is one, and if it is not a thing, it is not multiplicity. It is, however, multiplicity, and this is an impossible contradiction, and it is not possible for some things to be multiplicity only without unity.

/It is, moreover, clear from all these investigations that it is not possible for things to be multiplicity without unity, in that it is impossible for (even) some things to be multiplicity without unity.

Similarly, we shall now explain[1] that it is not possible for unity to occur without multiplicity, nor (may even) some things have unity without multiplicity.

We say: if there were unity only without multiplicity contrariety would not exist, for that which is /other than a contrary is (another) contrary, and otherness occurs in at least two things. Two things are multiple, and if there were no multiplicity there would be no contrariety, and if there is contrariety, there is multiplicity. Now contrariety exists, and therefore multiplicity exists; we had, however, postulated that multiplicity is not an existent. It would thus be an existent non-existent, and this is an impossible contradiction, and it is not possible for multiplicity not to occur.

If, furthermore, there were unity only without multiplicity, then there would be no exception, in that exception only occurs either to one or to more than one thing, disregarding
p. 137 things which are not excepted. /Thus, if there were exception, then multiplicity would exist. Now the exception and that which is excepted do exist, and multiplicity thus exists. We

[1]Reading نبين . AR تبين .

had, however, postulated that multiplicity does not exist. It would thus be an existent non-existent, and this is an impossible contradiction and it is not possible for multiplicity not to occur.

/If, also, there were unity only without multiplicity, then there would be no differentiation, in that two things are the least in which there is differentiation, and two and more things are a multiplicity. If there were no multiplicity, there would be no differentiation, and if there were differentiation, then multiplicity would exist. Now differentiation exists, and therefore multiplicity exists. We had, however,[1] postulated that multiplicity is not an existent.[2] It would thus be an existent non-existent; this[3] is an impossible contradiction, /and it is not possible for multiplicity not to occur.

If, furthermore, there were unity only without multiplicity, there would be neither agreement nor disagreement, conjunction nor separation. For two things are the least in which agreement, separation, disagreement and conjunction will occur, and two things are a multiplicity. If there were no multiplicity there would be neither agreement nor disagreement. /Now agreement and disagreement exist, and therefore multiplicity exists. We had, however, postulated that it did not exist. It would thus be an existent non-existent, and this is an impossible contradiction, (and it is not possible) for multiplicity not to occur.

If, furthermore, there were unity only without multiplicity, then it would have neither beginning, middle nor end; for this will not occur except in something which has parts,
p. 138 /and the one has neither beginning, middle nor end. However, the beginning, middle and end exist, and thus an object which has parts exists. Every object which has parts is more than one, and multiplicity exists in it. We had, however, postulated that multiplicity does not exist, and this is an impossible contradiction, and it is not possible for /multiplicity not to occur.

---

[1] وقد . AR وأيضا قد . Ms. originally as AR, but line through أيضا .
[2] Ms. ليست بموجودة , as AH. AR ليست موجودة .
[3] Ms. هذا . AR وهذا .

If, furthermore, there were unity only without multiplicity, then there would be no figure, for figures are made either from arcs or chords, or from that which is composed of arcs and chords, either from arched or chorded surfaces or from that which is composed of them both.

The circle and sphere have a center and circumference, and that which is composed of arcs or arched (surfaces), or /(of) a line or linear (surfaces), or of arcs or an arched (surface together), or of a chord and chorded (surface) together, has angles and sides, and has multiplicity. If figures exist, then multiplicity exists. But the figure exists, so multiplicity exists. We had, however, postulated that multiplicity does not exist. Multiplicity is thus an existent non-existent, and this is an impossible contradiction, /and it is not possible for multiplicity not to occur.

If, furthermore, there were unity only without multiplicity, then it would neither move nor rest; for that which moves moves by transference, either to another place, quantity, quality or substance; and this is multiplicity.

That which rests rests in a place. Moreover, some of its parts are within others. Place and parts /are each multiple, for parts are more numerous than a part, and a place has a high and low, front and rear, right and left.

Place by nature necessitates the existence of multiplicity, in that place is other than that which occupies a place; and place (necessitates the existence of) that which occupies a
p. 139 place, /(as) increase necessitates the existence of that which increases, decrease necessitates the existence of that which decreases, alteration necessitates the existence of that which is altered, generation necessitates the existence of that which comes to be, and corruption necessitates the existence of that which perishes. The negation as well of all these necessitates the existence of multiplicity. For (the terms) "not generating", "not perishing", "not increasing", "not dwindling", and "not altering", are subject and predicates: a subject of which negation is predicated for delimited things.

/If there is rest there is multiplicity, and if there were not multiplicity there would be neither rest nor motion. Now rest and motion exist. Therefore multiplicity exists. We had, however, postulated that multiplicity does not exist. It would therefore be an existent non-existent. This is an impossible contradiction, and it is not possible for there not to be multiplicity.

It shall now[1] be clear that it is not possible for even one thing not to have multiplicity in it; /for if multiplicity were not in it, it would be neither moving nor at rest, and nothing sensible or attached to the sensible can avoid the character of motion and rest. It is thus not possible for there to be one thing without multiplicity in it.

If, furthermore, there were unity only without multiplicity, there would be neither part nor all, for the all is an association of parts, and two is the least of that which may be associated, and two things are a multiplicity. If there were no /multiplicity there would be no all, and if there were no all, there would be no part, for the all and the part are related things in which each side is rendered necessary through the necessity of the other; or, either of them[2] being invalid, it invalidates, through its invalidity, the other. There would, then, be neither all nor part to things; however things are all and part. All and part would then each be an existent non-existent, and this is an impossible contradiction.

p. 140 /Furthermore, the part is one, so that if there is a part, there is unity; if, also, there is a part, there is an all, and if there were no part, there would be no all. If there were neither part nor all, there would not be anything. If there were nothing, then there would be no sensible or intelligible object at all, nor any unity in anything sensible or intelligible. /If, therefore, there were no part, and no unity, and, since there would be no part there would be no all, then there would be no unity (whatsoever). We had, however, postulated that there is unity. Unity would thus be an existent non-existent, and this is also an impossible contradiction, and it is not possible for there not to be multiplicity.

---

[1]Ms. وهنالك, as AH. AR وهناك.

[2]Reading أو أيهما, as the ms., rejecting AR's emendation to وأيهما.

It has now been clarified that it is not possible for any of the things which we have mentioned to have unity without multiplicity, for it would be neither part nor all, as we have stated previously. /Thus it is clear, from all these investigations, that it is not possible for there to be multiplicity without unity in any of the things which we have mentioned; while it is clear from some of these investigations that it is definitely not possible for there to be anything having unity without multiplicity in it.

It is thus evident that it is not possible for there to be unity only without multiplicity, or multiplicity only without unity, and nothing which we have mentioned can be free either from multiplicity or from unity.[1] /It is necessary, therefore, that the things which we have mentioned be multiple and one.

As, moreover, it is now clear that the nature of things has unity and multiplicity, the unity must be either separate from multiplicity or associated with it. If the unity were separate from the multiplicity, it would be necessary that there accompany unity only, that contradiction which accompanies the unity which we have mentioned previously; and (there would accompany) that which is multiplicity only, /that (contradiction) which accompanies the multiplicity which we have mentioned previously.

p. 141 /It remains, therefore, that unity is associated with multiplicity, i.e., associated with it in all of the sensible objects and whatever is attached to the sensible objects, in that whatever contains multiplicity contains unity, and whatever contains unity, contains multiplicity.

As it has now been explained that the association of multiplicity and unity is in every sensible object and that which is attached to /the sensible object, this association has to come about either through chance, i.e., coincidence, without a cause; or through a cause. If the association were through chance, then there would be a separation (between multiplicity and unity) which would be accompanied by the same

---

[1]Ms. ولا من وحدة, as AH. AR ولا وحدة.

absurdities which accompanied our investigations[1] concerning the existence of multiplicity without unity. How, furthermore, would it be possible for multiplicity and unity, being separate, to be together? Multiplicity is but the /multiplicity of units, i.e., a collection of single entities, and unity necessarily occurs with multiplicity and nothing else can be possible.

Moreover, assuming unity and multiplicity were separate things,[2] how would it be possible for there to be unity only, since they are two things, and two things are a multiplicity? It is thus not possible that these two things be like this (separate).

We may, then, return to that which is "caused" by the chance of separation, and (declare that) this is (composed of) two (things),[3] /and there accompanies it that contradiction which we mentioned previously. It is, therefore, not possible for there to be (things) which are separate which then come together by chance, i.e., without a cause.

It therefore remains that their association[4] is caused, from the beginning of the object's coming to be.

As it has now been explained that the association is caused, the cause must be either from itself, or the association will have another cause other than itself, outside of and separate from it. /If the cause of its association were from itself, then it would be part of it, and that part would be prior to the rest. As by itself the cause precedes the effect, as we have explained in our writing concerning the separation (between cause and effect), that (cause) which is one of the sensibles or is attached
p. 142 to the sensibles, i.e., to all things, /would be either unity only, multiplicity only, or an association of multiplicity with unity. Now there would be attached to unity only (and to multiplicity only) that which is attached to the multiplicity and unity which we have previously studied. /The unity and

---

[1]Reading الأبحاث اذ بحثنا , as AH. AR الاتحاد إذ بحثنا .

[2]Ms. as AH, إذ هما وهما متباينان . AR إذ هما متباينان , without noting necessary emendation.

[3]Reading إثنان . AR إنيات .

[4]Ms. اشتراكهما . AR اشتراكها .

multiplicity (of the cause) ought, then, to be associated, and their association may be either by chance or through a cause, either of their own or from something else.

There would be attached to an association by chance that contradiction which we have previously mentioned; while in an association caused by themselves, the association would be a cause (caused) by itself, this going on indefinitely, and there would be a cause of a cause and a cause of a cause until infinity. It has, however, been explained that it is impossible for there to be an actual infinite thing, and it is thus not possible that /the association of unity and multiplicity is caused by themselves.

Nothing remains, therefore, other than that their association have another cause, other than themselves, more illustrious, more noble and prior to them, since in essence the cause precedes the effect, as we have mentioned previously in the writings in which we have spoken of the separation (of cause and effect). This cause is not associated with them, for, as we stated previously, being associated requires, in the associated things, a cause outside of the associated things. If this were the case, however, causes would go on indefinitely, and an infinity /of causes is impossible, as we stated previously, since it is not possible for there to be an actual thing having infinity.

Furthermore, (the cause of the association of multiplicity and unity) is not in that which is generic to them, for things which are in one genus are not prior to one another in essence; as, for example, the human and equine (species) in the genus of living being, neither one preceding the other in essence. The cause, however, does precede the effect in essence, and therefore the cause of the association of multiplicity and unity with multiple-single things is not in the genus.

/As it is not with them in genus, it is not with them in (having) one likeness: for that which is alike occurs in one genus and in one species, as redness and redness, one figure and another figure, and similar things. Thus the cause of the association of multiplicity and unity with multiple-single things is neither in genus, nor likeness nor resemblance, but rather it is the cause of the association's generation and consolidation, more elevated, more noble and prior to it.

p. 143 /It has thus been explained that all things have a first cause, which does not have their genus, and has no resemblance nor likeness nor association with them. It is, rather, superior,[1] more noble and prior to them, being the cause of their generation and perdurance.

This cause must be either single or multiple: if it were multiple, then it would contain unity, since multiplicity is but a collection of units, and it would /then be multiplicity and unity together. The cause of multiplicity and unity would therefore be unity and multiplicity, and a thing would then[2] be the cause of itself. The cause, however, is other than the effect, and consequently a thing would be other than its essence. This is therefore an impossible contradiction, and the first cause is neither multiple nor multiple and single. Nothing remains, therefore, other than that the cause be single only, in no way accompanied by multiplicity.

It has, then, been shown that the first cause is one, and that the one exists in caused things. /We have, furthermore, previously discussed the number of ways one is predicated of sensible things and of things attached to sensible objects. Therefore we ought to explain, in that which follows this part, in which way unity exists in caused things, what is true unity and what is unity metaphorically and not truly; and let us now conclude this part.

---

[1]Ms. اعلا . AR أعلى .
[2]Ms. إذا . AR إذن .

THE FOURTH CHAPTER OF THE FIRST PART

Let us now speak of the way in which unity exists in the categories, of that which is /truly one, and of that which is one metaphorically and not truly; and let us accordingly discuss first that which has to take precedence. We say:

The large and small, long and short, much and little are never predicated absolutely of anything, but, rather, relatively; for "large" is predicated only in relation to something which is smaller than it, and "small" in relation to something which is larger than it. Accordingly, "large" is predicated of
p. 144 a misfortune /when it is compared to a misfortune smaller than it, while "small" is predicated of a mountain when it is compared to another mountain larger than it.

If the large—as, similarly, the small—were predicated absolutely of those things of which the large is predicated, the infinite would have no existence whatsoever, either in actuality or in potentiality, since it would not be possible for /another thing to be larger than that of which largeness had been predicated absolutely. The absolutely large will then not have infinity either in actuality or in potentiality, for if another object were larger than it in actuality or in potentiality, it would not be an absolutely large object, since it would have become small when another would be larger than it. If this is not possible, then that which is larger than it will be smaller or equal to it, and this is /an impossible contradiction; thus nothing may be larger than the absolutely large object, either in actuality or in potentiality.

There would then exist a large (object) of which nothing is double, either[1] in actuality or in potentiality. Now doubling

---

[1]Ms. لا ضعف له لا بالفعل . AR لا ضعف له بالفعل .

something is multiplying its quantity by two, and multiplying
p. 145 a quantity by two exists, in actuality or /in potentiality. Thus multiplying the absolute large by two exists, in actuality or in potentiality, and therefore the absolute large has a double. The double is all of that which has the double, while that which has the double is half of the double. Half is part of the all, and that which is doubled is part of the double.

Thus the absolute large would be both all and part. Furthermore, if /double the absolute large were not larger than the absolute large, it would be equal or smaller than it. If it were equal to it, an ugly absurdity would occur, *viz.*, the all would be equal to the part; and this is an impossible contradiction. Similarly, if double the absolute large were smaller than the absolute large, the all would be smaller than the part, and this is even more absurd and ugly.

As the all is larger than the part, double the large which was considered as absolute /would be larger than the large which is considered as the absolute large. However by the "absolute large" is meant simply that than which nothing is larger, and therefore the absolute large would not be an absolute large. Either, then, there will be no (absolute) large whatsoever, or there will be a relatively large, since the large is not predicated other than absolutely or relatively.

p. 146 /If the absolute large were not large (absolutely), it would be an existent non-existent, and this is an impossible contradiction; while if the absolute large were the relatively large, absolute and relative would be synonymous terms for the same thing, *viz.*, that another thing is smaller than it; since it has been explained that there can never be a thing which does not have something larger than it, either in potentiality or in actuality.

/In this manner it may be explained that there cannot be an absolute small, and that the small also occurs only relatively.

While the large and small are predicated of all quantitative things, the long and short are predicated of all quantitative things which are continuous, and they are specific to the continuous and not to other kinds of quantity. /They also are predicated relatively only, and not as an absolute predicate, and the explanation of this is like that which we explained previously regarding the large and the small.

As for the little and the much, they are the property of discrete quantity. That which occurs to the large and small, long and short will occur to the much, in that it will not be predicated absolutely, but relatively, and the explanation of this lies in that which we have explained previously, the method being the same.

/It may be supposed, however, that the little may be predicated absolutely, it being supposed so because if the first number is two, and every number other than two is greater than two, two is then the least of the numbers, and two is then the absolute little, since it is in no way at all "much", as no number is less than it.

If one were a number, nothing would be less than one, and one would be the absolute little. /This supposition, however, is not true, for if we were to say that one is a number we suppose something ugly and most shameful which would attach to us due to this. For if one were a number, then it would be a certain quantity, and if one were a quantity, then the property of quantity would be attached to it and accompany it, i.e., it would be equal and non-equal.

p. 147 /Moreover, if the one were to have units, some equal to it and others not equal to it, then the one would be divisible, for the "smaller one" would be inferior to the "larger one" or inferior to a portion of it, and the "larger one" would therefore be a part and the one would be divisible. Now the one is not divisible, and its division would then be an existent non-existent, and this is an impossible contradiction. /The one is therefore not a number.

Do not, incidentally, infer from our remarks concerning "one" that the *hyle* of the one, i.e., the matter which exists with the (numeral) one, is one. This existent is not one, and the things which are composed in this way are numbered and are not number. As in our saying "five horses", the horses are numbered by five, a number having no matter, the matter being only in the horses. Do not, therefore, take our remarks concerning "one" to refer to /that which is unified by "one", but rather to unity itself, and unity is never divisible.

Now if "one" were a number and not quantitative, while the remaining numbers—i.e., two and more—were quantities, then "one" would not be subsumed in quantity, but would be subsumed in another category; and "one" and the remaining numbers would then be said to be numbers homonymously only and not naturally. "One", then, would not be a number naturally, but homonymously, since numbers are not /predicated other than in relation to "one" thing, as medical things to medicine and recoveries to the cure.

How, however, could it be possible for this supposition to be true, i.e., that if "one" were a number, then the property of quantity, which entails being equal and non-equal, would have to accompany it, so that the one would have units, some equal to it and others larger or smaller than it? For if this
p. 148 were to accompany the one, then it would also /accompany every number, i.e., that it would have a namesake equal to it, a namesake smaller than it, and a namesake larger than it, and the three would (each) have three, some equal to each, and others smaller or larger than each; and this would be necessary in every number. Now, if this is not necessary in (all) numbers, of which there is no doubt, then it is not necessary in oneness.

/Furthermore, if the meaning of our remark, "the property of number and all quantity entails being equal and non-equal", were that every number has a number like it and a number not like it, *viz.*, larger or smaller than it, then "two" would not be a number, since no number is smaller than it, but only larger. If, however, it were necessary that two be a number, since it has an equal, *viz.*, another two; and a non-equal, *viz.*, more than two; then it would be necessary for "one" to be a number, since it has an equal, *viz.*, another one; and a non-equal, *viz.*, more[1] than /it, i.e., two and more. "One" would then be a quantity, and "one" and the rest of the numbers would be subsumed in quantity; and since "one" would

[1]Reading the ms. أكثر, as AH, and paralleling the previous line. AR there أكثر, here أكبر.

not be a number homonymously[1] it would be (one) naturally.

"One", in addition, cannot avoid being either a number or not a number, and, if a number, then either even or odd; if even, then it would be divisible into two parts of like onenesses, and "one" is indivisible. It would then be indivisible and divisible, this being an /impossible contradiction. Moreover, if it had units in it, it would be composed of units; and it is (also) composed of itself, so that it would be one and units. "One", however, is one only, and not units, and it would thus (both) be units and not units, and this is also an impossible contradiction.

If the one cannot be even, then it is odd. The odd is that of which each of the two sections into which it is divided is not of like onenesses. "One" would then be (both) divisible (and) non-divisible, and units (and) non-units, and /this is
p. 149 an impossible contradiction, /and one, therefore, would not be a number.

However, this definition whereby the odd number has been defined may be considered as not necessary except after it is clarified that "one" is not a number. For otherwise, what prevents one who says "one is a number" from defining the odd number as the number which, if divided into two parts, its two parts would not be of like /onenesses? "One" would then belong to the odd number, since the odd number does not have to be divided necessarily.

Since it does not appear as a necessary consequence of this investigation that "one" is not a number, we then say:

The element of something from which the thing is constructed, i.e., from which the thing is composed, is not the thing (itself), as the articulated letters from which speech is composed are not themselves speech, since speech is a compound sound, a convention indicating something temporal, while a letter is a /natural sound, not a compound. Now if number is acknowledged by all to be compounded from units,

---

[1] الاسم (باشتباه). AR الأيس , n. 5 suggests possibility of بالاسم. Ms. «الاسر», apparently corrupt.

and one is the element of number and not a number; and one does not have an element from which it is composed, which would also be the element for that which is composed from the one; then the one would be number, its element being the element of everything acknowledged to be numbers, and it would then be possible for one to be a number.

It might, accordingly, be considered that one is the element of two, and two the element of three, since /two exists in three. Therefore it might be considered that since two, which is a number, is the element of three, therefore one, being the element of two, could be a number. This supposition, however, is not true, since two, though considered as an element of three, has an element, which is one; while one, though the element of two, has no element (itself). One is not composite, and is thus distinguishable from two in being simple; while two is a composite composed of the simple one. It is not, of
p. 150 course, possible for /some numbers to be simple, *viz.*, the element, meaning by simple not composed of anything; and some composed of this simple (element).

It may, however, be thought that this sort of thing is possible with the substance of a composed thing, i.e., (with) the body which is composed of two simple substances, *viz.*, matter and form; in that it has been said that /substance is threefold, two simple substances which are the matter and the form, (and) that which is composed from them, *viz.*, the formed matter, i.e., body; and it may be thought that it is also possible for number to have on the one hand something simple, *viz.*, the one from which the acknowledged number is composed; and, on the other hand, the acknowledged number which is composed from the simple one.

This supposition is not, however, true, in that the comparison is the reverse (of that which it has been represented as being): for the /first simple substances from which a body is composed are matter and form; and the body, being composed of the substances of matter and form, happens to be a substance, since it is (composed of) substances only. It is, however, a body in its own nature, i.e., composed of matter and dimensions which are its form; and it will not occur either to the matter alone, or to the dimension which is form alone to be a body, since (only) that which is composed of them both is a body.

/Similarly it does not follow that one, since it is the element of an acknowledged number, should be a number. It is, rather, because number is composed of units that it is a unit; as body, being composed of substances, is a substance. Moreover, as regards things from which (other) things are composed, these elements being parts of that which is composed from them, nothing precludes our giving the composite entities the names and definitions of the elements, i.e., their substantial and not accidental names, as "alive" in "alive things" and "substance" in "substances". /One, therefore, is an element of number and not at all number.

Since, therefore, it is clear that one is not a number, the
p. 151 definition said of number shall then encompass /number fully, *viz.*, that it is a magnitude (composed of) onenesses,[1] a totality of onenesses, and a collection of onenesses. Two is, then, the first number. When, however, two is set apart[2] in its nature, and nothing else is considered, then it is not small, in its nature. Hence smallness is attached to two only when it is related to that which is more than it, and therefore[3] it is small only because all numbers are more than it. Consequently /it is small only when related to the numbers, but when its nature is considered, then it is double the one, the sum of two ones, and composed of two ones. Now that which is composite has parts, and is the whole of its parts, the whole being greater than the part; consequently two is not small, in its nature.

Since neither big nor little, long nor short, many nor few are predicated absolutely, (but rather) relatively, each one of them is related /to another only in the same genus, and not in another genus. For example, magnitude, if it is (predicated) of body, can be related only to (magnitude of) another

---

[1] الوحدانيات, AR. Ms., requiring emendation, has الواحدانيات.

[2] Emending the ms. to أفرد, as AH. AR قيل. The ms. apparently has اقول with لا above the و (and not above the ق, as AR, note 2); the لا, however, being crossed out.

[3] Ms. فاذا. AR فاذن.

body, and not to (that of an), area, line, place, time, number, or (any other) predicate. For one does not say that a body is greater or less than an area, line, place, time, number or (any other) predicate, but rather than (another) body; /and similarly for any other magnitude, its being said to be greater or less than something not in its genus would not be a true statement.

An area, likewise, is not said to be greater or less than a line, place, time, number or (other) predicate, but rather than (another) area. Nor is a line greater or less than a place, time, number or (other) predicate, but rather than (another) line; nor is place greater or less than time, number, or (other) predicate, but rather than (another) /place; nor is time greater or less than number or (another) predicate, but rather than (another) time; nor is number greater or less than (another) predicate, but rather than (another) number; nor is a predicate greater or less than (any) one of the rest of the magnitudes, but rather than (another) predicate (of its kind).

p. 152 /Similarly, it cannot be truly said that a body is longer or shorter than an area, line, place, number or (any other) predicate, and if it were supposed that a body is longer or shorter than an area, line or place, it would be a false supposition. For, if it is supposed that the length of a body is longer or shorter than the length of an area, /line or place, and if the length of each one of them is, of the dimensions related to it, a single dimension, and the single dimension is line; then, from the greater length or shortness of a body, area, line or place we infer only that the line of one is longer than the line of the other, all these belonging to continuous quantity.

Time too belongs to continuous quantity, but, because time has no line, it is completely apparent /that[1] one may not say, "a body is longer or shorter than time". It is evident that length and shortness are not predicated, in those things[2] of which length and shortness are predicated, other than for

[1] أنه, rejecting AR's emendation of فانه.

[2] بما. Ms. apparently as AR لما, but see his n. 5.

that which is in a single genus, i.e., in body only, or area only, or place only, or time only; and, regarding number and predicate, length and shortness do not occur to them essentially, but are predicated of them by virtue of the time in which they occur. Thus, one says "a long number", i.e., (one which occurs) in a long time; and similarly, one says "a long predicate", i.e., (one which occurs) /in a long time, and neither predicate nor number bears the names "long" and "short" in its essence.

"Many" and "few" are likewise not predicated, in that of which they are predicated, *viz.*, in that of which number and predicate are predicated, other than in a single genus; for "a predicate is more or less than a number" would not be said to be a true statement, nor would "a number is more or less than a predicate"; but rather, "a number is more or less than (another) number," /and "a predicate is more or less than (another) predicate."

p. 153 /The foregoing having been clarified, the True One, then, cannot be related to (another) thing in its genus, even if it had a genus, before being related to the (other) thing in its genus. Consequently, the True One has no genus whatsoever. We have already stated that what has a genus is not eternal, and that the eternal has no genus. Consequently the True One is eternal, and in no way whatsoever ever becomes multiple; and the One should not be spoken of /in relation to something other than itself. It therefore is that which has no matter in which it is divisible, nor form composed of genus and species, that which is so being multiple by that of which it is composed; neither is it at all a quantity nor has it quantity, that which is so being also divisible, since every quantity or quantitative thing is subject to addition and diminuition, and that which is subject to diminuition is divisible, the divisible being multiple in a certain way. Multiplicity has been said to be in every one of the predicables and in that which is attached to them, /as regards the genus, species, individual, (specific) difference, property, common accident, all, part and whole; and similarly "one" is predicated of every one of these;[1] consequently the True One is not "one" of these.

Motion is in that which belongs to these, *viz.*, the body, which is formed matter, since motion is either a transfer from place to place, increase or diminuition, generation or corruption, /or alteration. Motion is multiple, since place is a quantity and is divisible, and that which exists in parts is divisible through the divisions of the place. It is thus multiple, and therefore local motion is multiple.

Increase and diminution are likewise multiple; the motion of the limits of that which increases and diminishes is divisible, since it is found in the division of the place between that which was the limit of the body before the increase and that which is the limit of the /body at the end of the increase; and similarly between that which was the limit of the body before the diminuition and that which is the limit at the end of the diminuition.

p. 154 /Similarly, as regards generation and corruption, (the period) from the beginning of generation and corruption to the end of generation and corruption is divisible, by the division of the time in which generation and corruption occur; and the motion of increase, diminution, generation and corruption is all divisible. Similarly an alteration /to the contrary[2] and an alteration towards completion are divisible, by the divisions of the time of the alteration.

All motions are then divisible, and are also unified, in that the wholeness of every motion is one, since unity is predicated of the undetermined whole; while the part is (also) one, since "one" is predicated of the undetermined part. Since consequently multiplicity exists in motion, the True One is not motion.

/As every thing perceived through the sense or intellect either exists, in itself or in our thought, as a natural existence;

---

[1] هذه (من), as paralleled in the following line. Ms. (unpointed) as AR, من بعده (possibly a scribal error of بعـ(ـده) for هـ(ـذه) ?).

[2] للضد , following AR's emendation of "سديد" of ms.

or, in our speaking or writing, as an accidental existence, so motion exists in the soul; i.e., the thought passes from certain forms of things to others and among various dispositions and passions which accompany the soul, such as anger[1], fear, rejoicing, sadness and similar things. Thoughts[2] are, therefore, multiple and (also) unified, since every multiplicity has a whole and a part, in that it is numbered. /These are the accidents of the soul, and it is multiple also and unified in this manner, and the True One is not soul.

The end result of thoughts, whenever they proceed along correct paths, is (directed) toward the intellect. Intellect is the species of things, since the species is intelligible, as well as that which is above them. Individual things, on the other hand, are sensible, meaning by "individual", particular things which do not give the things their names nor their
p. 155 definitions. /When, however, they are united with the soul they are intelligible. Through the union of species with it the soul is an intelligence in actuality, whereas before their union with it the soul was an intelligence in potentiality. Everything which belongs potentially to something can be brought to actuality only by another thing. That which brings something from potentiality to actuality is itself in actuality, and that which brings the soul, which is an intelligence in potentiality, to be an intelligence in actuality, i.e., (that) there are united with it the species /and genera, the universals of things, is the universals themselves. It is through their union with the soul that the soul intelligizes, i.e., that it has a particular intellect, i.e., that it has[3] universal things. As universal things emerge from potentiality to actuality in the soul, they are the acquired intellect of the soul which the soul had in potentiality; and they are the intellect in actuality which has brought the soul from potentiality to actuality. The universals are therefore multiple, as we have stated previously, and consequently the intellect is multiple.

---

[1] كالغضب . AR كلغضت .

[2] فالفِكَر , as AH. AR فالفِكْر .

[3] لها , as AH. AR بها .

/It may be thought that the intellect is the beginning of that which is multiple, and that it is united in a certain way, since it is a whole, as we stated previously, and unity is predicated of the whole. However, the true unity is not intellect.

Since in our speech there are synonymous names, as *shafrah* (a large knife) and *madyah* (a butcher's knife), which are synonyms because of the slaughtering iron (common to them), "one" is predicated of the synonymous, and *madyah* and *shafrah* are said to be one. This one is also multiple, in that its matter and that which is predicated of its matter is multiple; for the slaughtering iron which is the /matter of the synonymous, *viz*., the *madyah*, *shafrah* and *sikkin* (knife), is divisible into parts, and is multiple, and the names predicated of the slaughtering iron are also multiple. The True One is, therefore, not (identifiable by) synonymous names.

Moreover, since in our speech there are homonyms as the animal who is called "dog" and the star which is called "dog", they are both, therefore, said to be one in name, *viz*., "dog". The matter of this "dog", however, is multiple, *viz*., the animal and the star. Neither of these homonyms is a cause of the other, in that the /star is not a cause of the animal nor the animal a cause of the star. Some homonyms, however, are found to be the cause of others, as that which is written, pronounced and thought of, and the actual quiddity; for the writing, which is a substance, is indicative of the pronounced term, which is (also) a substance; and the pronounced term, which is a substance, is indicative of that which is thought, which is (also) a substance; and that which is thought, which
p. 156 is a substance, is indicative of the quiddity, /which is a substance. "One" is predicated of all of these, i.e., of the quiddity in its essence, and in thought, speech and writing. The quiddity in its essence is a cause of the quiddity in the thought, the quiddity in the thought a cause of the quiddity in the speech, and quiddity in the speech a cause of the quiddity in the writing. This kind of one is also multiple, since it is predicated of many (things), /so the True One is not one by way of homonomy.

Since "one" would be predicated of things whose matter is

one, but for their differing[1] in a certain way, either being active, passive, related (to something else), or having other kinds of differences; as the door and the bed whose matter is one, *viz.*, wood, or any matter from which things of different forms are made; so it may be said that the door and the bed are one, through (their) matter. They are also multiple by virtue of their matter, since their matter is /multiple and divisible into parts; and by virtue of their forms. Those things, likewise, which are one through the first matter, i.e., through possibility, are multiple by virtue of the matter, since it exists for many forms.

Things predicated of something to which something else is necessarily attached may also be said to be one through matter: corruption, for example, which is predicated of that which undergoes corruption, has generation attached to it, since corruption of that which undergoes corruption is generation for another (substance). Thus it may be said that that which undergoes generation is that which undergoes corruption through the matter, this being in actuality. /This too is multiple, however, since the matter belongs to a number of forms.

This kind of one, *viz.*, one through matter, may also be spoken of in potentiality for those things predicated of something and to which something else is attached; swelling, for example, which is predicated of that which is swelling, has contraction attached to it, for that which has swelling has contraction in potentiality. The swelling, contracting thing is said to be one, i.e., that which swells is that which contracts. This is also multiple by virtue of the matter, since the matter, /as regards the forms, *viz.*, the swelling and contracting, belongs to several (things). The True One, however, is never spoken of by way of matter, and is not predicated as one[2] by the kinds of one which are (one) through matter.

p. 157 /One, as has been stated previously, may be predicated of that which is indivisible. The indivisible is indivisible either

[1] Ms., as AH, تغاير . AR تتغاير .

[2] Ms., as AH, بواحد . AR واحد , and see his n. 6.

in actuality or in potentiality: the indivisible in actuality is either like that which is indivisible because of its hardness, as a diamond, i.e., it is divisible with difficulty—this having parts necessarily, since it is a body, and it is multiple—; or like that which is very small, (too small to be divided by) a dividing instrument. Such a thing is said to be indivisible, /since there is no instrument which can divide it. It has, however, parts, for it is a certain magnitude, since smallness is attached to it, and it is therefore multiple.

That is also said to be indivisible in actuality which, even if continually divided, would not leave its nature for another; rather, each of its divisions would bear its definition and its name. Take, for example, all the continuous magnitudes, i.e., body, area, line, place and time: a division of body is body, /a division of area is area, a division of line is line, a division of place is place and a division of time is time. All of these are not divisible in actuality nor in potentiality into another species, and each one of them is continually subject to division and multiplication into its own species.

Body is also multiple through its three dimensions and six limits, area through its two dimensions and four limits, and line through its (single) dimension and two limits. /Similarly place is multiple according to the dimensions of that which occupies the place and its limits; and likewise time is multiple through its limits, which are two instants of time which define its limits, similar to the definitions of points for the limits of the line. Likewise everything which has similar parts is said to be one, in that it is indivisible, i.e., each of its sections bears its definition and its name. It is also multiple in that it is indivisible, i.e., each (section) /is continually subject (to division).

A thing is also said to be indivisible, in actuality and in potentiality, when if divided, its essence is nullified. As, for example, the single man such as Muḥammad and Saᶜīd, and
p. 158 the single horse such as the untethered and the tethered, /and whatever is like this as regards every natural individual provided with a form, or accidental individual of this sort, or species, genus, specific difference, property or common accident; if divided it is not itself. This thing is, however, multiple

through that of which it is composed, and through its continual separability also. All of these, moreover, are said to be one because of their continuity also.

/That which is indivisible, in that it is not divisible into another species since it is not continuous, is also said to be one. A thing of this sort is said (to be one) in two ways: one is because it is not continuous and has neither a position nor a common (factor), as the numerically one. It is not a continuous thing, i.e., such that it would have dimensions and limits, being thereby continuous; it, rather, is not divisible and not separable. This is also multiple by virtue of its subjects which we enumerate, for it is the numerically one which is the measure of all /things. The other (way in which this non-continuous category is said to be one can be seen from the example of) articulated letters: they are not continuous and (have) no position, for the reasons whereby the numerically one is indivisible; but (the letter) is the measure of words.

That which is of this sort (i.e., indivisible) in that it is not divisible into another species since it has no part like it nor any likeness other than itself, is (also) said to be one, and it is also (possessed of a) common (factor). That which is like this is said (to be one) in two ways: one is that it has /positions; as, for example, the point of a line, which is its limit, has no part, in that it is the limit of one dimension, and the limit of a dimension is not a dimension. It is multiple, however, in its subjects, i.e., past and future times, to both of which it is common.

That which is indivisible by virtue of its whole is (also) said to be one. One speaks of "one *raṭl*" since if something were separated from the whole of the *raṭl*, the *raṭl* would be negated and it would not be a whole for one *raṭl*. /For this reason it is said that the circular line is more deserving of the (predicate) "one" than are other lines, since it is all of the definition, having neither deficiency nor excess but rather a
p. 159 perfect whole. That which is like this /is also multiple, through its separability. Lastly, (it is such that) for all of which one is predicated, the indivisible is more deserving of unity than are all the other kinds of one, and its unification is more intense.

It has thus been explained from what we have said that the one is predicated either *per se* or *per accidens*. As regards (the one) *per accidens*, it is like the kind which is predicated (either) by homonym, or by synonyms or (by) including many accidents together; /as our saying, "the writer and the orator are one", when they are predicated of one man or of mankind; or, "the man and the writer are one", and whatever is like this.

As regards (the one) *per se*, it includes the rest of what the one is predicated of—(*viz.*) of those things of which we have mentioned that they are said to be one, i.e., all those things of which the substance is one. Its first division may occur either through continuity, which is in the domain of matter, or through form, which is in the domain of species, or through the name, which is in the domain of both together, or through the genus, which is in /the domain of the first.

The one through continuity is that which is one through matter or through attachment. It is that which is said to be one by number or by figure. The one through form is that whose definition is one. The one through genus is that the definition of whose predicate is one. That through the name, i.e., that which is in it through analogy, is one; and the one through analogy is that being whose relations are the same, as medical things /all of which relate to medicine.

Of all kinds (of one) which we have mentioned, i.e., the one through number, then the one through form, then the one through genus and then the one through analogy, the latter follow the former and the former do not follow the latter. I mean by this that what is one through number is one through form, and what is one through form is one through genus, and what is one through genus is one through relation; but /what is one through relation is not one through genus, and what is one through genus is not one through form, and what is one through form is not one through number.

p. 160 /It is clear that the opposite of unity is multiplicity, and multiplicity, therefore[1], is predicated of every one of these kinds: multiplicity is thus predicated of something either because it is not continuous, being discrete, (or) because its matter is divisible into forms, or its forms into a genus, or

[1]Ms. إذا . AR إذن .

(its genus) into that which is related to it. It is, moreover, clear that existence is predicated of everything whose cause is one, and that existence is predicated for that /which the types of the one enumerate.

It has thus been explained that the True One is not one of the intelligible things, and is neither matter, genus, species, individual, specific difference, property, common accident, motion, soul, intellect, whole, part, all or some. It is also not one in relation to anything else, but is an absolute one, neither augmentable, /composed (nor) multiple. Nor is it one of the sort which we mentioned in which kinds (of one) exist, (of) all the kinds of one which we mentioned, and that which is attached to their names is not attached to it. Since the things which we have mentioned are more simple and yet[1] do not belong to it, i.e., are not predicated of it, (things which are) more multiple are not predicated of it either.

The True One, therefore, has neither matter, form, quantity, quality, or relation, is not described by any of the remaining intelligible things, and has neither genus, /specific difference, individual, property, common accident or movement; and it is not described by any of the things which are denied to be one in truth. It is, accordingly, pure and simple unity, i.e., (having) nothing other than unity, while every other one is multiple.

p. 161 Unity, therefore, when an /accident in all things, is not the True One, as we stated previously: the True One being the one *per se* which is never multiple in any way, or divisible in any kind (of divisibility), neither by way of its essence nor by way of something other than it, neither time, place, subject, predicate, all or part, and neither into substance nor into accident,[2] nor /ever by any kind of divisibility or multiplicity.

As for all the kinds of one other than the True One, when they occur in whatever they are, it is *per accidens*. The cause of an accident, for everything which is in something *per accidens*, is other than the thing in which the accident is; this

[1] فا. AR ما. Ms., apparently as AH, لما.

[2] ولا للجوهر ولا للعرض, as the ms., and AH (and AR n. 1).

thing is in it either *per accidens* or *per se*. It is impossible for things to be infinite in actuality. Consequently the first cause of unity in unified things is the True One which does not acquire unity from another, as it is impossible for there to be things giving, one to another, without an initial limit.

/The cause of unity in unified things is accordingly the True One, the First, and everything which receives unity is caused, every one other than the One in truth being one metaphorically and not in truth. Every caused unity simply passes from its unity (that of the True One) to that which is other than its being, i.e., the True One is not multiple with respect to its existence. (The caused unity) is a multiple and not an absolute one, meaning by "absolute one" that which is not multiple at all and the unity of which is nothing other than its being.

/Inasmuch as unity and multiplicity together are in every sensible object and that which is attached to it, and the unity in it is entirely an effect from an agent which occurs accidentally in it and not through (its) nature, and multiplicity is, necessarily, a group of single units; then it is necessary that there would never be multiplicity if there were not unity. Accordingly every multiplicity comes to be through unity,
p. 162 and if there were no /unity the multiple would never have being. Hence[1] every coming to be is simply an affection which brings into existence what did not exist; and consequently[2] the emanation of unity from the True One, the First, is the coming to be of every sensible object and what is attached to the sensible object; and (the True One) causes every one of them to exist when it causes them to be[3] through its being. Therefore[4] the cause of coming to be is due to the True One, which does not acquire unity from a donor but is rather one /through its essence. Moreover, that which is made to be is not eternal, and that which is not eternal is created, i.e., it comes to be from a cause; consequently that which is made to be is created.

---

[1]and[2] Ms. فاذا . AR فاذن.

[3] يهوى . AR تهوى.

[4]Ms. فاذا . AR فاذن .

As the cause of coming to be is the True One, the First, so the cause of creation is the True One, the First; and it is the cause from which there is a beginning of motion, i.e., that which sets in motion the beginning of motion; meaning that "that which sets in motion" is the agent. As the True One, the First, is the cause of the beginning of the motion of coming to be, i.e., of the affection, it is the creator of all that comes to be. As there is no being /except through the unity in things, and their unification is their coming to be, the maintenance of all being due to its unity, if (things which come to be) departed from the unity, they would revert and perish, together with the departure (of the unity), in no time. The True One is therefore the First, the Creator who holds everything He has created, and whatever is freed from His hold and power reverts and perishes.

Inasmuch as that which we wanted to clarify concerning the distinction of ones has been explained—to show the True One, the Donor, the Creator, the Mighty, the Holder (of all together); and what the ones by metaphor are, *viz.*, (one) by benefit of the True One, /Who is greater and more exalted than the attributions of the godless—let us now complete this section and follow it with its natural sequel, with the assistance of Him who possesses complete power, perfect potency, and a lavish generosity.

The first part of the book of Yaʿqūb ibn Isḥāq al-Kindī is completed. Praised be God the Master of the worlds, and blessings upon both Muḥammad the prophet and all his people.

Commentary

97.3 "al-Muʿtaṣim Billāh": The son of Hārūn al-Rashīd and the slave girl Mārida, al-Muʿtaṣim succeeded his brother al-Maʾmūn as the eighth ʿAbbāsid caliph, reigning from A.H. 218/A.D. 833 to 227/842 (cf. the succinct summary of his life given by K.V. Zettersteen in *The Encyclopaedia of Islam*, 3: 784, and see the list of primary historical sources given there). Al-Kindī dedicated treatises to both caliphs, as well, particularly, to al-Muʿtaṣim's son Aḥmad, his pupil (cf. Walzer's enumeration of these treatises, "New Studies on al-Kindī", *Greek into Arabic*, p. 176 f.).

97.5 "May God grant you long life..." This opening phrase in particular (literally, "May Allah prolong your duration"), and the entire passage to 1. 7, "...and cleanse you from all the dirtiness of vice", is typical of the eloquence al-Kindī employs when addressing the caliph or his son; compare AR I: 244, II: 48 (and I: 214, which, from its many literal and stylistic parallels with the above, must also have been intended for a member of the royal household). When addressing friends or colleagues, al-Kindī's invocation is usually brief and to the point. Cf. AR I: 186, 194, 201, 265, 353, 363; II: 40, 64 and *passim* (cf. further other sources, assembled by Walzer, *Studi su al-Kindī II*, op. cit., p. 47, n. 2).

97.8 "Indeed, the human art which is highest in degree and most noble in rank is the art of philosophy": إن أعلى الصناعات الإنسانية منزلة وأشرفها مرتبة صناعة الفلسفة.

This sentence is similar in structure and wording to that below at 98.1, and like it is ultimately inspired by *Met.* VI: 1. 1026a 21-22 (though possibly also reflecting the influence of *Met.* I: 2. 982b 3f.). As Aristotle does in the *Met.* VI passage, al-Kindī proceeds to esteem philosophy above all other pursuits, and "First Philosophy" above all other kinds of philosophy. Between the opening and closing sentences of this passage, however, he follows another *Metaphysics* source, and this beginning sentence itself indicates additional sources upon which he drew.

In his treatise "On the Definition and Description of Things" (AR I: 173), al-Kindī presents a description of this sort as one of the "ancients" (*qudamāʾ*) *definitions* of philosophy: وحدوها أيضا من جهة العلة فقالوا : صناعة الصناعات وحكمة الحكم. Together with al-Kindī's five other definitions of philosophy (ibid., pp. 172, 173), this has been translated by S.M. Stern: "They also defined it from its pre-eminence (*sic*), saying: Art of arts and science of sciences." (cf. *Isaac Israeli*, op. cit.,

p. 28). As Stern remarks there, this "On Definitions" passage "derives mostly from the Alexandrian commentators of Aristotle, among whom it became a convention to include in the introduction to their commentaries on the *Isagoge* an enumeration of the various definitions of philosophy". Thus this definition is found in Ammonius as Τέχνη τεχνῶν καὶ ἐπιστήμη ἐπιστημῶν (cf. "In Porphyrii Isagogen", *CAG* iv/3, p. 6; and cf. as well the "Prolegomena" of Elias, *CAG* xviii/1, p. 8, and David, *CAG* xviii/2, p. 20). While this definition, attributed to Aristotle, is said to be derived from the "pre-eminence" of philosophy (ὑπεροχή), al-Kindī says that it is due to its causal aspect (العلة), alluding possibly to the Alexandrian treatment of philosophy under this definition as the "mother of sciences".

Al-Kindī here, moreover, qualifies the philosophical art as "human", though the immediately following definition carries a similar qualification (see below). This emphasis serves to distinguish philosophy from the "Divine science", العلم الالهي i.e., prophecy; a distinction al-Kindī makes explicit in his treatise "On the Number of Aristotle's Books..." (AR I: 372, and cf. Richard Walzer, *Una Scritto Introduttivo allo Studio di Aristotle*, op. cit., p. 395). It is philosophy as a science which—without supernatural intervention or theological assumptions—slowly yields knowledge to the person intensely trained and persistent, with which al-Kindī is here concerned (cf. *FP* 102.15). Though he is far from denying the validity of prophetic knowledge (cf. Richard Walzer, "New Studies on al-Kindī", *Greek into Arabic*, pp. 177 ff.), al-Kindī attempts in this treatise, as in most of his philosophical writings, to prove his case without resort to extra-philosophical means.

97.9[1] "The definition of which is knowledge of the true nature of things, insofar as is possible for man": التي حدها علم الأشياء بحقائقها بقدر طاقة الإنسان. Cf. Aristotle's description of philosophy in *Met.* II:1. 993b 20 as a "knowledge of the truth", ἐπιστήμη τῆς ἀληθείας, translated by Asṭāt (Bouyges, I: 11) as علم الحق .

That Aristotle here understands "the truth", ἡ ἀλήθεια, as equivalent to the ultimate nature of things, the first principles of being, is clear from the sequel to this passage as well as from his use of the term the same way elsewhere. Cf. e.g. *Met.* I: 3. 983b 2 (when it is used synonymously with τῶν ὄντων), 7. 988a 20 (when it occurs with τῶν ἀρχῶν), and elsewhere (see Ross, *Met.*I: 3. 983 b 2n.).

Such an ontologically oriented definition is also found in the Alexandrian commentaries to the *Isagoge* mentioned above, and al-Kindī is reading Aristotle here through their eyes; consulting, in the process, his adaptation of an Alexandrian source in "On Definitions" (Abū Rida I: 173). Thus the two definitions of philosophy said by the commentators to be taken from "its subject", "the knowledge of beings *qua* beings (or "the real nature of beings"), γνῶσις τῶν ὄντων ᾗ ὄντα ἐστί; and "the knowledge of divine (i.e., eternal) and human affairs", γνῶσις θείων τε καὶ ἀνθρωπίνων πραγμάτων (cf. Ammonius, op.

cit., pp. 2, 3; Elias, op. cit., p. 8; David, op. cit., p. 20), are apparently conflated by al-Kindī in "On Definitions" (ibid.) into one definition (the mortal aspect of the second definition apparently being viewed *sub species aeternitatis*): "Philosophy is the knowledge of the eternal, universal things, of their existence, essence and causes, insofar as is possible for man", إن الفلسفة علم الأشياء الابدية الكلية ، أنيتها ومائيتها وعللها ، بقدر طاقة الإنسان (and cf. Stern, op. cit., p. 29). This definition now appears in abridged form in *FP* as above, with the "true nature of things" representing all the adjectives used in the longer definition, and the tag "insofar as is possible for man" retained.

Throughout *FP*, al-Kindī is actually following the first of the above Alexandrian definitions, as his formulation of the definition here indicates; though he is doubtless convinced that from the study of being *per se* there emerges whatever knowledge we may have of the Divine and of "eternal" things.

97.9[a] "insofar as is possible for man" : بقدر طاقة الانسان . As noted above, the reason for al-Kindī's use of this term here is probably because of its occurrence in the equivalent "On Definitions" definition of philosophy. The reason for its appearance there, furthermore, may be traced with some certainty, and bears upon al-Kindī's further composition of this *FP* passage.

The phrase in question is actually used by al-Kindī in "On Definitions" in another definition of philosophy as well, that which al-Kindī says is taken from its "activity" (فعل). Philosophy is resemblance to the actions of God, may He be exalted, insofar as is possible for man" (إن الفلسفة هو التشبه بافعال الله تعالى بقدر طاقة الإنسان, AR I: 172). This is a translation of one of the Alexandrian definitions (said to be taken from the "aim", τέλος, of philosophy), incorporating as well part of their explanation of the definition. The definition itself, going back to Plato's *Theaetetus* 176 B, is of philosophy as "becoming like God insofar as is possible for man", ὁμοίωσις Θεῷ κατὰ τὸ δυνατὸν ἀνθρώπῳ; which resemblance (Stern, op. cit., p. 29, "assimilation") is then qualified as being not to God directly but to His actions (Stern, ibid. p. 30, "works") or faculties, ἐνέργειαι and δυνάμεις. (It is apparently this emphasis upon God's actions, ἐνέργειαι / افعال, which accounts for al-Kindī's description of this definition as being from its "activity", فعل). These actions are viewed, broadly, as His knowledge and benevolent action, πρόνοια, which man is to imitate. Yet neither man's knowledge nor his deeds can be the same as God's, since the substance (οὐσία) and perfection (τελειότης) of the two beings differ. God, e.g., knows all simultaneously and eternally, man does not (cf. Ammonius, op. cit., pp. 3, 4; Elias, op. cit., pp. 8, 16f.; David, op. cit., pp. 2, 34f. See too Stern, op. cit., pp. 29, 30 and Altmann, ibid., pp. 197 ff., for the widespread use of this definition among Hellenistic and Islamic, as well as Jewish, authors).

It appears, therefore, that as the resemblance to God is understood by al-Kindī's source to be achieved in part through knowledge, which knowledge is considered as limited by man's very nature, al-Kindī gives the definition of philosophy which involves knowledge, in both "On Definitions" and here, that qualification which he also appends, following his source, to the definition of philosophy involving resemblance. Moreover, al-Kindī reads the next line of the *Metaphysics* with this resemblance-definition in mind (see the following note), and it is this qualifying phrase which serves to bridge the two definitions for him.

97.9[3] "The aim of the philosopher is, as regards his knowledge, to attain the truth, and as regards his action, to act truthfully": غرض الفيلسوف في علمه إصابة الحق وفي عمله العمل بالحق . Cf. *Met.* II:1. 993b. 20, "the end of theoretical knowledge is truth, while that of practical knowledge is action", θεωρητικῆς μὲν γὰρ τέλος ἀληθεία, πρακτικῆς δ'ἔργον. This is translated misleadingly by Asṭāt (Bouyges, p. 11), "the end of knowledge is to attain the truth, and the end of virtue (*sic*, probably a scribal error for "action", الفعل, as Bouyges suggests, n. 2) is to act truthfully," غاية العلم اصابة الحق وغاية الفضل (!) العمل بالحق . Al-Kindī is apparently following Asṭāt's text, explicitly considering both knowledge and practice of the truth as the "aim" of philosophy. In this he (and possibly Asṭāt) is influenced by the two-fold division of philosophy into θεωρητικὸν καὶ πρακτικόν common in the Alexandrian prolegomena (cf. Ammonius, op. cit., p. 11; Elias, op. cit., p. 26; David, op. cit., p. 55); which division constitutes the two ways man is thought to resemble God (and cf. Franz Rosenthal, "From Arabic Books and Manuscripts VI: Istanbul Materials for al-Kindī and as-Saraḫsī," *JAOS* vol. 76, no. 1 [1956]: 27 f., for the further subdivision of these pursuits common in late antiquity, which subdivision al-Kindī is reported elsewhere to have made). As mentioned in the preceding note, the resemblance-definition is said by the Alexandrians to be from the "aim" of philosophy, and al-Kindī's sentence here emphasizes this term, giving the essential part of the explanation of this definition without explicitly referring to it. It appears likely, therefore, that al-Kindī is incorporating yet another "definition" of philosophy into this paragraph, managing to utilize three of the four Alexandrian kinds of definitions, those from the "pre-eminence", "subject" and "aim" of philosophy, omitting only that definition taken from its etymology (cf. Stern, op. cit., p. 29).

97.10 "not that the activity is endless, for we abstain and the activity ceases, once we have reached the truth": لا الفعل سرمدا، لان نمسك ويتسرم الفعل إذا انتهينا الى الحق .

This sentence, and particularly its first part, probably originates in Asṭāt's translation of *Met.* II: 1. 993b 22, "practical men study not the eternal but what is relative and in the present", οὐ τὸ ἀΐδιον ἀλλ' ὃ πρός τι καὶ νῦν Θεωροῦσιν οἱ πρακτικόι. Asṭāt, partly following a reading preserved by Alexander of Aphrodisias, renders this in a way which could be understood as follows: "their aim (*sc.* that of practical men, though Asṭāt's reference to them is awkward) is not (to study) activity *per se*, nor is the duration of the activity endless; rather, their aim is to act for another reason (viz., for that which is) relative and timely; لم يكن غرضهم لنفس الفعل ولا المداومة على الفعل سرمدياً، بل غرضهم أن يفعلوا لعلة أخرى مضافة زمانية (Bouyges, p. 11).

Al-Kindī's sentence, unlike Asṭāt's, may well refer to theory (*ᶜilm*) as well as practice (*ᶜamal*), viewing the activity (*fiᶜl*) of philosophy in all its aspects as of limited duration. This would reflect the Alexandrian comparison (in their explanations of the resemblance-definition) of the "actions" of man with those of God, in which man's knowledge (and certainly his acts) is deemed non-eternal (cf. the two preceding notes). Al-Kindī has been alluding to the explanation of this resemblance-definition just before, and it is likely that he is still under its influence; moreover, his use of *fiᶜl* here may not be simply borrowed from Asṭāt's text, since it is this term which he says characterizes the resemblance-definition of philosophy. Al-Kindī may, therefore, be emphasizing in this manner the absence of any permanent conjunction or union with God through the philosophical endeavor. He does not, we know, assert such a relationship elsewhere, but his contemporary coreligionists would have been reassured to hear that he did not envision any such religious or mystical role for philosophy.

97.12[1] "We do not find the truth we are seeking without finding a cause": ولسنا نجد مطلوباتنا من الحق من غير علة. This sentence closely follows *Met.* II: 1.993b 23, "now we do not know a truth without its cause", οὐκ ἴσμεν δὲ τὸ ἀληθὲς ἄνευ τῆς αἰτίας; faithfully translated by Asṭāt (Bouyges, p. 12) as (ولسـ)نا نعرف الحق من غير علة.

97.12[2] "the cause of the existence and continuance of everything is the True One": وعلة وجود كل شيء وثباته الحق. Cf. *Met.* II: 1. 993b 27-30, "that is most true which causes subsequent truths to be true. Hence the principles of eternal things must be always most true...nor is there any cause of their being, but they are the cause of the being of other things" (ἀληθέστατον το τοῖς ὑστέροις αἴτιον τοῦ ἀληθέσιν εἶναι. δεῖ τὰς τῶν ἀεὶ ὄντων ἀρχὰς ἀναγκαῖον ἀεὶ εἶναι ἀληθεστάτας... οὐδέ ἐκείναις αἴτιον τί ἐστι τοῦ εἶναι, ἀλλ' ἐκεῖναι τοῖς ἄλλοις).

The shift in subject number and thus in concept from Aristotle's first principles to al-Kindī's Principle, from truths to The True One (or Truth), may be accounted for in part by Asṭāt's translation of the above *Met.* passage, l. 27 (Bouyges, p. 13): فمعلوم أن الحق الأول علة لحقيقة الأشياء الأخيرة.

This would ordinarily have been read, "it is known that the first truth is the cause for the truth of subsequent things", a reading that would have been reinforced by Asṭāt's translation of the following line (28) of the *Metaphysics:* وباضطرار أن تكون أول علة الأكوان واجبة حقا ابدا. This would probably have been understood to mean that "the principles (أول) of the cause of beings must necessarily be true and eternal", again conveying to the reader the notion of basically one cause of beings. (Compare with this Isḥāq ibn Ḥunayn's more accurate translation of the Greek text (Bouyges, loc. cit.): فيجب من ذلك أن يكون اولى الأشياء بالحق الشيء الذي هو علة

لحقيقية الأشياء التي بعده ولذلك قد يجب ضرورة ان تكون مبادىء الأشياء الموجودة دائما هي دائما في الغاية من الحق .

Al-Kindī, of course, needed little prompting for his view of creation as dependent ultimately on one source, which is the major theme of the treatise, though it was convenient for him to "find" the doctrine in his Aristotelian model. Similarly, al-Kindī was quite familiar with the term *al-ḥaqq*, the "True One"/"The truth", used as an epithet for and description of God in the Qur'ān (cf., e.g., Suras 20: 114 and 18: 44) and in philosophical sources (cf. the second n. below). He himself uses the term in this context a number of times throughout his writings (cf. AR I: 160-162, 182-183, 215, 373).

97.13[1] "in that each thing which has being has truth" : لأن كل ما له أنيه له حقيقة . Cf. *Met.* II: 1.993b 30, of which al-Kindī's passage could well be a literal translation; "so that as each thing is in respect of being, so it is in respect of truth" (ὥσθ ἕκαστον ὡς ἔχει τοῦ εἶναι, οὕτω καὶ τῆς ἀληθείας). Asṭāt's translation of this passage (Bouyges, ibid.) is not actually as precise as al-Kindī's: "the truth of everything must necessarily be like its being", فواجب أن حقيقة كل واحد من الأشياء مثل أيسيته, though in light of al-Kindī's sentence this partly illegible last word could well have been originally (*pace* Bouyges, n. 5) أنيته .

Al-Kindī's use of *annīyah* for being here is thus in all probability taken from Asṭāt's translation of εἶναι; a translation which Asṭāt uses elsewhere in the *Metaphysics* as well (cf. *Met.* 1041a 15; 1042b 28; 1043a 1 and 1047a 20). Al-Kindī uses the term here as a synonym for the previous sentence's "existence", وجود ; which duplication may be accounted for by the fact that in the next sentence al-Kindī needs both terms to express his idea.

97.13[2] "The True One exists necessarily, and therefore beings exist": فالحق اضطرارا موجود إذا لأنيات موجودة . Al-Kindī is led to this conclusion by the foregoing paraphrase of the *Metaphysics* (particularly 11.28-30). As worded, however, this sentence and the entire paragraph has a decidedly Neoplatonic coloration, the existence of beings seen as deriving from the (necessary) existence of the True One.

Al-Kindī would have found support for an interpretation of the *Metaphysics* in these terms in the *Theology of Aristotle*, where, e.g., the statement is found that the Creator is "the first being, the true one" (الأنية الأولى الحق), the cause of all other beings, both immaterial and material (cf. A. Badawī's edition of the *Theology* in his *Plotinus Apud Arabes*, p. 26; translated by G. Lewis in *Plotini Opera*, ed. P. Henry and H.R. Schwyzer, II: 231. See also Badawī, p. 122 [Lewis, p. 271], equivalent to *Enn.* V: 1. 5, 4). In his treatise "On Explaining the Active, Proximate Cause of Generation and Corruption" (AR I: 215), al-Kindī actually describes God as "the true Being", الأنية الحق (literally, "The Being, the True One"), referring to our treatise for elaboration.

The various meanings of *annīyah* (and not *innīyah*, as AR prefers; cf *FP* 97, n. 2) and its possible derivations have received much attention;

cf., e.g., the studies of M.Y. D'Alverny ("Anniyya-Anitas", in *Mélanges offerts à Étienne Gilson* [Toronto, 1959], pp. 59-91), Richard Frank ("The Origin of the Arabic Philosophical Term انّية", *Cahiers de Byrsa*, 1956, p. 181-201), and S. Van den Bergh (*The Encyclopaedia of Islam*, new ed., 1:513). These and other scholars have shown that the term was used in both a narrow and broad sense. The narrow sense was first discussed by S. Munk (in his French edition of Maimonides' *Guide of the Perplexed* [Paris, 1860], I: 241). He suggested that "quoddity" be used to express *annīyah* when it denoted the existence of a particular thing, an x that is (used in Mlle. D'Alverny's words, "*avec un sens d'affirmation existentielle*", op. cit., p. 73); without regard to determining *what* the x is, its definition (i.e., *annīyah* as opposed to *māhīyah*, the Scholastic *existentia* and *essentia*). Al-Kindī uses both these terms in "On Definitions" (AR I: 173), reflecting —via the Alexandrian commentators—the distinction Aristotle makes in *Anal. Post.* II: I 89b 24 between τὸ ὅτι and τὸ τί ἐστιν, translated by Abū Bishr Matta as أنه يوجد and ما هو (*Manṭiq Aristū*, ed. ᶜAbd al-Raḥmān Badawī [Cairo, 1949], II: 407).

The broad sense of *annīyah*, however, denotes not only being in general, the equivalent of *huwīyah* and *wujūd*; but also, at times, "essence" (which latter translation Lewis chooses for the *Theology* passage quoted above; and cf. further A.M. Goichon, *Lexique de la Langue Philosophique D'Ibn Sīnā* [Paris, 1938], pp. 9 ff., and Soheil M. Afnan, "*Philosophical Terminology in Arabic and Persian*" [Leiden, 1964], pp. 94 ff.).

It does not appear that al-Kindī is using *annīyah* in its narrow sense here, nor again at p. 120, though he may be so using it at pp. 101 and 130. He seems rather to be saying that beings in general owe their nature to God, the source of being.

98.1 "The noblest part of philosophy and the highest in rank is the First Philosophy, i.e., knowledge of the First Truth who is the cause of all truth": وأشرف الفلسفة وأعلاها مرتبة الفلسفة الأولى ، أعني علم الحق الاول الذي هو علة كل حق. While *Met.* II: 1. 994a 1ff. speaks of the need for a first cause, and 993b 27 asserts that "that which causes derivative truths to be true is most true" (Ross), it appears that al-Kindī is digressing briefly from his *Alpha Elatton* source here, returning to it at p. 102 with a paraphrase of the earlier section of II: 1. 993a 31-b 19.

The short section which this sentence introduces is a fitting conclusion and sequel to that which precedes it, and like it is also composed of an adaptation of the *Metaphysics* in a Neoplatonic direction, and the incorporation (at p. 101) of remarks from the Alexandrian *Isagoge* commentaries (for which cf. Stern, op. cit., pp. 13 ff.). The actual sections of the *Metaphysics* which al-Kindī may be paraphrasing in the above sentence—as at 97.8 above—could be *Met.* I: 2 982a 21-b 10 or (and?), more probably, *Met.* VI: 1. 1026a 18-31. While the former passage is not extant in any of the medieval Arabic translations, the contents of the latter passage and Asṭāt's translation contains some of the very terms al-Kindī uses, or their equivalents.

Thus 1026a 21: "and the most noble science (or philosophy, *sc.* Theology) must deal with the most noble genus" (καὶ τὴν τιμιωτάτην δεῖ περὶ τὸ τιμιώτατον γένος εἶναι), which Asṭāt renders (Bouyges, op. cit., II: 707) وينبغي أن يكون العلم الشريف للجنس الشريف; while at lines 29 f. "first philosophy" (πρώτη φιλοσοφία, الفلسفة الأولى Bouyges, p. 713) is related to an "immovable (and separately existing) substance" (τις οὐσία ἀκίνητος, جوهر ما غير متحرك). Though Aristotle is refcrring to substance in a generic sense (cf. there above, 11. 16 ff.), it is easy for al-Kindī, having read the *Theology*, to regard Aristotle's "divine" substances as a singular and unique entity, the "First Truth", prior and thus, to al-Kindī, the cause of all subsequent truth.

This relating of priority to causality could have followed from familiarity with the quest for the causes of being with which *Met.* VI: 1 is concerned; as well, perhaps, from the somewhat ambiguous remark in l. 30 that the science of the immovable substance will be "universal in this way, because it is first", καὶ καθόλου οὕτως ὅτι πρώτη. This is translated quite ambiguously by Asṭāt, p. 713 Bouyges, as الكلية أيضاً فهو أول بهذا النوع. While *fa-huwa awwal* (for which there are variant readings of *wa-huwa* ...) may be understood as a circumstantial clause, and thus faithful to the Greek, Averroes for one understood the sentence to read فهو أول بهذا النوع, "and it is first in this way" (ibid., p. 714). Al-Kindī may well have so read, seeing the "way" in which theology is first as causal.

98.2 "Therefore it is necessary... its cause". Compare here *Met.* I: 1. 981b 27 ff.

101.3[1] "Every cause... thing is". Assuming al-Kindī is paraphrasing *Met.* I: 2. in the preceding sentence, he could have been led by the opening of *Met.* I: 3. (983a 24-32) to this remark; which is, however, common enough in Aristotle and subsequently. (Cf., e.g., *Physics* II: 3. 194b 16 ff., *Met.* V: 2. 1013a 24 ff., and see the following note.) Stern has, in fact, shown that a reference to the four causes is given in a Hellenistic interpretation to *Posterior Analytics* II: 1. 89b 24 which links them with the four types of inquiry in a manner similar to that given below (cf. *Isaac Israeli*, p. 18). This interpretation (preserved by the late Greek commentator Eustratius, *CAG*, xxi/1, p. 9) was probably relocated fully in an introduction to philosophy of the sort which al-Kindī has been using in this section, though extant Greek texts speak only of the four types of inquiry (cf. the note to 101.5[1] below). Then again, al-Kindī could have learned of this relationship from a commentary on the *Posterior Analytics*, though we have no evidence of an Arabic translation of such a work, or of the *Post. An.* itself, in his time. Yet al-Kindī must have been familiar with the Aristotelian work, if not with commentaries upon it, even if only in a second-hand, incomplete way, for he is reported to have written one if not two commentaries of it. (Cf. the *Fihrist*, pp. 249, 256, 257; Walzer, "New Light on the Arabic Translations of Aristotle", *Greek into Arabic*, p. 98; Peters, op. cit., pp. 17-20.) Whether or not al-Kindī is here showing a familiarity with a *Post. An.* commentary tradition, his use elsewhere of this Aristotelian work, to which he had no direct access, supports our conjecture that the preceding sentence may well be a paraphrase of *Met.* I, knowledge of which he would also have acquired indirectly. Thus superficial familiarity with a text did not, it seems, deter al-Kindī from paraphrasing it or commenting upon it.

101.3[2] "matter, form, agent, final": عنصر، صورة، فاعلة and متممة. Compare G. Lewis' translation of the similarly worded *Theology of Aristotle*, op. cit., II: 486: "the. . .causes of the universe are four, namely Matter (*al-hayūlā*), Form, the Active Cause and Perfection" (*al-tamām*; Arabic edition by ᶜAbd al-Raḥmān Badawī, op. cit., p. 4).

101.3[3] "that for the sake of which the thing is: ما من أجله كان الشيء, rendered as "at which a thing aims" by S.M. Stern in his translation of this and the following passage, to l. 14, op. cit., p. 13.

101.5[1] "Scientific inquiries are four": والمطالب العلمية أربعة. Cf. Elias, op. cit., p. 3, David, op. cit., p. 1. Stern has analyzed this entire passage and traced its history from Aristotle, through the Alexandrian introductions to the *Isagoge*, to Islamic and Jewish sources, op. cit., pp. 13-23.

101.5[2] "as we have determined elsewhere in our philosophical treatises": كما حددنا في غير موضع من أقاويلنا الفلسفية. Al-Kindī is possibly referring to his commentary (possibly commentaries) on the *Posterior Analytics*, for which cf. above, n. to 101.3; or (and ?) to his treatises based upon the *Isagoge*. He is reported to have written a number of such treatises, all unfortunately still lost, dealing explicitly or implicitly with the themes of the *Isagoge* and of its commentators; cf. *Fihrist*, I: 256, and cf. Flügel, *Al-Kindī*, pp. 36-38, nos. 7, 8, 25, 27, 32 (and see Baumstark, op. cit., p. 161, and Stern, op. cit., p. 31, n. 1). The four epistemological categories are also referred to in al-Kindī's work on the *Almagest*, كتاب في الصناعة العظمى (cf. Franz Rosenthal, "Al-Kindī and Ptolemy", op. cit., p. 441), a work with which *FP* has also other points in common (cf. below, nn. to 102. 15-19, 103. 9).

101.7 "only of the existence (of something)": عن الأنية فقط, which might be rendered as the "quoddity", whether there is an X. Cf. above, n. to 97.13[2]. While his commentators treated of this question, as noted above, Porphyry himself incorporates only the "what" and "which" queries into his discussion of predicables, the "whether" (and "why") things exist being the sort of ontological question he deliberately excludes from consideration in the *Isagoge* (cf. A. Busse, *Isagoge et in Aristotelis Categorias Commentarium*, *CAG* iv/1, p. 1; missing in the MS. from which the Arabic translation of the *Isagoge* has been edited, but supplied by Stern in his article "Ibn al-Ṭayyib's Commentary on the *Isagoge*", *BSOAS*, vol. 19, no. 3 [1957]: 424).

101.8-10 "what" investigates the genus. . . "which". . . its specific difference. . . "what" and "which" together. . . its species" : الما تبحث عن جنسها، وأي تبحث عن فصلها، وما وأي جميعاً تبحثان عن نوعها. These correlations are found already in the *Isagoge*, Porphyry being followed in this by the commentators: for "genus", predicated of τί ἐστιν, cf. Busse, op. cit., p. 2 (Arabic *mā huwa* in translation of Abū Uthman al-Dimashqī [d. ca. 900], edited by ᶜAbd al-Raḥmān Badawī, *Manṭiq Arisṭū* [*Organon Aristotelis*, Cairo, 1952], III: 1024; following Aristotle, *Topics*, I. 5. 102a 31ff., rendered into Arabic by the same al-Dimashqī, ed. Badawī, op. cit., II: 476); for the "specific difference", literally just difference, διαφορά/فصل, predicated of ποῖόν τί ἔστιν/أي شيء هو, cf. Busse, op. cit., p. 3 and 11; Badawī, op. cit.,: 1026, 1046. (Al-Dimashqī also translates the τί ἔστιν and ποῖόν τι of 17.10 Busse as *māhīyah* and *kayfīyah* respectively, Badawī, p. 1058). At 15.2 Busse (1054 Badawī), both types of the above sentences are mentioned together; while species is spoken of as a result of the determinations of genus and differentia at various places in the work (cf. Busse, 9.3, 13.23, 20.7, equivalent to Badawī 1038, 1052, 1064).

101.12 "matter... genus;... form... species": عنصر، جنس، صورة، نوع. Cf. the *Isagoge*, 11.15 Busse (1047 Badawī), where man's genus is said to be analogous to his matter (ὕλη / *mādda*), the specific difference to his form μορφή / *ṣūra*. When this is repeated at 15.6 Busse (Badawī 1054), μορφή is rendered as *khilqah*. At 3.22 Busse (Badawī 1027), however, the species is said to be predicated of form; the interdependent nature of species and difference permitting both expressions, as al-Kindī proceeds immediately to explain.

101.13[1] "knowledge of the specific difference ... species" : وفي علم النوع علم الفصل, literally, "knowledge of the specific difference being in the knowledge of the species". Cf. *Isagoge*, 10.1 ff. Busse (1041 Badawī).

101.13[2] "When, therefore, we obtain full knowledge of its matter, form and final cause, we thereby obtain full knowledge of its definition" : فاذا أحطنا بعلم عنصرها وصورتها وعلتها التمامية فقد أحطنا بعلم حدها. That the complete definition of a thing includes both its subject matter (ὑποκείμενον, rendered here by al-Kindī in terms of matter and form) and aim (τέλος, equivalent to al-Kindī's final cause), is asserted by Elias, op. cit., p. 5.19 ff., and David, op. cit., 17.31 ff. (and cf. Ammonius, op. cit., 1.18 ff.). Al-Kindī thus again refers, obliquely, to the two most important definitions of philosophy which the Alexandrians had discussed (cf. above, notes to 97.9), and again emphasizes the goal as well as the subject matter of philosophy. Though ordinarily—and in actual practice even for al-Kindī—the definition of a thing does not require more than knowledge of its genus and specific difference, the larger perspective within which al-Kindī views philosophy requires acknowledgement of a teleological force as part of the very definition of an object. Al-Kindī is thus led naturally to speak next of the first cause.

102.1-4 "The truth requires... obtaining." Al-Kindī returns here to *Met.* II: 1, from which he drew his remarks above at 97.8-14. As his previous statements were based upon the latter part of that chapter (993b 19-31), this passage as well as 11. 10-12 below are paraphrases of its middle section (993b 11-14, 16-19). At *FP* 102. 5-9 al-Kindī borrows from the beginning of this chapter (993a 31-b 4), and then at 103.1-3 he returns again to its middle (993b 15-16). A chart of these comparable passages is as follows:

FP	*Met. II:* 1.
97.8-14	993b 19-31
102.1-4, 10-12	993b 11-14, 16-19
102.5-9	993a 31-b 4
103.1-3	993b 15-16

Met. 993b 11-14 enjoins gratitude for those whose views we might share, as well as for those who have expressed more superficial (ἐπιπολαιότερον) views. Asṭāt's translation (op. cit., pp. 8, 9), which al-Kindī follows, makes this explicit: "it is not right for us only to thank one who has uttered an important remark (قولا جزلا), of those with whose views we may be associated; rather is it also right for us to thank those who have uttered a small insignificant remark (قولا يسيرا نزرا)".

Aristotle stresses that one should be grateful even for superficial thinkers with whom one does not agree, since their views at least helped train the mind. To al-Kindī it is the major benefactors of the truth (as well as the minor) who have performed this service. This change of subject —accomplished in part by inverting the sentence order of his source— renders al-Kindī's text different from Aristotle's. The Stagirite appears to be saying that, while knowledge of the truth is a collective effort, some views are philosophically valid and should be accepted, while others have a kind of historical validity only. Al-Kindī ignores this distinction, apparently believing that in general previous philosophy is true, though not complete. This total though qualified acceptance of past philosophy is of a piece with al-Kindī's non-historical approach in other treatises; an approach characterized by a broad, purportedly harmonizing compilation of views, rather than by a critical analysis of them (cf. his various definitions of philosophy, AR I: 172 f.; and of the soul, AR I: 272-282. See also Walzer, "New Studies on al-Kindī", *Greek into Arabic*, p. 201).

102.1-2 "The truth requires that we do not reproach... serious benefits to us" ومن اوجب الحق ألا نذم... منافعنا... الجدية. This sentence paraphrases Asṭāt's translation quoted in the preceding note, reversing the style of its presentation.

102.3 "Kindred and associates": أنساب وشركاء. Cf. Asṭāt's use of مشاركة (for κοινώσαιτο of 993b 12) in the phrase translated above, 102.1-4 note, "of those with whose views we may be associated".

102.3-4 "they benefited us ... approaches and instruments": أفادونا ... سبلا وآلات. This statement is an elaboration of 993b 14: οὗτοι συνεβάλοντό τι· τὴν γὰρ ἕξιν προήσκησαν ἡμῶν ("these ... contributed something, by developing before us the powers of thought", i.e., following Ross, *Met.* I: 215, "they formed our ἕξις by practice"). Asṭāt's translation (Bouyges, 9.2) is as follows: إنهم اعانونا بتقدمهم في الفحص قبلنا, "they have helped us by their prior progress in inquiry." Al-Kindī's explication of this passage indicates more than a slavish dependance upon Asṭāt's written work. Al-Kindī may also have consulted Asṭāt for explanations of difficult passages, having commissioned him to translate the *Metaphysics*. To the degree that our text amplifies Asṭāt's translation, it might be (or be taken from) the "report" (*khabar*) of the *Metaphysics* which al-Kindī is said to have written (cf. *Fihrist*, op. cit., p. 251). Cf. further below, 103.1-3.

Al-Kindī's usage of *afādūnā*, which he again employs in the related passage below at l. 11 (and cf. n. there), probably comes from Asṭāt's translation of παρειλήφαμεν there (l. 18) as استفدنا (op. cit., l . 4).

102.4 "the real nature of which they fell short of obtaining" : مما قصروا عن نيل حقيقته . This emphasizes the essential failure of prior philosophical attempts more than Aristotle does in the corresponding *Metaphysics* passage; and may also allude to al-Kindī's subject—*al-ḥaqq*, the Real one—whose "real nature", *ḥaqīqa*, has not, in al-Kindī's estimation, been fully understood. Al-Kindī is probably following what he takes to be the intention of Asṭāt's rendering of *Met.* 993b 18, "for from some thinkers we have inherited certain opinions (τινας δόξας)", as "for we have benefited from the limited views (literally "small views", آراء يسيرة) of some of them" (Bouyges, I: 9,4).

102.5[1] "to the distinguished philosophers before us": عند المبرزين من المتفلسفين قبلنا, particularly Aristotle (and cf. below, 103.1), whose view in 993a 31-b 4 al-Kindī now in effect quotes (with modifications) to l. 9, following Asṭāt's translation. As the ms. of this section of Asṭāt's work is in poor condition (op. cit., p. 3, ll. 2 and 3), we may reconstruct it from al-Kindī's passage, and further verify the latter's use of Asṭāt by comparing al-Kindī with Isḥāq b. Ḥunayn's later translation. The one significant difference from the translation may be assumed to be al-Kindī's own contribution.

102.5[2] "our co-linguists": أهل لساننا, following the translation suggested by Rosenthal ("Al-Kindī and Ptolemy", op. cit, II: 445). As Rosenthal has pointed out (based upon remarks in the ك. في الصناعة العظمى and our text), al-Kindī considers himself largely as an interpreter of Greek learning to the Arabic speaking (and reading) world.

102.6[1] "no man... has attained the truth": لم ينل الحق ... أحد من الناس . Asṭāt (ibid.), لم يقدر واحد من الناس with the rest mutilated. Cf. Isḥāq's translation, Bouyges 3.7, لم يقدر أحد من الناس على بلوغ فيه , translating 993a 31, μηδένα δύνασθαι θιγεῖν αὐτῆς (τῆς ἀληθείας).

102.6[2] "that which the truth deserves": بما يستاهل الحق , reflecting Aristotle's ἀξίως of 993a 31; given by Isḥāq (Bouyges, 3, 7, 8) بقدر ما يستحق .

102.6[3] "nor have the (philosophers as a) whole comprehended it" : ولا أحاط به جميعهم . The translation of 993b 1, μήτε πάντας ἀποτυγχάνειν, "nor do we collectively fail", is missing in the extant Asṭāt version. Isḥāq renders it ولا ذهب على الناس كلهم , "nor (does the truth) depart from all men collectively". This negative phrase, containing both a negation and a negative-value verb, may have confused al-Kindī (and possibly Asṭāt), as it might have the anonymous author of the marginal notes to the extant ms. (Cf. Bouyges, *Notice*, op. cit., p. *L*, 2°). This person wrote ambiguously

—in what Bouyges calls "une traduction paraphrasée"—أيضا الحق على الناس جميعهم (ibid., p. LVII). This could be translated either "moreover, the truth (is attained) collectively", which gives *aiḍan* a converse meaning in the total context but which represents the original meaning of the Greek; or straightforwardly as "likewise the truth (is not attained) collectively", which would be similar to al-Kindī. On this latter reading, however, there is ostensibly a glaring discrepancy between this statement of al-Kindī's and the following sentence but one, which affirms that man does, collectively, achieve considerable truth (l. 9). This may be resolved by assuming that al-Kindī is distinguishing between collective knowledge which does not know *all* the truth (احاط به in the sense of comprehensive truth), and collective knowledge which knows "something of great worth".

102.10[1] "It is proper that our gratitude be great" : فينبغي أن يعظم شكرنا , using a nominal form of *shkr,* which root Asṭāt employs verbally in the sentence which serves as the base for this passage (cf. above, n. to 102. 1-4); al-Kindī paraphrasing both Asṭāt and his own parallel sentence above, 102. 1 f.

102.10[2] "even a little (of the truth)... much (truth)" : يسير الحق ... كثير من الحق. Following but inverting the order of Asṭāt's translation to *Met.* 993b 11-13 (Bouyges, pp. 8, 9): قولا جزلا ... قولا يسيراً نزراً.

102.11-12 "since they have shared with us... approaches to the truth". This paraphrase of *Met.* 993b 14 corresponds to that given above at ll. 3 and 4, though the terminology is mostly different. Al-Kindī's اشركونا and سهلوا لنا are equivalent to Asṭāt's اعانونا ; the former's فكر and مطالب like the latter's فحص; while المقدمات echoes بتقدمهم (and cf. the note to 102.3-4 above for أفادونا).

102.12 "If they had not lived": فانهم لو لم يكونوا, following Asṭāt on *Met.* 993b 15 (op. cit., p. 9.2). However, while Asṭāt goes on to translate Aristotle faithfully, referring the subject to "Ṭimā'ūs" (Timotheus), al-Kindī makes this a general remark concerning all those who have contributed to the truth; and then he paraphrases the Timotheus reference below, at 103.1 f.

102.13-14 "principles ... conclusions" : الأوائل ... الأواخر. Whereas Aristotle in *Met.* 993b 18 is speaking of "some" philosophers to whom we are indebted, who in turn are yet indebted to "others" (آخرون in Asṭāt), al-Kindī here speaks of principles and conclusions, literally "firsts" and "lasts" (أواخر). He thus converts Aristotle's reference to a chronological order of philosophers into a statement concerning the logical order of philosophical knowledge.

102.15-19 "intensive research, necessary perseverance and love of toil in that ... subtle speculation and fondness for perseverance": شدة البحث ولزوم الدأب وإيثار التعب ... وإلطاف النظر وإيثار الدأب . Cf. the similar terminology al-Kindī employs, in his treatise on the *Almagest,* كتاب في الصناعة العظمى , to describe what is necessary for an understanding of astronomy (as quoted by F. Rosenthal, op. cit., II: 444). He also acknowledges there the successive labors and cumulative knowledge of prior scholars, an acknowledgement which Rosenthal calls "daring" for the challenge it represented to the traditional view of knowledge as that received by inspiration. Rosenthal, however, finds that this view of al-Kindī's was current in his time and afterwards, among Muslim scientists (and philosophers); and traces it for al-Kindī to Theon of Alexandria's *Commentary on the Almagest* (ed. A. Rome, *Studi e Testi* 72 [1936]: 325; for which compare Ptolemy's *Syntaxis Mathematica*, ed. J.L. Heiberg, *Opera* [Leipzig, 1898] I: 1, 7.25; English translation by R. C. Taliaferro in the series *Great Books of the Western World* [Chicago, 1938], XVI: 6; see also Rosenthal, op. cit., pp. 445-446). We thus have here an example of al-Kindī expanding upon an Aristotelian text with material borrowed from another Greek source. Cf. further below, 103.9 f.

103.1 "Aristotle, the most distinguished of the Greeks in philosophy, said": فاما ارسطوطالس ، مبرز اليونانيين في الفلسفة ، فقال, using the same adjective as above, 102.5. While the passage there, particularly 11. 7-9, is essentially an unattributed quotation from Aristotle's work (cf. n. to 102.5), the following is actually a paraphrase (however different) of the *Metaphysics*, though claiming to be a quotation. Taking such liberties with sources is not unusual in medieval writers, and is, as we have already seen and will see, quite characteristic of al-Kindī's method.

103.1-3 "We ought to be grateful to the fathers ... attaining the truth". This particular paraphrase of *Met.* I : 993b 15-16 uses a similar opening phrase as at 102.10 above, the source of which passage, at *Met.* 993b 11, precedes the *Met.* source of this sentence. In inserting remarks between these sentences, al-Kindī has lost the *Metaphysics* thread of continuity, so he begins, as it were, again. Aristotle wrote, at 11. 15 and 16, as follows: εἰ μὲν γὰρ Τιμόθεος μὴ ἐγένετο, πολλὴν ἂν μελοποιίαν οὐκ εἴχομεν· εἰ δὲ μὴ Φρῦνις, Τιμόθεος οὐκ ἂν ἐγένετο ("If there had been no Timotheus, we should not have much lyric poetry; and if there had been no Phrynis, there would have been no Timotheus"). Asṭāt translates this quite accurately (Bouyges, p. 9) ... فإنه ، لو لم يكن طيماوس لم يكن لنا معرفة بتأليف اللحون ، ولو لم يكن أفرونيس لم يكن طيماوس, understanding μελοποιία in the general sense of "musical composition", (تاليف اللحون, literally "composition of melodies"). Al-Kindī is in the dark (as was, no doubt, Asṭāt) concerning the identity of Phrynis and Timotheus, whom he apparently regards as father and son (they were not related, though both were fifth century Athenians associated with the development of the *nome* form of poetry; and cf. further, regarding them, the entries in Pauly-Wissowa, *Real-Encyclopädie der Classischen Altertumswissenschaft,* Zweit Reihe VI: 1331, no. 9 and XX: 1, p. 925). Al-Kindī's view of their relationship may well be based on his understanding of Asṭāt's use of *kāna*—for *gignomai*—as connoting "to be born"; which is a meaning of the Greek verb when predicated of persons. This again raises the possibility that al-Kindī consulted with Asṭāt to determine the possible meanings of difficult passages in the Greek (cf. above, 102.3-4 n.).

103.9 "our practice in all our compositions": عاداتنا في جميع موضوعاتنا, as, e.g., in his treatise on the *Almagest*, in the introduction to which (fol. 56b) Al-Kindī makes the same type of statement as that which follows (cf. Rosenthal, op. cit., p. 445). This method is one which Ptolemy says he practiced (cf. sources listed in note to 102.15-19 above), and while al-Kindī admits there that he is following Ptolemy's example, he omits this attribution here. It may well be that he assumes his auditors—and readers—are familiar with the Ptolemy work and/or method, having heard him lecture on it; and that mention of Ptolemy here is superfluous. Moreover, that this is (also) al-Kindī's method is indisputable, as evidenced from both these works and many others, in which predecessors' ideas are presented both with and without proper attribution.

103.11 "insofar as is possible for us" ; بقدر طاقتنا . Cf. 97.9 (and the second note there) above.

103.13 "acclaimed for speculation" : المتسمين بالنظر . "*Naẓar*" here is used to express the dialectical process, "speculation" in the sense of general reasoning, the sense which is implied also in the terms *ra'y* and *ijtihād* below, 1. 15 (cf. *The Encyclopaedia of Islam, s.v. naẓar*, 3: 889). Though he does not mention by name the people against whom he is inveighing here, it is not difficult to deduce their identity from this and the following lines. They must be the *muᶜtazilah*, sometimes called *ahl al-naẓar* (cf. J. Schacht, *The Origins of Muhammadan Jurisprudence* [Oxford, 1950], pp. 128, 258); men well known for their relatively extreme acceptance of the validity of reason in religious argument. As he does not go into detail, here or elsewhere, it is difficult to be certain what in particular al-Kindī objected to in the Kalām method (and cf. above, introduction pp. 32 ff., for further discussion). He is most certainly *not* criticizing the use of reason, but rather what appears to him as its misuse.

103.14 "even if they are enthroned undeservedly with the crowns of truth": وإن تتوجوا بتيجان الحق من غير استحقاق . This evoking of monarchic imagery is repeated in the following line and below at 104.4. Clearly, al-Kindī is referring to intellectuals who are in positions of authority (and cf. 104.5) and who enjoy royal approval, however unworthy of it they may be. The only theologians who were in this favored position at the time of al-Kindī's composition of this treatise were the *muᶜtazilah* (cf. above, introduction, p. 4). Therefore, barring the possibility that this is a later interpolation, the *muᶜtazilah* must be the objects of al-Kindī's indignation. This is, moreover, confirmed by internal evidence in the following lines.

103.14-104.1 "because of their narrow understanding of the methods of truth and their scant knowledge of what befits the august (scholar) as regards opinion and judgement in those common usages which are all pervasive: لضيق فطنهم عن أساليب الحق وقلة معرفتهم بما يستحق ذو الجلالة في الرأي والاجتهاد في الأنفاع العامة الكل الشاملة لهم .

Al-Kindī refers here to terms with which the *Muᶜtazilah* method of reasoning is associated. While "opinion" (*raʾy*) and "judgement" (*ijtihād*) may be seen in the *Muᶜtazilah* scheme as synonyms for individual reasoning in general (cf. Schacht, op. cit., pp. 98, 99), as used by al-Kindī both should be contrasted with "knowledge" (*ma^{c}rifah*), bearing in mind his definitions of *ma^{c}rifah* and *ra^{ɔ}y* elsewhere. In his treatise "On Definitions and Descriptions of Things", we read that "knowledge" (or "cognition", as Stern translates, *Isaac Israeli*, p. 54) is "an opinion which does not cease": المعرفة رأى غير زائل (AR I: 176) ; while "opinion" is an "estimation which appears in word or writing. It is also said that it is a type of psychic belief, in one of two contradictory things, which can cease; and it is also said that it is estimation with the judgement established for the person judging, opinion thus being the resting of estimation": الرأي هو الظن الظاهر في القول و الكتاب، ويقال إنه اعتقاد النفس أحد شيئين متناقضين اعتقاداً يمكن الزوال عنه ، ويقال إنه الظن مع ثبات القضية عند القاضي، والرأي إذن سكون الظن. (AR I: 168, and compare Stern's translation, ibid.).

To these definitions should be added that of "estimation," said to be "a judgement of the apparent nature of a thing; not, it is said, of its true nature; and an explanation without proofs or demonstration, so that the person judging it may cease his judgement: الظن هو القضاء على الشيء من الظاهر ، ويقال لا من الحقيقة، والتبيين من غير دلائل ولا برهان ، يمكن عند القاضي بها زوال قضيته . (AR I: 171, and compare Stern's translation and comments, op. cit., pp. 63, 64.)

To al-Kindī, then, "opinion" is a kind of articulated "estimation", an expressed view which may be strongly, but not necessarily correctly, held; and certainly not a view for which the holder has a logical demonstration. On the other hand, as "an opinion which does not cease", "knowledge" undoubtedly derives its permanence from conformity with the truth; a truth, it may be assumed, which can be rendered into "proofs or demonstration". In this connection it is worth noting that Isaac Israeli (c.A.D. 855-955), who follows al-Kindī quite closely in these definitions, has one for "true knowledge" not found in the al-Kindī treatise extant, but which is certainly Kindian in derivation; "Definition of true knowledge: True cognition confirmed by syllogism and established by demonstration" (following Stern, op. cit., p. 54). This is rendered in Judaeo-Arabic, as discovered by H. Hirschfeld, ("The Arabic Portion of the Cairo Genizah at Cambridge", *JQR* XV, [1903]: 690) as: *ḥadd al-^{c}ilm al-ṣādiq ma^{c}rafah ṣādiqah yuḥaqiquhā al-qiyās wa-yuthbituhā al-burhān.* Al-Kindī himself discusses "scientific syllogisms", المقاييس العلمية elsewhere, describing the apodictic as those which are always true (تجمع صدقاً ظاهراً ابدا وهذه هي البرهانية, cf. "On the Number of the Books of Aristotle...", AR I: 380, 381, also edited by Michelangelo Guidi and Richard Walzer, "Studi su Al-Kindī I", op. cit., pp. 400, 401 Arabic, 415, 416 Italian; and translated into English by Nicholas Rescher, "Al-Kindī's Sketch of Aristotle's Organon", op. cit., pp. 54, 55).

Al-Kindī's criticism of the *mu^{c}tazilah*, therefore, is that they scant demonstrative proofs and are not sufficiently aware of the logical limitations of their own kind of reasoning.

104.1 "due to the dirty envy which controls their animal souls" : ولدرانة الحسد المتمكن من أنفسهم البهيمية . Al-Kindī here begins to level a series of rather personal charges against his opponents, for which unfortunately we have little specific corroborating evidence. That the *mu'tazilah* were generally intolerant and capable of cruel, inhuman acts has been mentioned in the introduction, as has the later indignity which al-Kindī suffered under al-Mutawakkil (see above, p. 5 f.). Clearly, the environment was such that suspicion and charges of deviationism, encouraged by personal slander, were rife. Al-Kindī attributes such behavior to a combination of jealousy, vested interests, and wrong ideas.

In referring to the "animal soul", al-Kindī is alluding to the tripartite Platonic division of the soul, which he discusses at greater length in his "Treatise on the Soul: A Summary of the Writing of Aristotle, Plato and Other Philosophers" (AR I: 273-280). There the parts of the soul (called at p. 273 both "faculties" and "souls") are divided into the "rational", "spirited" and "appetitive", القوة العقلية ، الغضبية و الشهوانية, the Platonic λογιστικόν, θυμοειδής and ἐπιθυμητικόν (cf. *Republic* IV: 439d 5 ff. and elsewhere). The "appetitive" faculty is then compared to a pig and the "spirited" to a dog, while the rational faculty is likened to an angel (AR I: 274, a passage which has also been retained among the sayings of al-Kindī collected by al-Sijistānī; cf. Atiyeh's edition of the *Muntakhab Ṣiwān al-Ḥikmah*, no. 5, pp. 218 Arabic, 240 English). Again, at the end of the treatise (p. 279), emotional indulgence is associated with animal behavior (طبع البهائم). Envy, one of such emotions, and as such a function of the "animal soul", is specifically referred to in al-Kindī's treatise *On Definitions*, where it is described as a consequence of an intemperate possessive desire (AR I: 178, 179, and cf. the *Republic* IX : 580d 10ff.; see too the second note below).

104.2 "the light of truth": نور الحق. Cf. the "Treatise On the Soul", AR I: 274-276, where al-Kindī speaks of "the light of the Creator", نور البارى, from which the individual soul comes and to which it goes, when it separates itself from the body, i.e., from non-theoretical objects. The rational soul thus has as its natural object the radiant world of eternally true entities, and ultimately the Source of all truth.

104.3 "human virtues": الفضائل الانسانية, by which al-Kindī would think of the four Platonic cardinal virtues (and probably subdivisions of them as well), which he gives as the meaning of this term in his treatise *On Definitions* and elsewhere; describing each with its excesses and deficiencies, and advocating for each observance of an Aristotelian mean, الاعتدال (cf. AR I: 177-179, and al-Sijistānī, op. cit., nos. 104, 108, pp. 236, 238 Arabic 256, 257 English). For Plato's σοφία, ἀνδρεία, σωφροσύνη and δικαιοσύνη, al-Kindī has الحكمة، النجدة، العفة and العدل (and cf. Richard Walzer, "Some Aspects of Miskawaih's Tahdhīb al-Akhlāq," *Greek into Arabic*, p. 224). These terms reappear in one saying attributed to al-Kindī (cf. al-Sijistānī, op. cit., no. 26, pp. 227, 228, English translation pp. 247, 248) which incorporates both his combined Aristotelian and Platonic moral philosophy and his Platonic trichotomy of the soul.

104.5[1] "for the purpose of gaining leadership and traffic in religion" : للترؤس

والتجارة بالدين . As al-Kindi makes clear here and in the following lines, his opponents are in power, and apparently he is prepared to call for their ouster, accusing them of corruption, hypocrisy, intolerance and opposition to the truth. The very boldness of this attack upon the *Muᶜtazilah*, however brief and unsustained it may be, raises the possibility that this entire section may be a later insertion, written by al-Kindī after their fall from power and his fall from favor, in an attempt to ingratiate himself with the new religious officialdom. Against this view, however, it should be noted that there is no peculiarly *kalām* position taken in these remarks, nothing said either for or against the eternity of the *Quʾrān*, Divine attributes, etc. Moreover, al-Kindi's criticisms are equally valid against the *Muᶜtazilah* and their theological opponents, since they largely shared the same methods of reasoning and had common attitudes to a state religion and to dissent.

There is, therefore, no reason why al-Kindī should not have so spoken against the *Muᶜtazilah* while they were in office, particularly since he too enjoyed at that time the protection of the caliph and would not have been suspected of actually plotting politically against the official religion. In addition, as an advocate of tolerance for diverse ideas, al-Kindī would have been incensed by the charges of heresy and unbelief, *Kufr*, which the *Muᶜtazilah* threw at their opponents (cf. Goldziher, *Vorlesungen*, op. cit., pp. 114-116); and though the charge was officially proferred only against those who did not accept the createdness of the *Quʾrān* and other theological dogmas, we may gather from al-Kindī's response that many *Muᶜtazilah* had neither a kind word for philosophy proper nor for a particular philosopher.

104.5[2] "for one who trades in something sells it": لأن من تجر بشيء باعه , reflecting the material as well as social benefits normally enjoyed by those holding state-supported religious office. Al-Kindī apparently spurned such official perquisites, and was reportedly taken to task for not trying, among other places, to earn a living at court (cf. al-Sijistānī, *op. cit.*, pp. 221 Arabic, 242 English).

104.8-9 "The knowledge of the true nature of things.... with precautions against it." The benefits of true knowledge for both moral philosophy and metaphysics are also proclaimed in *On the Soul* (AR I: 275, echoed by al-Sijistānī, op. cit., pp. 218, 219 Arabic, 240 English), showing again the influence of that treatise on al-Kindī's thinking in this section.

104.10 "the true messengers": الرسل الصادقة *viz.*, the prophets (and particularly, of course, Muḥammad), whose message which follows is simplified so as to be compatible with philosophy. In this accommodation al-Kindī is apparently prepared to minimize the particular dogmas and "principles of faith" which the theologians and traditionalists emphasized. His very formulation of religious "essentials" shows a rational bias.

105.2 "and that which we shall say now": ولما نحن قائلون الآن. The following argument was attributed in antiquity to Aristotle's *Protrepticus* (cf. Richard Walzer, *Aristotelis Dialogorum Fragmenta* [Florence, 1934], no. 2, pp.

22-24; English translation by Sir David Ross, *The Works of Aristotle*, Vol. VII, *Select Fragments* [Oxford, 1952], no. 2, pp. 27-29), and is found in a number of late Greek as well as Syriac writers (cf. Walzer, "Un Frammento Nuovo di Aristotele", *Greek into Arabic*, p. 45 n. 5). Al-Kindī undoubtedly came across it in the same introduction to philosophy which has served him above, 97.8 ff. (cf. Elias, op. cit., p. 3. 17-23, David op. cit., 9.2-12); he thus returns at the end of this chapter to the source under which influence he began it.

CHAPTER II: NOTES

106.1-2 "Chapter Two of the First Part of *On First Philosophy*" :الفن الثاني وهو الجزء الأول في الفلسفة الأولى (literally, "The Second Article, Being the First Part in *The First Philosophy*"), following the phrasing of chap. 3 above, p. 76. *Fann*, which I translate as "chapter" and, more literally, as "article" (for the more usual "kind" or "species"), is probably a translation of *technē;* it might be used to connote the introduction of another system or "art" of discussing the subject, a "treatise", though not a totally independent one, on the theme.

106.3[1] "that which ought to precede" : ما يجب تقديمه, viz., an introduction which has contained a definition of philosophy and an enumeration of the various types of causes; as well as a general appreciation of previous philosophers and of philosophical endeavor.

106.3[2] "let us follow this with what follows naturally" : فلنتل ذلك بما يتلوه تلوا طبيعياً, viz., specific arguments employing philosophical methods and definitions.

106.5-6 "there are two kinds of human perceptions, one of which is nearer to us and further from nature": الوجود الإنساني وجودان أحدهما أقرب منا وأبعد عند الطبيعة. Cf. *Post. An.* I: 2 72a 1-5, "I mean that objects nearer to sense (τὰ ἐγγύτερον τῆς αἰσθήσεως; أقرب الى الحس in the translation of Abū Bishr Mattā, ed. ᶜAbd al-Raḥmān Badawī, *Manṭiq Arisṭū* [Cairo, 1949] 3: 314) are prior and better known to us; objects without qualification prior and better known are those further (from sense, τὰ πορρώτερον, أكثر بعدا). The greatest universals (τὰ καθόλου μάλιστα ; الأمور الكلية خاصة) are furthest from sense, while particulars are nearest." Compare this with *Physics* I: 1 184a 16, "the natural way (of determining the principles of Physics) is to proceed from the things which are more knowable and clearer to us, to those which are clearer and more knowable by nature" (πέφυκε δὲ ἐκ τῶν γνωριμωτέρων ἡμῶν ἡ ὁδὸς καὶ σαφεστέρων ἐπὶ τὰ σαφέστερα τῇ φύσει καὶ γνωριμώτερα ; ومن شأن الطريق أن يكون من الأمور التي هي أعرف وابين عندنا ، إلى الأمور التي هي أبين وأعرف عند الطبيعة, in the translation of Isḥāq ibn Ḥunayn, ed. ᶜAbd al-Raḥman Badawī [Cairo, 1964], I:3).

Al-Kindī's statement is compounded terminologically of elements of both these sources, even as his ensuing remarks draw upon both books as well as portions of the *De Anima* and *Metaphysics* (and see, in this particular connection, *Met* I: 2 982a 21). It is likely that he was helped to this eclectic approach by some commentary to one or more of these books, rather than by direct familiarity with them all. Indeed, the *Posterior Analytics* and *De Anima* would have been known only by second hand to an Arab reader in al-Kindī's time (see Peters, op. cit., pp. 17 ff, 31 ff. and 40 ff.).

106.7 "from the beginning of our development" : منذ بدء نشونا . Cf. e.g., *Met.* I: 1 980a 28, "by nature animals are born with the faculty of sensation".

106.9[1] "due to the motion": لزوال , in the sense here, and at l. 11 below, of an evanescent, fleeting motion.

106.9[2] "its change in every case being through one of the kinds of motion": وتبدله في كل حال بأحد أنواع الحركات, literally "movements," *viz.*, alteration, and cf. *De An.* II: 5 416b 33. Al-Kindi uses "change" and "motion" here in a loose, synonymous sense, as below at 118.19 (and cf. n. 118.19[2]).

106.10 "Its quantity is differentiated by 'more' or 'less', 'equal' and 'unequal', while its quality is contrasted by 'similar' and 'dissimilar', 'stronger' and 'weaker'": وتفاضل الكمية فيه بالأكثر والأقل والتساوى وغير التساوى ، وتغاير الكيفية فيه بالشبيه وغير الشبيه ، والأشد والأضعف , i.e., one object of sensation as perceived is compared with another by various criteria. "Equality" and "inequality", τὸ ἴσον καὶ ἄνισον (مساوي وغير مساو in K. Georr's edition of Isḥāq ibn Ḥunayn's translation, *Les Categories D'Aristote*... [Beirut, 1948], p. 332) are particularly predicated of quantity by Aristotle in *Cat.* 6. 6a 27, while at 5b 14 "much" and "little", τὸ πολύ and ὁ ὀλίγος (الكثير والقليل , Georr, p. 330) are considered applicable as relative predicates. At *Cat.* 8. 11a 15 Aristotle mentions the "similar" and "dissimilar", ὅμοια καὶ ἀνόμοια (الشبيه وغير الشبيه , Georr, p. 344) as the distinctive predicates of quality; while the predicates of "more" and "less", τὸ μᾶλλον καὶ τὸ ἧττον (الأكثر والأقل ibid.) are also used, in 10b 26, as general predicates of quality. Al-Kindī mentions "little" and "much" (القليل والكثير) among the predicates of quantity below at 146.12, while in "On Definitions" (AR I : 167) he defines quantity and quality by their distinctive above-mentioned Aristotelian predicates. Al-Kindī is reported to have written two works on the *Categories* (cf. *Fihrist*, p. 256, and see Peters, op. cit., p. 11), and, in his brief description of its contents in *On the Number of Aristotle's Books*, he mentions similarity and dissimilarity as predicates of quality (cf. AR I: 365; ed. M. Guidi and R. Walzer, *Studi I*, pp. 391 Arabic, 405 Italian; N. Rescher's English translation, "Al-Kindī's Sketch of Aristotle's Organon", op. cit., p. 51, reading "shape" [*shakl*] for "shade").

Thus, if al-Kindī did not find these various remarks already brought together in a commentary, it could have occurred to him naturally to elaborate on the nature of perception by using criteria taken from the *Categories;* even as his next association, dealing with the internal mechanics of sensation, could have come to him from familiarity with the *De Anima* tradition.

106.12-13 "It (sc. sensory perception) is that the forms of which... the living being": i.e., both men and animals perceive along similar lines, animals too having an imaginative faculty, الصورة (literally الصور in the ms.), and related memory, الحفظ (cf. *De An.* III: 10 433a 11, *De Mem.* 1 450a 12-15; and see H. Wolfson's classification of the various terms used to describe the imagination and memory in their various aspects, in "The Internal Senses in Latin, Arabic and Hebrew Philosophic Texts", *Harvard Theological Review* 28 [1935]: 130-133). In comparing the lists of Arabic terms with al-Kindī's usages here and elsewhere (see below), we may conclude that his classification is along broad, general lines, though he probably understood the functions of the various internal senses as multiple. It is, in fact, the "sensational" aspect of imagination, φαντασία αἰσθητική, which animals share with men, to which al-Kindī is particularly referring in this sentence, apparently ignoring its more "rational" or "deliberative" character, φαντασία λογιστική or βουλευτική (cf. *De An.* III: 10 433b 29, 11 434a 5; though, as S. Van den Bergh points out, in *Averroes' Tahāfut al-Tahāfut* [London, 1954], II: 189, note to p. 334.6, Aristotle recognized that sensation is never completely without a rational element); and it is the latter function which in man prepares his perceptions for comprehension by the intellect. That al-Kindī was familiar with this rationalizing role of the imagination is evident from his definition of *tawahhum* (ordinarily rendered as "estimation" but used by al-Kindī as the equivalent of "imagination" in the broad sense) in *On Definitions* (AR I: 167): "it is *fanṭāsīyā*, a psychic faculty which apprehends sensory forms in the absence of their matter. It is also said that *fanṭāsīyā*, which is the imagination, is the presenting of the forms of sensible things in the absence of their matter" (التوهم هو الفنطاسيا ، قوة نفسانية ومدركة للصور الحسية مع غيبة طينتها ؛ ويقال الفنطاسيا ، وهو التخيل ، وهو حضور صور الأشياء المحسوسة مع غيبة طينتها). This point is repeated in his treatise *On the Essence of Sleep and Vision*, في ماهية النوم والرؤيا (AR I: 295, Latin translation by Gerard of Cremona, *Liber de sommo et visione*, ed. A. Nagy, *Die Philosophischen Abhandlungen des Yaᶜqūb ben Isḥāq al-Kindī* [Münster, 1897], pp. 13, 14), where the imaginative faculty (القوة المصورة, *virtus formativa*) is differentiated from the senses by its role as an abstracting agent ("despoiler" in the terminology used by A. Altmann, who translates this passage in his and Stern's *Isaac Israeli*, p. 144; cf. the entire discussion of the history of this faculty there, and of al-Kindī's influence on others in dream theory, pp. 142-145.)

Thus it is probably not insignificant that al-Kindī here chooses to refer to a view of sense perception which ostensibly has nothing to do with the intellect; and that he mentions two of the "internal senses" but omits the third and, for man, the most important, *viz.*, the rational faculty, in which perceptions normally culminate. This omission may be due to his desire to draw a sharp contrast between sensory and intellectual perceptions; and to construct a philosophy along lines that are "purely" logical and demonstrative.

107.1 "and in a body": وبالجرم, possibly a scribal error for او بالجرم, "or in a body"; or this word may have begun a separate two word phrase (as AH), since the ms. has a blank space after it.

107.2-4 "The other ... universal and particular". See above 106.5,6, and the quotation from *Post. An.* I: 2 72a 4 quoted in the note there. Cf. too *De An.* II: 5 417b 22, "actual sensation apprehends individuals, while knowledge apprehends universals".

107.4 "things are universal and particular": الأشياء كلية وجزئية, i.e., the totality of things is composed of universal and particular objects; alternatively, and more probably, al-Kindī's intention is to say that objects are *either* universal or particular.

107.4-5 "I mean by 'universal' the genera of species and the species of individuals; while I mean by 'particular' the individuals of species" : أعني بالكلي الأجناس للأنواع ، والأنواع للأشخاص ، وأعني بالجزئية الأشخاص للأنواع. Al-Kindī is interested in defining his terms with logical precision; and he refers naturally to the relationship between genus, species and the specific difference constitutive of the individual with which he was familiar from his acquaintance with the *Isagoge* and/or a commentary to it (cf. above, pp. 97.8, 101.5).

107.6-8 "Particular, material individuals ... human intellect." Cf. below, p. 154.17: "(Intellect) is the species of things... as well as that which is above them. Individual things, on the other hand, are sensible"; and see the commentary there.

107.11 "for all representation is sensible", لأن المثل كلها محسوسة. This is a tautology, in al-Kindī's use of the term "representation". As remarked above in the note to 106. 12, 13, al-Kindī apparently deliberately avoids acknowledgement of the traditional role of sensory perception, or "representation", in intellection. It appears that there is for him no epistemic bridge from genuine sensory perception to intellectual cognition. A similar impression is received from his treatise *On the Intellect* (AR I: 354, edited as well by Richard J. McCarthy in *Islamic Studies* [1964] iii, pp. 112 Arabic, 126 English); as Stern remarks in assessing al-Kindī's treatment of the process of intellection there (*Isaac Israeli*, p. 38): "Al-Kindī explains how the objects of intellection present in the 'intellect in actuality' are communicated to the 'intellect in potentiality', and does not deal at all with the process of apprehension passing through the senses."

107.12 "Rather the concepts are verified in the soul, validated and rendered certain through the veracity of the intellectual principles which are known necessarily": بل مصدق في النفس محقق متيقن بصدق الأوائل العقلية المعقولة اضطراراً. Al-Kindī is thinking of universal propositions and the principles by which they are verified. He confuses the issue by referring to all intelligible forms, many of which are ideas derived by induction, generalizations based upon the particular perceptions of our senses. Aristotle discusses both topics separately (cf. *Post. An.* I: 2, 3, *De An.* III: 3, 4, 7, 8), distinguishing in effect between the process of acquiring ideas, and that of validating statements about such ideas, in which latter process the "scientific knowledge" obtained is essentially independent of sense perception (cf. *Post. An* I: 31 87b 27, and see W. Hammond's discussion of the role of sensory perception and logical premises in Aristotle's view of intellection, *Aristotle's Psychology*, London, 1902, pp. *LXXVIII-LXXXII*). Al-Kindi apparently blurs this distinction, despite his remarks below at 111.14 ff.; and the impression is that he seems to be reading the *De Anima* with a *Posterior Analytics* bias.

107.13 "as that 'it is' and 'it is not' cannot both be true of the same thing without its changing": كهولا هو غير صادقين في شيء بعينه ليس بغيري. Cf. *Met.* IV: 3 1005b 19, "(the firmest of all first principles is) that it is impossible for the same thing to belong and not to belong to the same thing at the same time and in the same respect": τὸ γὰρ αὐτὸ ἅμα ὑπάρχειν τε καὶ μὴ ὑπάρχειν ἀδύνατον τῷ αὐτῷ καὶ κατὰ τὸ αὐτό (in Asṭāt's translation, Bouyges I: 346, لا يمكن أن يكون شيء واحد في شيئين معا بكل جهة). Contradiction is, moreover, defined in *Post. An.* I: 2 72a 12 as "an opposition which of itself excludes any intermediate": ἀντίφασις δὲ ἀντίθεσις ἧς οὐκ ἔστι μεταξὺ καθ' αὑτήν, of which the awkward last part of al-Kindi's sentence above— بعينه ليس بغيرى — could well be an echo. Interestingly, the Arabic translation of Abū Bishr Mattā (d. A.D. 940) is corrupt here (unless we have an editorial lapse), reading واما المناقضة فهى انطيثاسس ، أعني التقابل الذي الأوسط له بذاته (ed. Badawī, *Manṭiq Arisṭū* II: 314). It may thus be that this passage was never clearly transmitted to the Arabs.

108.1 "This is a perception of the soul which is not sensory, is necessary, (and) does not require an intermediary": فان هذا وجود للنفس لاحسى ، اضطراري ، لا يحتاج إلى متوسط. Cf. *Post. An.* I:2 71b 20. At 72a 8 Aristotle explains that an "immediate" premiss, (ἄμεσος , غير ذات الوسط , Badawī, op. cit., p. 314) is one to which no other is prior.

108.4 "the common sense will represent it in the soul": يمثله الحس الكلى في النفس. Al-Kindi refers here and at line 8 below to the "common sense", κοινὴ αἴσθησις, and from such meagre sources it is difficult to be certain how he understood this faculty, or if he saw it at all *as* a separate faculty. Apparently he makes no claim for the common sense other than as a medium of perception in the soul. He refers only to its function in the perception of sensibles and the "common sensibles" (cf. the following note), ignoring its other functions (for which cf. D. Ross' introduction to the *De Anima*, pp. 33-36). As he has already acknowledged the role of the senses and of imagination in sense perception, it would seem that his common sense is either identical with one or the other, or, as its name implies, functions between them. It is this latter role which Isaac Israeli gives to common sense: "It is intermediate between the corporeal sense of sight and the imaginative faculty, which resides in the anterior ventricle of the brain and is called *fanṭāsīya*. It is for this reason that it is called "common sense' (*ha-ḥūsh ha-meshūtāf, sensus communis*), for it receives from the corporeal sense, i.e., that of sight, the corporeal aspects of things and transmits them to the spiritual sense, i.e., the imaginative faculty" (*ha-meẓayyer, formatum,* following Altmann's translation of Israeli's "Book on the Elements", pp. 53, 54, in *Isaac Israeli*, pp. 135, 136; Latin and Hebrew passages given by H. Wolfson, "Isaac Israeli on the Internal Senses", *Jewish Studies in memory of George A. Kohut*, ed. S. Baron and A. Marx [New York, 1935], p. 584, n. 9). As Israeli is often indebted to al-Kindī, the master's understanding of common sense might be reflected in the disciple's explanation, hitherto described as "unique" (cf. Wolfson, op. cit., p. 585, Altmann, op. cit., p. 141).

On the other hand, the Israeli passage quoted above has the common sense transmitting corporeal images to the imagination, which faculty is to refine them further into intelligibles. Al-Kindī, however, is opposed here to this view of intellection (cf. 1. 10 below). Thus, our knowledge of his understanding of the common sense remains at present incomplete; while his reticence freed Israeli to expound his own explanation, which he probably thought was in keeping, at least in part, with al-Kindī's opinion.

108.5 "while everything which is immaterial may exist with the material, as shape which is perceived through color" : وكل ما هو لاهيولانى وقد يوجد مع الهيولانى ، كالشكل الموجود باللون . For the common sense's perception of (composite) corporeal images, involving discrimination between the objects of diverse senses, cf. *De An.* III: 2 426b 12 ff., *De Sensu* 7 449a 3 ff.; while for its perception of the "common sensibles" of rest, motion, number, shape, magnitude and time—which al-Kindī is apparently referring to as "everything immaterial"—cf. *De An.* II: 6 418a 17, III: 1 425a 16, 3 428b 22 and *De Mem.* 1 450a 10.

108.8 "It is sometimes believed that it (*sc.* the immaterial) is represented in the soul through the common sense's acquiring of it": وقد يظن أنه يتمثل في النفس باجتلاب الحس الكلى له. This is the Aristotelian view (cf. the preceding note), that the common sensibles are perceived with and through the perceptions of particular sensible objects. Though their being perceived is a function of the general perceptive faculty of the sense, and not, e.g., of sight *qua* sight (cf. Ross, op. cit., p. 33), the common sensibles are considered as perceived representationally.

108.10 "(However) the perception of the limit, which is the shape, is an intellectual perception which occurs through sensation but is not really sensible": فوجود النهاية التي هي الشكل ، وجود عقلى عرض بالحس لا محسوس بالحقيقة . This goes beyond Aristotle's position, as outlined in the preceding note, and effectively transforms the sense (when functioning as a common sense with common sensibles) into an intelligent faculty. This is quite the opposite of Aristotle's teaching that the soul never thinks, at least at first, without an image (cf. *De An.* III: 7 431a 16, 8 432a 3). From the beginning, al-Kindī appears to be saying, there are no genuine images, i.e. representations, of ideas; and the function of the intellect is extended into the senses.

109.4 "it is something which only the intellect necessarily perceives": وإنما هو شيء يجده العقل اضطراراً, though not immediately. Al-Kindī's choice of example is interesting, since it assumes quite a familiarity with questions of physics and cosmology; nor are the reasons with which he verifies the statement as self-contained and obvious as he might have wished. His interest in the subject matter of the example probably led him to get ahead of himself at this point. In another treatise, رسالة...أن العناصر والجرم الأقصى كرية الشكل, "That the Elements and the Outermost Body (of the Universe) Are Spherical in Form", al-Kindī uses this same statement as a premise with which to prove the sphericity of the universe (cf. AR II: 49 f.; translated by Haig Khatchadourian and Nicholas Rescher, *Isis* 56 [1965], pp. 190 f., reprinted in the latter's *Studies in Arabic Philosophy*, p. 10).

109.6 "the meaning of 'void' is a place without any spatial object in it": الخلاء مكان لا متمكن فيه. Al-Kindī has a word play not found in the original Greek definition (*Physics* IV: 7 213b 31, τὸ κενὸν τόπος εἶναι ἐν ᾧ μηδέν ἐστι, in Isḥāq ibn Ḥunayn's translation, ed. ʿAbd al-Raḥmān Badawī [Cairo 1964], I: 347: الخلاء هو مكان ليس فيه شيء أصلا). In the *Physics* passage cited, Aristotle proceeds to reject the existence of a void, showing that it is incompatible with the movements of bodies. In *De Caelo* I: 9 279a 11 ff., he argues against the existence of a void outside the heaven—understanding void as the place of a potential body—on the grounds that the properties (such as place, void and time) of a body which cannot itself exist outside the heaven (as explained in *De Caelo* I: 9 278b 21 ff.) cannot exist either. Al-Kindī ignores this distinction between potential and actual body, and the relative sense in which "void" is a meaningful term, though one which may be rejected on physical grounds. He is rather thinking of the void in some absolute logical sense; which allows him to establish an immediate self-contradiction of terms.

109.7 "Now 'place' and 'a spatial object' are in that type of relation where one does not precede the other". Cf. *Physics* IV: 4 210b 34 ff., and particularly 212a 20, in which place is defined as "the innermost motionless boundary of what contains", τὸ τοῦ περιέχοντος πέρας ἀκίνητον πρῶτον.

109.11 "if the plenum is a body": والملاء اذا كان هو جسماً (following AR's emendation of جسم). Cf. *De Caelo* I: 9 278b 21 ff. Aristotle argues that "there neither is nor can there come into being any body outside the heaven", since the physical movements of all bodies, which are briefly mentioned, preclude such a possibility. In contrast, al-Kindī offers no physical argument in support of this statement, that there is no body outside the universe. He concentrates rather upon the logical entailments of "infinite body"; which is, for reasons he has yet to give (cf. below, 155.1 ff.,), a self-contradictory term.

110.7 "beyond nature" فوق الطبيعة, i.e., metaphysical objects; compare al-Kindī's use of ما فوق الطبيعى in his *Almagest* paraphrase, as discussed by Rosenthal in "Al-Kindī and Ptolemy", op. cit., p. 440.

110.9 "Preserve... this preface": فاحفظ . . . هذه المقدمة. This appeal does not conclude al-Kindī's general remarks, which continue until 112.19. He may have inserted this paragraph both for didactic and/or rhetorical, stylistic purposes, and to serve as well as a transition to a theme which, while related to the foregoing, may well be taken from a different source.

110.12 "By these two ways is the truth on the one hand easy and on the other hand difficult": فان بهاتين السبيلين كان الحق من جهة سهلا ومن جهة عسرا. Cf. *Met.* II 1 993a 30, "the investigation of truth is in one way difficult, in another easy", ἡ περὶ τῆς ἀληθείας θεωρία τῇ μὲν χαλεπὴ τῇ δὲ ῥᾳδία (أن النظر في الحق من جهة عسر ومن جهة سهلا ... in Asṭāt translation, Bouyges I: 3). Aristotle, however, goes on to explain that it is difficult to be precise about a particular part of the truth which is being studied, though it is easy to say something true in general. Al-Kindī, however, intends something else in referring to "two ways" by which the truth is easy and difficult, *viz.*, the right way by which it is easy (use of the intellect), and the wrong way, by which it is difficult (use of the senses).

110.13 "as the eye of the bat is blind . . . in the rays of the sun", كعشاء عين الوطواط . . . في شعاع الشمس. Cf. *Met.* II: 1 993b 8, "for as the eyes of bats are to the blaze of day", ὥσπερ γὰρ τὰ τῶν νυκτερίδων ὄμματα πρὸς τὸ φέγγος (apparently translated by Asṭāt as فكما حال عيون الوطواط عند ضوء النهار, Bouyges I : 4, while Isḥāq ibn Ḥunayn translates يشبه حال عيون الخفاش عندضياء الشمس). Al-Kindī, however, again modifies his source, since Aristotle's simile compares the bat's natural difficulty of seeing during the day with the intellect's natural difficulty of comprehending the causes and principles of all things; while for al-Kindī, the bat's daytime vision is to our vision as our sensory perception of intelligibles is to our intellection of them. Philosophy is not difficult, for al-Kindī, if properly pursued.

110.17 "Instruction is easy only in customary things": فان التعليم إنما يكون سهلا في المعتادات. Cf. *Met.* II: 3 994b 32, "the way we receive a lecture depends on our custom", αἱ δ' ἀκροάσεις κατὰ τὰ ἔθη συμβαίνουσιν (والتعليم المسموع إنما يكون على ما أعتدنا, in Asṭāt's translation (Bouyges I: 42). Al-Kindī deviates from the following Aristotelian passage by mentioning only traditional Islamic forms of instruction, not, e.g., mathematics, which is introduced as a separate subject.

110.19—
111.1 "mathematical investigation... is suitable only in what has no matter": الفحص التعليمي . . . ينبغي أن يكون فيما لا هيولى له. Cf. *Met.* II: 3 995a 15, the Arabic of which (Bouyges I: 49), though in a damaged state, is similar in its use of الفحص التعليمي.

111.1 "matter is a substratum for affection": الهيولى موضوعة للانفعال. This is similar to al-Kindī's definition of matter in his treatise *On Definitions* (AR I: 166): "matter: a faculty which is a substratum for the bearing of forms; an affection" (الهيولى – قوة موضوعة لحمل الصور ، منفعلة). Cf. *Met.* VIII: 1 1042a 32.

111.2 "and nature is the primary cause of everything which moves and rests" : والطبيعة علة أولية لكل متحرك ساكن. With this may be compared al-Kindī's definition of nature in *On Definitions* (p. 165): "nature is the principle of motion and of rest from motion. It is the first of the faculties of the soul" (الطبيعة – ابتداء حركة وسكون عن حركة ، وهو أول قوى النفس). In his treatise *An Explanation That the Nature of the Sphere is Different from the Natures of the Four Elements* (AR II: 40, 41), terrestial nature is defined in terms similar to those in our treatise. This definition of nature may be found in Aristole's *Physics* II: 1 192b 13.

111.4 "mathematical investigation": الفحص الرياضي, used as a synonym for الفحص التعليمي just above, indicating al-Kindī's inconsistent usages.

111.9 "The Principles of Physics": أوائل الطبيعة, a missing work of al-Kindī's, possibly equivalent to his "Book on the Action and Affection of First Natures" (كتاب في الفاعلة والمنفعلة من الطبيعيات الأولى), or the "Book on the Principles of Sensible Things" (كتاب في أوائل الأشياء المحسوسة) mentioned in the *Fihrist* I: 256. The work is perhaps, at least in part, a summary of *Physics* III 1-3. Cf. 1 200b 12 ff.

111.11 "For it is not possible that something should be the cause of its own generation, as we shall explain shortly": لأنه ليس يمكن أن يكون الشيء علة كون ذاته كما سنبين بعد قليل. Cf. below. 123.3 ff.

111.14[1] "an apodictical perception": الوجود البرهاني, literally, a demonstrative "finding" or apprehension. This intellectual apprehension is the sense of "perception" for *wujūd* in 106.5, 107.2, 112.2, etc. Cf., for the following lines in the text, *Anal. Post.* I: 3 72b 18 f.

111.14[2] "pursuit": مطلوب, literally, "desideratum."

112.1-2 "If there would be a demonstration for every demonstration, then there would never be perception of anything": إن كان لكل برهان برهان فلا يكون لشيء وجود البتة, since one cannot traverse an infinite series (cf. *Anal. Post.* I: 3 72b 10), and thus there would never be a demonstration, or premise, which could be known.

112.4 "he being that which is living, speaking and mortal": الذي هو الحي الناطق الميت, the ζῷον λογικὸν θνητόν of Porphyry (cf. the *Isagoge*, ed. Busse, *CAG* iv/1, 10.12, 11.16, pp. 1041, 1047 in Badawi's edition of Al-Dimashqī's translation, *Manṭiq Arisṭū* III; which appears, naturally, among Porphyry's commentators [cf. Elias, op. cit., 4. 17, 44. 14; David, op. cit., 2.4, 11.22]). Al-Kindī defines mankind, الانسانية, in these same terms in *On Definitions* (AR I: 179). As is made clear there by definitions of the angelic and animal realms, mortality distinguishes man from the angels ("gods" in Porphyry, op. cit., 10.13, missing entirely from the Arabic translation, p. 1041).

112.6 "we should not seek probable (literally 'persuasive') arguments in mathematical sciences": ينبغي أن [لا] نطلب الاقناعات في العلوم الرياضية. This remark and the following two paragraphs have their origin in *Met.* II: 3, to which other sources may have been added. Thus in *Eth. Nich.* I: 3 1094b 25 Aristotle states that "it is equally foolish to accept probable reasoning (πιθανολογοῦντος) from a mathematician, and to demand scientific proofs from a rhetorician" (and cf. the *Theaetetus*, 162e 7).

112.10 "some proceeding in accord with parables, some proceeding in accord with historical witness": وبعضهم جرى على عادة الأمثال ، وبعضهم جرى على عادة شهادات الأخبار. Cf. *Met.* 2: 3 995a 7, which may be translated as "(some people do not accept statements...) unless they are expressed by way of examples, while others demand that a poet be quoted as a witness": οἱ δ' ἂν μὴ παραδειγματικῶς, οἱ δὲ μάρτυρα ἀξιοῦσιν ἐπάγεσθαι ποιητήν (in Asṭāt's translation, Bouyges I: 44, 45 : ومنهم من لا يقنع إن لم يكن القول بأمثال ، ومنهم من يريد أن يوتى بشهادة شاعر على ما قيل). Al-Kindī has here rendered Aristotle, with a minimum of modification, in cultural terms which would have been familiar to a Muslim audience. Thus, Aristotle's "examples" taken from everyday life (in which sense the *paradeigma* should be understood; cf. Ross' note to his edition of the *Met.* I: 220) is probably understood by al-Kindī as denoting "parables" or possibly "proverbs", genres of literature and instruction common in Islam. Though *amthāl* can mean either "example" or "proverb" and "parable", and as such it is a fortuitous choice for translation of *paradeigma*, it would appear that the Arab reader, unfamiliar with the Platonic Dialogues or other examples of "paradigmatic discussion", would have understood the term in the latter sense. That this may have been the intention of Asṭāt is rendered possible by the second translation of this passage, that by the normally careful Isḥāq ibn Ḥunayn. He translates (Bouyges I: 44) the παραδειγματικῶς of the above passage as شهادة الجماعة, "collective witness"; which could only have meant, to a Muslim, the *ijmā*ᶜ or "agreement" of the community of believers.

This Islamicization of the text is more evident in al-Kindī's use of "historical witness", literally "witnesses of events" (or of the "stories" of these events), for Aristotle's "poetic witness". Al-Kindī's audience would have understood the phrase as alluding to reports of individual events, rendered as stories or anecdotes; and to the chain of transmitters which precedes the story and testifies to its accuracy. In this form, well delineated by al-Kindī's time, the *akhbār* genre of literature resembles that of the *ḥadīth*, and like it often dealt with stories of the Prophet or of battles fought (cf. Franz Rosenthal, *A History of Muslim Historiography* [Leiden, 1952], pp. 10-11, 59-63). It was common too to include poetic insertions in the prose story, and this element, in which the authority of the poet is in effect subordinated to that of other (prosaic but pious) witnesses may have served al-Kindī as the bridge for his translation of a Greek cultural norm into an Islamic one.

112.15 "nor sensation or exemplification in the science of the metaphysical": ولا في العلم الإلهي حسا ولا تمثيلا, i.e., there should be no sensory representation of any kind, neither directly nor by way of metaphor or parable, in the pursuit of metaphysics, العلم الإلهي; literally "theology", used as a synonym of "metaphysics" (cf. *Met.* VI: 1 1026a 19, Bouyges II: 707).

112.19 "we ought to set forth beforehand the canons the employment of which we require in this craft": فينبغي أن نقدم القوانين التي نحتاج إلى استعمالها في هذه الصناعة. Al-Kindī now proceeds to give a number of attributes of the eternal, which he considers to be a unique being. Understood as an allusion to the True One, i.e., God, these remarks anticipate in part the conclusions of this treatise, pp. 161f. The remarks are presented here as logical propositions from which the subsequent discussion of things which are not eternal derives (and cf. the use of قوانين العقل in the Plotinian-based رسالة من العلم الإلهي, *Epistola de Scientia Divina*, ed. Badawī, *Plotinus apud Arabes* p. 171; translated by Lewis, op. cit., p. 299: 4.16). The statements themselves spell out in somewhat redundant detail a number of mostly Aristotelian conclusions about the eternal, as well as a notion of the uniqueness of the eternal which may have come from Neoplatonic reflections upon the One or from John Philoponus' attitude to eternity. Declarations of the unique, uncaused, unchanging, self-sufficient One, or God, are of course scattered throughout the writings of the Church Fathers and *mutakallimūn*. It would seem, however, that al-Kindī is following a philosophical rather than theological formulation of the eternal, since his description lacks the more personal and volitional themes of the latter (cf., for example, al-Ashʿarī's *Maqālāt al-Islāmīyīn*, ed. by Hellmut Ritter, op. cit., p. 177).

113.1-114.8 "the eternal is . . . perfect". The information contained in these three paragraphs may be summarized as follows: the eternal has always existed and will always exist; it is independent of any cause; its being is simple and unique, changeless and perfect. With this description may be compared the definition of the eternal given in *On Definitions* (AR I: 169): "the eternal is that which has never been non-existent; it does not require another for its subsistence, and that which does not require another for its subsistence has no cause, while that which has no cause endures forever": الأزلي – الذي لم يكن ليس وليس يحتاج في قوامه إلى غيره ؛ والذي لا يحتاج في قوامه إلى غيره فلا علة له ، وما لا علة له فدائم أبداً . While there is overlapping of these concepts in the sources, cf. nevertheless, the view of the ungenerated and imperishable nature of the eternal in *Physics* IV: 12 221b 2, *De Caelo* I: 12 281b 25, *Met.* XII: 7 1072a 21, *Eth. Nich.* VI: 3 1139b 24; for the view of the eternal as self-sufficient and uncaused, *Met.* XII: 7 1072b 28, XIV: 4 1091b 18, *Enneads* V: 4 1 (ed. Henry and Schwyzer II: 332, and cf. Lewis' translation there, p. 333, of the equivalent passage in the Arabic Plotinus corpus, ed. Badawī, op. cit., p. 179), al-Ashʿarī's *Maqālāt*, p. 484, and al-Khayyaṭ's *Kitāb al-Intiṣār*, ed. by Albert Nader, op. cit., p. 80; for the view of the eternal as the one, unique, changeless, perfect being, cf. the last mentioned sources, as well as—in a tradition that may be traced to Parmenides' reflections upon the nature of being (preserved in Simplicius' commentary on the *Physics* *CAG* ix. 145, 1 ff.; as quoted by Kirk and Raven, *The Pre-Socratic Philosophers* [Cambridge, 1966] p. 273)—the Arabic Plotinian passages in Badawī, pp. 112 and 186 (Lewis pp. 271 and 474); and see too John of Damascus' *De Fide Orthodoxa* (ed. Migne, *PG* 94), I: 4, English translation by F. Chase Jr., *Saint John of Damascus: Writings*, The Fathers of the Church, vol. 37 (New York, 1958), p. 170 f.

Now, Neoplatonic thought depicts the One as not the only eternal being, though its nature is beyond all comprehension and comparison, even with the other eternal hypostases; while *kalām* and Christian sources discuss the essence of God in relation to His attributes; and these are themes to which al-Kindī is not addressing himself. His depiction of the eternal as unique generically might, however, be an echo of John Philoponus' view of God as the only ungenerated being. We know that Philoponus attacked Aristotle on this point and rejected his doctrine of the eternity of the world (cf. Simplicius' commentary on the *Physics*, *CAG* x: 1141.11, 19 ff., 1144.25, "only the First is ungenerated and uncaused, μόνον τὸ πρῶτον ἀγένητόν ἐστι καὶ ἀναίτιον; and see Walzer, *Greek into Arabic*, p. 192). As we are approaching a section in which al-Kindī is clearly indebted to Philoponus, it is probable that these remarks already show his influence.

113.1 "which must never have been a non-existent being": الذي لم يجب ليس هو مطلقاً . *Huwa*, as *huwīyah*, often represents "being", as the fifth form *tahawwaya* of pp. 123 and 162 can stand for "coming to be"; while *laysa* as "non-existent (being)", contrasted with *aysa* as "existent (being)" is used, e.g., in p. 123. Cf. below, note to 119.16.

113.3-4 "subject", "predicate", "agent", "reason": موضوع، محمول، فاعل، سبب . These four terms relate, as the allusion at l. 4 tells us, to the four types of causes mentioned above at 101.3. Al-Kindī, if not simply presenting a partially different set of synonyms of causal terms, is here stating the physical correlates of causation; i.e., he is saying that the eternal is not caused since it has nothing with which causation is associated.

113.5 "a species being composed of its genus, which is common to it and to others, and of a specific difference which does not exist in others": والنوع مركب من جنسه العامي له ولغيره ومن فصل ليس في غيره . At 107.4 f. above, al-Kindī has referred in passing to the relations between genus, species and individuals, and here he elaborates somewhat on this theme, using material found ultimately in Porphyry and his commentators (cf. the *Isagoge*, CAG iv/1, 4.2, 13.23; in the Arabic edited by Badawī, op. cit., pp. 1027, 1052). Al-Kindī's view of the eternal as unique is, as has been mentioned in the note to 113.1-114.8, his point of departure from Aristotle's world view and his point of affinity with that of John Philoponus. It is worth remembering here that al-Kindī does, however, agree with Aristotle elsewhere that the heavenly spheres as well as the basic elements of matter are "permanent", i.e., ungenerated and imperishable (cf. AR I: 220, 246; II: 45). Al-Kindī, however, does not consider them as eternal, but clearly states that they endure only for as long as God so wills. As, therefore, the world is ultimately not imperishable, one may assume that it is, in his view, originally created, though since — and now — "ungenerated".

This distinction is brought out in al-Kindī's terminology: *Azalīy* stands simply for the eternal, with no distinction between the eternal *a parte ante* and the eternal *a parte post* (cf. Van den Bergh, *Averroes' Tahafut al-Tahafut* [London, 1954], II: 1); while the objects which endure like the eternal are said to "remain" (باقية) for "a period of time", أيام مدة (cf. AR I: 220, II: 45). Thus it would appear that al-Kindī's unique eternal being is indeed God, and not any of the physical objects which might seem to qualify for the term.

113.11[1] "perishing being but the changing of the predicate": الفساد إنما هو تبدل المحمول. Though the argument at lines 13 f. below favor a reading of *tabaddul* as "alteration", it is translated as "change" since the argument here concerns the physical components of substance, viz., form ("predicate"/*maḥmūl*, for which cf. above, line 7) and (first) matter (cf. the following note), the coming into being and perishing of which are properly called "changes", μεταβολαί, while "alteration", ἀλλοίωσις, is the change of qualities within substance; cf. *Physics* V: 1 225a 15, V: 2 226a 26, and *Met.* XII: 2 1069b 9 (in the latter text Asṭāt, al-Kindī's colleague, renders the ἀλλοίωσις of 1. 12 as *al-taghyīr*, as he did for the plural form in *Met.* V: 21 1022b 19, Bouyges p. 641; while Abū Bishr Mattā translates it as *al-istiḥālah*, Bouyges, p. 1436 f.).

That *tabaddul* is used by al-Kindī as the generic equivalent of μεταβολή, much as *taghayyīr* is found in *Metaphysics* (cf. Bouyges 3: Index 258), is further seen below at 114.3 and 117.8, at which latter citation we read at 1. 11, وتبدل جوهره هو الكون والفساد, "and the change of . . . substance is coming to be and perishing".

113.11[2] "the primary substratum": الحامل الأول. حامل is the subject as substratum, and as such cannot be the eternal, which has no subject and is not involved with forms in any way. The term is an apparently literal translation of τὸ πρῶτον ὑποκείμενον, used as the definition of "matter" in *Physics* I: 9 192a 31 (translated, however, by Isḥāq ibn Ḥunayn, ed. Badawi, op. cit. I: 75, as الموضع الأول); which chapter also establishes the permanence of matter viewed as potentiality (1. 27). This notion helped lead to the concept of an indeterminate "first matter" (for which cf. H. Wolfson, *Crescas' Critique of Aristotle* [Cambridge, Mass., 1929] pp. 581 ff.), which may be implied by الحامل الأول, said in the following line to be *al-ays*, i.e., being (or existence, i.e., existent being; al-Kindī does not distinguish between the two) pure and simple, unformed, therefore unactualized and theoretically purely potential. Al-Kindī, however, ignores here this aspect of first matter, emphasizing merely the permanence of its existence. Cf., however, the passing reference of 156.10 below.

113.11-13 "as for the primary substratum . . . of its being". This is essentially a parenthetical remark probably prompted by the distinction of the preceding sentence between *al-maḥmūl* and *al-ḥāmil*. Al-Kindī's main argument in this paragraph is that the eternal does not perish, since perishing is predicated of forms/predicates which are contraries of a common genus; hence perishable objects belong to a genus, while the eternal clearly does not. In saying that "the perishing of a perishable object does not involve the being of its being", الفاسد ليس فساده بتأييس أيسيته, he means that it does not affect its ontological substratum, the first matter which to Aristotle is eternal and to al-Kindī ostensibly endures as long as God maintains His creation.

113.13[1] "every change is into its nearest contrary": وكل متبدل فانما تبدله بضده الأقرب . By "nearest contrary", al-Kindī may be thinking of the intermediate stages of the contraries, "into which that which changes must change first" (*Met.* X: 7 1057a 21). Cf., moreover, the *Cat.* 5 4a 10 discussion of the effect of contrary qualities upon *substance;* and the linking of contrariety to the primary substratum of bodies in *De Gen. et Corr.* II: 1 329a 24. See too *Physics* V. 2 225b 10.

113.13[2] "that which is with it in one genus": الذي معه في جنس واحد, which is said to occur with contraries and their intermediates in *Met.* X: 7 1057a 20; and see too *Met.*X: 4 1055a 4 for Aristotle's discussion of contrariety.

113.15 "related contraries": الأضداد المتقاربة , literally "near" or "successive" contraries, by which al-Kindī is, again, probably alluding to the intermediates of contraries, which are themselves contraries.

114.3 "Motion is change": والاستحالة تبدل . Cf. *Physics* V 1 225a 34, πᾶσα κίνησις μεταβολή τις. While *istiḥālah* is translated below at 117.11 as "alteration", I have translated it here as "motion", assuming an inconsistency of terminology on al-Kindī's part, and this I do for two reasons. Firstly, *istiḥālah* is qualified both in terms of *tabaddul*, of which it is a species; and of *intiqāl*, of which it is the genus. *Intiqāl*, like the more common *nuqlah*, is probably a translation of φορά, and likewise probably denotes spatial motion, which will best explain 11. 5 ff. below. (For φορά as spatial motion or "locomotion", cf., e.g., *Physics* V: 2 226a 32. Abū Bishr Mattā translates *Met.* XII: 1 1069b 12, φορὰ δὲ ἡ κατὰ τόπον, as والنقلة في المكان ; and *Met.* XII 7 1072b 9, φορὰ γὰρ ἡ πρώτη τῶν μεταβολῶν, as هى أول (!) التغيرات though Asṭāt, it should be noted, renders these passages respectively as والحركة في المكان and فان الحركة أولى التغيرات ; cf. Bouyges 3: 1437, 1608.) We thus have a descending order of *tabaddul*/change, *istiḥālah*/motion, and *intiqāl*/locomotion.
Secondly, al-Kindī has just discussed the impossibility of the eternal being perishable, which we saw relates to change of substance. Now he is about to make the point that the eternal is equally incapable of the remaining kinds of change, all of which entail motion, the primary kind of which is locomotion (cf. *Physics* VIII: 7 260a 28 f.). In these two examples al-Kindī thus establishes that the eternal does not change in any sense of the word. While this is true of Aristotle's unmoved mover, it is of course not true of the eternal circular movement of the spheres; movement which is perfection but nevertheless *is* motion (cf. *Met.* XII: 6 1072a 21, *De Caelo* I: 2, 3). Al-Kindī elsewhere accepts this unique, circular nature of celestial movement, which elevates the spheres out of the customary cycle of generation and corruption (cf. AR II: 44 f., 48 f.), but he does not therefore grant them the status of eternal being, reserved, as here, for that which does not move at all.

114.8 "Now, inasmuch as a body": وإذ الجرم . This sentence, whose beginning seems to follow the preceding remark, is entailed by it only generally and indirectly, belonging more naturally to the discussion above at 113.5-10. It therefore appears that al-Kindī has digressed somewhat and is now getting back into his major theme, that of corporeal finiteness and infinity.

114.10 "eternal body": جرم ازلي, an object whose existence, we had just learned, is theoretically impossible; therefore al-Kindī must be saying that not even an eternal body, if it could exist, could be infinite in actuality.

114.11 "I say, moreover...": فأقول. The following section, from 114.12 to 117.12, appears again practically *verbatim* in al-Kindī's treatise, "On the Unity of God and the Finiteness of the Body of the World", AR 1: 202.4-204.15 (*UG* in later references), affording us a basis for verifying the text here. Moreover, essentially the same basic mathematical points involving equality, addition and subtraction, and their application to finite and infinite bodies, are made in al-Kindī's two other treatises on this theme: formulated in more abstract mathematical fashion in the رسالة... في ايضاح تناهي جرم العالم ("Epistle... Explaining the Finiteness of the Body of the World," to be abbreviated as *EF*), pp. 188 ff.; and in a manner more like our treatise in the رسالة...في مائية ما لا يمكن أن يكن لا نهاية وما الذي يقال لا نهاية له ("Epistle...on the Essence of That Which Cannot Be Infinite and That of Which Infinity Can Be Predicated", *OE* in later references), pp. 194 ff. H. Davidson ("Creation", op. cit., p. 379), in noting most of these parallel versions (omitting mention of the "Epistle ... Explaining the Finiteness of the Body of the World"), shows that the ensuing argument for the finiteness of all body (and thus for the "body" of the universe as well), which follows from these mathematical premises, FP 115.1-116.5, is an elaboration and slight modification of an argument by John Philoponus against eternal motion; viz., that an infinite cannot be increased, whereas in an eternal universe there would have to be just such an addition of movements (cf. Simplicius' Commentary on the *Physics*, CAG X 1178.13, 14, 1179.12-14, and see Davidson, op. cit., p. 367).

114.12[1] "the true first premises": من المقدمات الأول الحقية; *UG*, 202:4, المقدمات الأولى الواضحة, "the evident first premises".

114.12[2] "which are thought with no mediation": المعقولة بلا توسط (*UG* 202.4, ... بغير متوسط, "without a mediator"), i.e., as intellectual intuitions, free of prior logical, as well as physical, mediation; the former being emphasized by al-Kindī's choice of *ma^cqūl*, the action of *^caql*, intellect. This same claim is not repeated in the other two treatises, and, indeed, *OE* follows its statements of premises with demonstrations which "prove" (in circular fashion) their truth.

114.12[3] "all bodies, of which one is not greater than the other": كل الأجرام التي ليس منها شيء أعظم من شيء, literally, "all bodies of (i.e., in) which nothing is greater (in one) than anything (in another)", understanding the reciprocal relation of bodies ("in one" and "in another") as implied by *minhā*, "of which" (since otherwise equality could be seen as referring to each particular body only). Alternatively, and more simply, the Arabic text translates "of which one is not greater than the other", if we understand *shay'* in the sense of *ba^cḍ*, "some", i.e., "one", as is actually given in the first premise of *EF*, 188.4.

114.13 "(dimensions) . . . are equal": *mutasāwiyah*, *UG* 202:6, *wāḥidah*, "the same", as also below, at 115.14.

114.14 "is not infinite": ليس لا نهاية ; *UG* 202:7, ليس لا نهاية له , "has no infinity".

114.15 "when a body is added... and greater than what it had been before that body was added to it": This fourth premise is expressed in a slightly different fashion in the second premise of *EF* (188.11), viz., that if something is added to one of two equal magnitudes, then they are no longer equal; while the first premise of *OE*, 194.18, makes the same point in an obverse way, viz., that which remains after something has been subtracted from it is less than it had been originally.

114.16[1] "before": *qabla; UG* 202.9, *min qabli.*

114.16[2] "whenever two bodies of finite magnitude are joined ...": وكل جرمين ... متناهى العظم ، إذا جمعا . This fifth premise resembles the fourth of *EF* 190.9, and the third premise of *OE*, 195.1; with the exception that the two latter treatises employ the plural number, while our treatise uses the dual.

114.17 "as well as in": في ... ايضاً; *UG* 202.11, omitted.

114.18 "the smaller of every two... things is inferior to the larger or inferior to a portion of it": وان الأصغر من كل شيئين ...وبعد الأكبر منهما أو بعد بعضه , and disparate sizes are finite. The Mu^{c}tazilite al-Naẓẓām (d. 845) is reported to have made this point, "that in which the little and the much (i.e., less and more) participate is finite" (فما دخلته القلة والكثرة أيضاً متناه); after also having implied, regarding the movements of the stars, that the addition of different magnitudes results in a finite sum (cf. *K. al-Intiṣār*, op. cit., p. 33 f., French translation, p. 32, and see Davidson, op. cit., p. 376). This sixth premise here is like the last part of the third premise in *EF* 189.9, and the fourth premise of *OE* 195.2; except that for the above terms *al-asgharu* and *al-akbaru* the other two treatises employ the equivalent terms *al-aqallu* and (as AR) *al-aktharu* (closer to the terms used by al-Naẓẓām).

114.19 "the larger": *al-akbaru; UG* 202.12, *al-a^{c}ẓamu*, the "greater".

115.1 "Now if there is an infinite body . . . ": فان كان جرم لا نهاية له. Cf. the last part of the note to 114.11 above, and see too the parallel versions of *EF*, 191.6ff. and *OE*, 195.4ff. (besides the identical—minus scribal variants—version of *UG* 202.14ff.). Cf. Davidson, op. cit., p. 379, for authors after al-Kindi who employ this argument.

115.2-3 "that which remains of it": الباقي منه ; *UG* 202.14 and 16 omit *minhu.*

115.4 "the body which comes to be from them both together is a finite magnitude": كان الجرم الكائن عنهما جميعاً متناهى العظم , as the fifth premise above, 114.16, states; which premise is specifically referred to in the *EF* presentation of this argument, 191.10.

115.6 "It is thus finite and infinite, and this is an impossible contradiction": فهو إذن متناه لا متناه، وهذا خلف لا يمكن, as well as stated explicitly as al-Kindi's third premise above, 114.14.

115.7 "whenever that which was taken from it is added to it, it will either be greater than or equal to...": إذا زيد عليه ما أخذ منه، صار أعظم مما كان... أو مساويا. The *FP* version of this argument is the most fully presented of the three (cf. *EF* 191.13 ff.), *OE* 195.9 ff. approaching the argument from the perspective of the "lesser" and not the "greater" of the infinities (possibly in keeping with its own formulation of the premise at 194.18, which is equivalent to *FP* 114.15, and see note there).

115.9 "will be greater than that which has infinity": صار...أعظم مما لا نهاية له. The impossibility of one infinite being less than another is given as (the first part of) the third premise of *EF* 189.9, followed by reasoning similar to that in our treatise.

115.10[1] "the greater": *aᶜẓamihimā*. "The larger", *al-akbaru*, as given above at 114.19 (al-Kindi's sixth premise, here repeated), would seem to be more appropriate, and this testifies to al-Kindi's indifferent use of terminology; for which cf. further the note to 114.18.

115.10[2] "a portion": *baᶜḍ*, used here synonymously with *juzᵓ*, "part", which is used in the parallel passages of *UG* 202.23 f.; and as evidenced below in 116.3 f., where *juzᵓ* takes over for *baᶜḍ*. The distinctions between these two terms drawn in 128.1f. are ignored here.

115.12 "—if the smaller body is inferior to the greater then it most certainly is inferior to a portion of it—": وإن كان بعده فهو بعد بعضه لا محالة, literally, "and if it comes after it ..." This sentence is omitted in *UG* 203.1 except for *la maḥālah*, "most certainly", which there follows the preceding sentence. The omission is perhaps best explained as a scribal error due to the homoteleuton of بعد بعضه in ll. 11 and 12. The "portion" to which the smaller body is inferior is that part of the larger body in excess of the part which is equal to the smaller body.

115.13 "a portion (of the greater)": *baᶜḍ; UG* 203.1, *li-jirm*, "to the body", which is probably a copyist's error for *li-juzᵓ*.

115.16[1] "one part": جزء واحد, as at *UG* 203.3, assuming again, though now in our text, that *jirm* (as AR) is a copyist's error for *juzᵓ*.

115.16[2] "is numbered the same": يعدها... عدداً واحداً. *UG* 203.3 missing.

115.16[3] "abundance or quality": بالكثرة أو الكيف; *UG* 203.4, بالكم والكيف, "in quantity and quality".

116.3 "and to its (own) part, which two (parts) join," ولجزئه اللذين اجتمعا. *UG* 203.8 omits this phrase.

116.4 "the all": *al-kull*, i.e., "the whole", though, following the Arabic semantic distinction, the latter term is reserved for *jamīᶜ*, as above in 1. 2. The two terms are not meant here as more than synonyms (as with *juzᵓ* and *baᶜḍ*, and cf. above, the note to 115.10), the distinction of 127.7 f. below being ignored, probably due to its irrelevance to this discussion. In terms of al-Kindi's above premises, that the part cannot be equal to the whole follows directly from the second, fourth and sixth statements above, p. 114 ll. 13, 14 and 18; and indirectly from the first premise as well, 114.12. At this point, with the remark that the body of the universe and all bodies therein are consequently finite—equivalent to the statement below at 116.12—*EF* in effect draws to a close (192.3). *OE* continues to present al-Kindī's other arguments against actually infinite things, but in a different and more succinct order than in *FP*.

116.5-8 "and in this manner—a finite beginning": Omitted in *UG* 203.9.

116.5 "it is impossible for a body to have infinity, and in this manner... any quantitative thing...": لا يمكن أن يكون جرم لا نهاية له . وبهذا التدبير (تبين أنه لا يمكن شيء) من الكميات. Besides possessing magnitude, body is defined elsewhere in this treatise in terms of a number of other quantifiable elements: cf. above, 114.8 (genus and species); below, 117.3 ff. (time and motion); and 120.7 ff. (substance and tri-dimensionality, matter and form).

116.7 "time is quantitative": والزمان كية, viz., as the number of motion, for which cf. below 117.5; and see Aristotle, *Physics* IV: 11 219b 2 ff., and *Met.* V: 13 1020a 29.

116.9 "Things predicated of a finite object are also, of necessity, finite": والأشياء أيضا المحمولة في المتناهى متناهية اضطراراً. Cf. *Physics* VIII: 10 266a 24-26, concluding οὐδὲν ἄρα πεπερασμένον ἐνδέχεται ἄπειρον δύναμιν ἔχειν, "nothing finite can have an infinite power" (translated by Isḥāq b. Ḥunayn as فليس يمكن إذن أن يكون متناهياً أصلا له قوة غير متناهية, ed. Badawī, op. cit., II: 927). Both this *Physics* passage (and the ones before and after it) and the preceding paragraphs in *FP* prove that an infinite thing always performs actually in a finite way: Aristotle showing here the (finite) effect of an infinite force on a finite body, and al-Kindī—following John Philoponus—demonstrating the (equally finite) effect of a finite magnitude on an infinite magnitude (also discussed—in different though related terms—by Aristotle, op. cit., 266b 6 ff.). Philoponus' lengthy comments upon *Physics* 266a 24 (probably in his treatise "Showing That Every Body Is Finite and Has Finite Power"), as preserved by Simplicius (*in Physicorum* 8: 10, p. 1326.38 ff.) are not specifically reiterated in the above remark and ensuing paragraph (cf., however, *ibid.*, 1327.17), though al-Kindī uses—albeit tersely—some of Philoponus' arguments from this section below at 120.7 ff. It is possible that al-Kindī's source here and in what immediately follows is Ibn Nāʿimah's translation of the *Physics*; which translation, being done from John Philoponus' commentary (cf. *Fihrist*, p. 250, and see Peters, op. cit., p. 30 ff.) probably incorporated some of the Grammarian's views into the translation (which may be the reason al-Nadīm disapproved of it). It is more likely, however, that al-Kindī used a compilation of Philoponus' arguments for finiteness, which compilation would have been based on a number of the Alexandrian's works, including, and particularly, his commentary to the *Physics*.

116.10[1] "Every predicate": فكل محمول ; *UG* 203.19, وكل محمول.

116.10[2] "motion or time": حركة أو زمان (*UG* 203.11, ... *al-zamān*). Cf. *Physics* VIII: 10 266a 12-24, concluding with the statement that it is impossible for the finite to cause motion for an infinite time, οὐκ ἐνδέχεται τὸ πεπερασμένον ἄπειρον κινεῖν χρόνον (Isḥāq b. Ḥunayn, op. cit., p. 925, لا يمكن أن يحرك المتناهي زماناً بلا نهاية).

116.10[3] "segmented through motion": مفصول بالحركة, i.e., measurable into *fuṣūl*, divisions or segments of time (cf. below, 121.5, for *faṣl* in this sense, and compare line 6 there, مدة مفصولة, "segmented interval"). *UG* 203. 11 has فاصل الحركة, "the segmenting agent (or divisor) of motion", instead of مفصول بالحركة as in our text, and the two statements appear at first to be opposed (cf. a similar paradoxical juxtaposition of statements in our text below at 117.5). The reciprocal relation of time and motion, in which each is the measure of the other (cf., e.g., *Physics* IV: 12 220b 15), renders both our versions "correct". The point of our two versions here and of the text in 117.5 below is the same, viz., that time in this context is significant as related to movement and dependent upon it (rather than vice-versa), and, as movement is a predicate of body, so too is time.

116.11 "in actuality": بالفعل; *UG* 203.12, missing.

116.12 "inferior: بعد, emended by AR to بعده; *UG* 203.13, missing.

116.13-16 "As it is possible... will occur": This statement (and compare the similar argument in *OE* 198.2 ff.) raises a number of problems concerning al-Kindī's use of the terms "possible" and "potential". Aristotle has said in *Met.* IX: 3 1047a 24 that "a thing is capable of doing something if there will be nothing impossible in its having the actuality of that of which it is said to have the capacity", ἔστι δὲ δυνατὸν τοῦτο ᾧ ἐὰν ὑπάρξῃ ἡ ἐνέργεια οὗ λέγεται ἔχειν τὴν δύναμιν, οὐθὲν ἔσται ἀδύνατον. Elsewhere Aristotle has argued that bodies, and the universe as a whole, cannot even theoretically be expanded to infinity without contradicting their very nature and definition (cf. *Physics* III: 5 204b 5 ff., *De Caelo* I: 3 270a 13, 5 271b 27 ff., 9 278b 21 ff.). Thus in positing the possibility of an infinitely increasing universe, al-Kindī considers an impossibility as possible.

Now Aristotle does admit that a magnitude is potentially infinite, but by way of division; while it is number (and time) which are potentially infinite by way of addition (cf. *Physics* III: 6 206a 16 ff., 7 207b 2 ff.). If al-Kindī is not being careless or ignorant of Aristotle's teachings, he apparently is indifferent to all these distinctions, and this despite the fact that he has himself shown above, following Aristotle, that there can be nothing outside the body of the universe (cf. 109. 1 and n. there). That this may well be indifference could be deduced from his use of the terms "possible through the imagination", ممكن بالوهم, by which "imagination" he apparently means a fanciful possibility; something teasingly like a real possibility but basically just a creature of whimsy (and cf. the following note). This possibility is "just" imagination, as an infinite universe is "nothing other" than a possibility, i.e., not a real existent. The potentiality of certain things is "only" a possible existent, and to al-Kindī this kind of possible existence is not to be taken seriously. Therefore he need not be concerned with distinguishing between kinds of non-existents.

This deprecating of potential existence as related to infinite entities is fundamental to al-Kindī's position, and goes to the heart of his difference with Aristotle. For the Stagirite viewed time, motion and magnitude as infinite, each in its own way, but all potentially so, understanding their potentiality as a necessary and not merely possible type of existence, part of the process of becoming which characterizes the eternally moving world (cf. *Physics* III: 6 206a 18ff., *Met* IX: 6 1048b 9 ff. and Ross' notes there, 2: 252). Indeed, this acceptance of the ontological legitimacy of potential existence enables Aristotle to consider the universe as eternal, though in actuality we perceive only finite time, movements and magnitudes. In treating potential existence as a mere fancy, therefore, al-Kindī rejects this view of the world, and is left solely with an actual finite world, which he apparently considers as dependent upon an external agent more than in the Aristotelian view.

116.13 "through the imagination": بالوهم ; cf. the preceding note and see the use of *wahm* in comparable statements in Saadya Gaon's *K. al-Amānāt wa-l-Iᶜtiqādāt*, ed. S. Landauer (Leiden, 1880), I: 1, p. 37, (*maḥshabah* in Hebrew, *S. ha-Emunot we-ha-Deᶜot* [Josefov, 1885], p. 60, "virtually" in the English translation of S. Rosenblatt, *The Book of Beliefs and Opinions* [New Haven, 1948], p. 45, and as "a matter of imagination" by A. Altmann, *The Book of Doctrines and Beliefs* [Oxford, 1946] p. 57); and in Maimonides' *Dalālat al-Ḥaᵓirīn*, ed. S. Munk (Jerusalem, 1929), I: 74, p. 155 (*umūr wahmīyah*, translated into Hebrew [*S. Moreh Nebukhim* (New York, 1946), p. 129r] as *ᶜinyanīm maḥshābīyīm*, and in the recent English translation of Shlomo Pines, *The Guide of the Perplexed* [Chicago, 1963], p. 222, as "matters of fantasy").

Both these other authors consider the proofs of infinity—be they infinite divisibility or increase—which they reject as based on mere imaginary, not real, states of being. But where Saadya's argument against what is recognizable as a Zenonian paradox accepts the Aristotelian idea of a potentially infinite divisibility, but, like al-Kindī, minimizes its significance, Maimonides' critique—attributed by him (loc. cit.) and by Averroes ("Epitome of the Metaphysics", *Rasaᵓil Ibn Rushd* [Hyderabad, 1947], pp. 128-29) to Alfarabi's "On Changeable Beings" (and cf. Davidson, op. cit., p. 380 f. for their as well as Avicenna's similar remarks)—is founded on an Aristotelian understanding of the nature of the infinite as a succession of things and moments; i.e., the members of such an infinity are seen to succeed each other (accidentally) but not to co-exist in actuality, and therefore are not numerable as a whole (cf. *Physics* III: 6 206a 27; Simplicius' commentary on the *Physics*, p. 1179 ff.; Averroes' *Tahāfut al-Tahāfut* I: 18, 19, and Van den Bergh's *Tahāfut*, 2: 7, 8; and Wolfson, "Kalām Arguments for Creation", op. cit., p. 222 f.).

Maimonides and the other Aristotelians would therefore view al-Kindī's (and Saadya's) refutations of infinity—which Maimonides attributes to the *mutakallimūn*—, positing as they do actual infinities, as spurious, their basic assumption concerning potential infinity being unnecessarily restrictive. Al-Kindī would thus be counted out by the Aristotelians on two counts: for dismissing the significance of potential existence as merely imaginative fancy; and for not realizing the extent of fanciful imagination, i.e., impossible assumptions, in his own refutations of infinity.

116.16 "said to be in potentiality": المقول هو بالقوة ; *UG* 203.17 *huwa* missing.

116.17 "is also": هو أيضا ; *UG* 203.17, فهو أيضاً .

116.18 "in actuality": بالفعل ; *UG* 204.1 في الفعل .

116.19 "for (reasons) which we have given previously": لما قدمنا . Cf. above, 115.1-116.5.

117.4 "the being": *annīyah;* "being" rather than "existence" (cf. above, notes to 97.13), to emphasize, as al-Kindī may well intend, that the very basic nature, the "quoddity", of body is finite. Davidson has shown that part of al-Kindī's arguments for finiteness from composition (cf. 120.7 ff. below) may be traced to John Philoponus (cf. Simplicius' commentary on the *Physics* pp. 1329.20 and 1331.20, and see Davidson, "Creation", op. cit., pp. 363 and 371). The Alexandrian, however, asserts that the universe has only finite "power" and is therefore generated, since infinite power (ἀπειροδύναμα) cannot be present in a finite body (cf. the n. to 116.9 above); while al-Kindī argues for generation from the finite "being"—*annīyah*—of the (body of the) universe. Davidson therefore believes that al-Kindī's "being" is equivalent, in its function within the structure of the argument, to Philoponus' "power". This equivalence is detected again at 120.4, where an ostensibly superfluous use of the finite-being (of the body of the universe) clause in an argument based on the coexistence of time, motion and the universe, is seen as evidence of a Philoponus influence (cf. Davidson, ibid., p. 372). Thus Davidson would seem to assert that there exists a formal structural resemblance, in this section of "First Philosophy" at least and in passages such as the present one, between al-Kindī's "being" and Philoponus' "power".

While Davidson may well be right historically, two facts ought to be noted: al-Kindī explicitly defines "being" in this section (cf. below 120.17, and compare 119.16) in such a way that it ignores the notion of "power" (which notion *is* implicit above at 116.9); and the major thrust of the following chapters of this book, which these remarks may be seen as foreshadowing, is to assert the composite and hence dependent nature of every aspect of being, understood as here in terms of its basic nature or substance.

117.5 "(time is but) the number of motion, i.e., it is a duration counted by motion": عدد الحركة، أعني أنه مدة تعدها الحركة ... , literally, "... which motion counts". The first definition above is Aristotelian, inadequately abbreviated (cf. *Physics* IV: 11 219b 1, ἀριθμὸς κινήσεως κατὰ τὸ πρότερον καὶ ὕστερον, "for time is this, the number of motion according to prior and posterior"); the second, equally common to al-Kindi's contemporaries and Neoplatonic predecessors, to whom *muddah* is διάστημα or διάστασις, and by whom the universe is regarded as the body whose motion is enumerated by time, considered as an extension or duration, was attributed by the latter to Plato and to the Stoics (cf., *inter alia*, *Crescas*, p. 638 ff., *Israeli*, p. 74 ff.). It is the second definition, somewhat amplified, which al-Kindī uses in his treatise *On Definitions* AR I: 167, and this seems to be the one which he favors, judging by its place in the structure of this sentence and above at 117.3 and 116.10 (and cf. as well *OE* 196.6); though it is clear that he considers both definitions as essentially the same (as evidenced further below at line 12 in the fusion of terms). As such, al-Kindī should be seen as subscribing to the (Aristotelian) view of the continuous nature of time, which he acknowledges below, at 122.10 (and cf. *Categories* VI: 4b 22, *Physics* IV: 11 219a 13 ff.) Cf. however, below, 121.5, and n. there.

117.7[1] "Motion is . . . of a body only": والحركة إنما ... الجرم. Cf. *De Caelo* I: 9 279a 15, κίνησις δ'ἄνευ φυσικοῦ σώματος οὐκ ἔστιν, "without natural body there is no motion."

117.7[2] "and otherwise": وإلا , *UG* 204.8, وإن لم يكن جرم, "and if there were not body".

117.8[1] "Motion is some change": والحركة هي تبدل ما ; *UG* 204.10 والحركة هي تبدل الأحوال , "motion is a change of states" (which description includes substantive change, following al-Kindi's discussion of 113.11). Cf., e.g., *Physics* V: 1 225a 34, and, in general for what follows, *Physics* V: 2 226a 24 and *Met.* XII: 2 1069b 9. Al-Kindī uses here the more suitable *ḥarakah* for κίνησις, instead of the *istiḥālah* of 114.3, and cf. the note there.

117.8[2] "the change only of place": فتبدل مكان ... فقط , following AR in emending the MS. from *q d* (*qad*) *b d l* (not, as in AR note 4, *q d t b d l*).

117.8[3] "...of the parts of a body and its center or...": أجزاء الجرم ومركزه أو ; *UG* 204.10 missing (so AR, though in n. 4 to our text *UG* is quoted as containing this clause).

117.9 "the change of place, to which the body is brought by its limits": وتبدل المكان الذي ينتهي إليه الجرم بنهاياته ; *UG* 204.11, وتبدل مكان نهاياته, "the change of place of its limits".

117.10 "or farness': وإما بالبعد ; *UG* 204.11, أو البعد .

117.11 "alteration": *al-istiḥālah*. Cf. above, the first n. to 113.11.

117.12[1] "counting of the number": عاد عدد ; *UG* 204.14 omits ᶜ*adad*. Cf. n. to 117.5 above.

117.12[2] "of the body": *al-jirm; UG* 204.14 المتبدل أي الجرم , "of that which changes, i.e., body".

117.12[3] "that which is temporal". There now follows in our text a section which is not found in *UG*, which (at 204.16) parallels our text again at 120.7.

The omitted material is mostly a deductive elaboration of the argument for the interdependence of (time) body and motion, outlined above at 117.3-7, an elaboration which is also missing, together with the argument from composition at 120.7 ff., from *OE*. This latter text (at 196.6 ff.)

rather resembles *FP* 117.3-7 and its reiterations at 119.13-20 and 120. 15-20, being limited to the argument for the interdependent finiteness of time, body and motion; which argument was probably the original one, based upon the finiteness of magnitude. The relationship of body and motion, and the argument for composition as we have them in *FP*, and partially in *UG*, were apparently seen as variations upon this argument (and cf. below, n. to 120.5 and 6).

117.15 "or it would not be": وإما أن لا تكون, i.e., in actuality, as al-Kindī makes explicit immediately and again below at 118.5; though he uses this formulation of non-actual motion in the sense of absolute non-motion in the contradiction he establishes below at 118.9.

117.17 "However, since body exists, motion is an existent": وإذ الجرم موجود هي موجودة . Motion is an existent since body is, on the assumption that we know, by our common sense perceptions, that there are bodies and that motion does occur; and it has just been asserted above that where there is motion, it is of a body. This appeal to fact within a logical proof is typical of the type of argument al-Kindī uses.

118.2-7 "Now motion necessarily exists in some bodies. . . in the simple body": This paragraph shows the influence of Aristotle's viewpoint on the priority of actuality to potentiality in species and substance, as expressed, e.g., in *De Anima* II: 4 417a 22 ff. and *Met.* IX: 8 1049b 18 ff.

118.2 "motion necessarily exists in some bodies, for that which is possible is that which exists in some possessors of its substance": فان الحركة بالاضطرار موجودة في بعض الأجرام لأن الممكن له الشيء هو الموجود ذلك الشيء في بعض ذوات جوهره . At 116.13 above the possible was treated as an imaginative absurdity because the proposed infinite was "only" potentially possible; whereas, we may now deduce, the truly possible for al-Kindī is that which is realized in actuality by some member of its species. To him motion is probably a necessary fact for the species of bodies — accepting as he does the priority of actuality to potentiality and the impossibility of an infinite regress — but a contingent fact for each member of the species. To claim that any substance moves of its own necessity would ostensibly draw al-Kindī towards Aristotle's view of such substances as eternally actual beings. See, however, 118.7 below and n. there.

118.4 "As the (art of) writing which may be affirmed as a possibility for Muḥammad, though it is not in him in actuality, since it does exist in some human substance, i.e., in another man": كالكتابة موجبة بالامكان لمحمد ، وليست فيه بالفعل ، إذ هي موجودة في بعض جوهر الانسان ، أعني في آخر من الناس . Cf. *De An.* II: 5 417a 21 ff., with the term *kitābah* a translation of *grammatikos* (though this cannot be compared with the extant Arabic manuscript of this translation, ʿAbd al-Raḥmān Badawī, ed., *Arisṭūṭālis fī al-Nafs* [Cairo, 1954] p. 42, due to its corrupt or unsatisfactory nature here; cf., however, Isḥāq's translation of this term in *Cat.* 11a 1, K. Georr. ed., *Les Catégories D'Aristote Dans Leurs Versions Syro-Arabes* [Beirut, 1948] p. 344). I have rendered *kitābah* as "(the art of) writing" in the sense of literacy, reflecting, as our context demands, more than is usually understood by the philosophically common literal translation of the Greek term as related to things "grammatical".

It is not, I believe, accidental that al-Kindī chooses this particular example of possible and actual being, using an illustration from a text that was probably not his primary one in this section; nor is it surprising that he employs Muḥammad in his example. It would, in fact, be natural for a pious Muslim to take the Prophet's life as a paradigm of universal truth. Moreover, in this instance the belief in Muḥammad's illiteracy (understood in Islamic tradition from passages in the *Qurʾān* such as VII: 157, 158; and cf. *The Encyclopaedia of Islam*, s.v. *ummī*, IV: 1016)—which it was considered necessary to assert as a support for the dogma of the inimitable, miraculously revealed *Qurʾān* (cf. W. Montgomery Watt, *Muhammad At Mecca* [Oxford, 1960], p. 46)—would seem to receive al-Kindī's blessing. Thus he would appear to be asserting, even if only in passing, the compatibility of religious belief and philosophical truth.

It should be noted, however, that Muḥammad's possible literacy is not, at least directly, due to God's Will, but rather due to the priority of actual literacy in the human species, to which the Prophet belongs. This actuality is, in addition, conceived of as necessary; part, in some sense, of what being human entails. The religious dogma, in other words, is put into a philosophical perspective which is antithetical to conservative religious theology, that held, e.g., by the more anti-rational *mutakallimūn;* though al-Kindī's view may have been more compatible with that held by the more rational *muʿtazilah.* The more conservative theologians are understood to have felt on the one hand that all is possible for God, acting completely unilaterally; and, on the other, that nothing is innately possible for created things (i.e., everything else), all of whose states of being are dependent on God and as such may be considered as necessary. Certain members of the *muʿtazilah*, however, were apparently prepared to allow for independently possible existents, among which God was in a sense obliged to act (cf. the elaboration of these two points of view in E. Fackenheim, "The Possibility of the Universe in Al-Farabi, Ibn Sina and Maimonides", *PAAJR* 16 [1946-47]: 49 f. and for an expression of the orthodox *kalām* view, as represented by Maimonides and Averroes, cf. H. Wolfson, "The Kalām Arguments For Creation...", op. cit., p. 234 f., and see particularly S. Van den Bergh's *Averroes' Tahafut Al-Tahafut* II: 37 ff.).

Thus to the *muʿtazilah* God asserted Himself constantly but not, as it were, arbitrarily, upon the universe; while we may assume that to al-Kindī Divine action is apparently even more restricted, in the normal course of events, functioning mainly as the ultimate source and cause of the universe. He apparently views nature, in spite of its ultimate theoretical contingency, as functioning independently on a mundane level; which level, he seems interested to single out, includes that of the Prophet's life.

118.7 "(motion) existing necessarily in the simple body": موجودة إضطرارا في الجرم المطلق. The "simple body" is Aristotle's "first heaven", ὁ πρῶτος οὐρανός, the outermost sphere of the universe, that in which the fixed stars reside (cf. *Met.* XII: 7 1072a 23); probably so called because its movement is unceasingly "simple" (ἁπλοῦς), i.e., circular (cf. *De Caelo* II: 6 288a 11-288b 1, and see the Arabic translation there, ed. ᶜAbd al-Raḥmān Badawī, *Arisṭūṭālis fī as-Samā*ᵓ [Cairo, 1961], pp. 248 ff.).

The use of *al-jirm al-muṭlaq* here is of course quite different from the more widely used term *al-jism al-muṭlaq*, commonly translated as "absolute body", that which denotes the "second matter", i.e., the combination of "first matter" and "corporeal form" (for which cf. H. Wolfson, *Crescas*, pp. 578 ff., and see further for the *Ikhwan al-Ṣafā*ᵓ, Seyyed Hossein Nasr, *An Introduction to Islamic Cosmological Doctrines* [Cambridge, Mass., 1964], p. 58 f.). *Jirm* is used by al-Kindī elsewhere, in such expressions as *al-jirm al-aqṣā*, *al-jirm al-kull* and *al-jirm al-ᶜālam*, to denote a heavenly body or sphere, and the universe (cf. AR I: 186, 192, 201, 203, 244, 252). *Al-jirm al-muṭlaq* may be seen as a synonym of the former term, and probably as entailing the latter terms as well.

Al-Kindī's intention in saying that motion exists necessarily in the simple body is something of a puzzle. He may have wished to offer a logical remark, that the whole of which certain parts move also—and necessarily—moves, viz., insofar as its parts move; or, he may have wanted to assert (however inadequately presented) not that the universe or "first heaven" moves necessarily, due to the fact of motion within it, but that it moves of necessity, by itself.

Though al-Kindī would have been hard put to justify the nature of this latter necessity philosophically, since he denies the eternal nature of the spheres which renders them necessary beings in Aristotle's view, he could have felt that God gave the celestial substances necessary movement, even as in al-Kindī's view He rendered them ungenerated and incorruptible; and that this state would last as long as God wished, resulting in effect in a kind of autonomous, "necessary" motion.

While this latter interpretation is well in keeping with al-Kindī's modified Aristotelian view of the nature of heavenly substances, the former interpretation is supported more by our text, and tends to enhance al-Kindī's philosophical credibility. Cf., however, 132.8 and note there.

118.12 "and it is not possible for there to be body and not motion": فليس يمكن أن يكون جرم ولا حركة. As a categorical remark this statement is misleading, for it ignores the actual states of rest and potential movements of sub-lunar objects, which al-Kindī refers to above, 1. 3. He apparently is thinking here of "body" as a member of a species, and even more probably of body in the sense of heavenly bodies, or of the universe as a whole, which he next considers.

118.14-17 "It is sometimes assumed. . . a generation from nothing or eternal": This is to be read, as Davidson suggests ("Creation", op. cit., p. 371), "against the background" of *Physics* VIII: 1. There is, however, a basically different orientation to the two texts. Aristotle asks essentially whether the motion of a movable thing comes from nothing or is eternal (cf.

250b 11-15; 251a 9-17), and the answer is eternal; while al-Kindī more specifically inquires whether a universe which is assumed to have been at rest originally and then to have moved can be said to be generated from nothing or to be eternal—and the answer is neither.

118.14 "It is sometimes assumed that it is possible for the body of the universe to have been at rest originally. . ." : وقد يظن (not نظن as AR) أنه يمكن أن يكون جرم الكل كان ساكناً أولا . This is the view Aristotle attributes to Anaxagoras at *Physics* VIII: 1 250b 24. Al-Kindī's use of it here is not directed against his contemporaries but rather against the very idea of divorcing body from movement. This particular formulation leads directly to the thesis that al-Kindī wishes to refute, viz., that the universe can be eternal. He has already established, and will argue again, that movement is finite (cf. above, 116.10 and see below, 119.14 ff. and 120.15 ff.); now he wishes to foreclose the possibility of another kind of infinity, viz., rest.

118.19[1] "in accordance with our previous classification": كما قدمنا حيث صنفنا ; literally, "as we have said previously where we classified".

118.19[2] "that generation is one of the species of motion": أن أحد أنواع الحركة هو الكون . At 117.11 above generation and corruption are said to be species of change (*tabaddul*), not motion (*ḥarakah*), which term is reserved at 1. 9 for locomotion; and indeed the whole classification is of kinds of "change", not "motion". It would thus seem that al-Kindī is using *ḥarakah* here in a general sense, as equivalent to *tabaddul* though without really bearing the distinction between the two terms in mind (something like his reversion to *istiḥālah* in the general sense of motion below at 119.7, after having defined it in the more limited meaning of "alteration" in 117.11). He may well be thinking of the classification of 117.8, "motion is a kind of change", in the sense of the variant given in *UG* 204.10, "motion is a change of states", which would include as motions the substantive changes of generation and corruption as described above at 113.11. Yet that discussion posits changes of contraries within a genus, the very opposite of substantive change into (and out of) nothing. This latter type of change (using even "change" equivocally) ought thus not to be called "generation", as al-Kindī has just blithely done, for in doing so he assumes what he ought to prove, viz., that *ex nihilo* "motion" is not unique. This assumption is made out of a strong conviction that all really possible kinds of physical change are contained in the Aristotelian classification of the subject.

119.1 "body is not prior (to motion, motion) is (of) its essence": لم يسبق الجرم (الحركة) كانت (الحركة من) ذاته , following AR in emending this sentence, though preferring *al-ḥarakah* to his *al-kawn*, and *min dhātihi* to his *dhātahu*, since motion, in al-Kindī's terms the genus of generation, could more properly be said to be essential to body.

119.7 "will have moved": فقد استحال , following the usage of *istiḥālah* in 114.3, and cf. the n. there.

119.8 "as we have explained previously": كما قدمنا بيان ذلك. Cf. 114.3 f.

Al-Kindī thus disposes of this possibility as well by showing it to be a self-contradiction. Aristotle's own argument here against eternal rest is again quite different from al-Kindī's. The Stagirite's objection is based on his view of rest as the "privation of motion", στέρησις κινήσεως (*Physics* VIII: 1 251a 26), thus assuming prior motion and an actual cause of the change. The eternally movable can't be originally at rest, Aristotle is implying, because "originally" there is movement, actual and eternal, of a body; the very antithesis of al-Kindī's position.

It appears inaccurate, therefore, for Davidson ("Creation", op. cit., p. 371) to paraphrase this argument of al-Kindī's as follows:: "If... the universe is eternal, it must always have been in motion, for if it were ever completely at rest, it could never have begun moving." Al-Kindī feels the universe can easily be shown not to have been eternally at rest originally, given the definition of the eternal (and the fact of motion); but he does not want to infer that if the universe were eternal, it would have to be in constant motion. That couldn't happen, he has shown, due to the finiteness of motion. Al-Kindī is here eliminating the last possible chance for an eternal universe; while Aristotle is pointing the way to just such a conclusion.

119.14 "It has been explained previously": وقد تقدم . Cf. 117.5.

119.16 "since duration is that in which its being is, i.e., that in which there is that which it is": إذ المدة هي ما هو فيه هوية ، أعني ما هو فيه هو ما هو (following AR's pointing and addition of a final *huwa*), by which al-Kindī is apparently saying that time is essential to body, even as motion is so declared to be above, at 119.1; and cf. below, l. 18.

Huwīyah denotes the being of a thing, its being an entity, sometimes termed "ipseity" (cf. Soheil M. Afnan, *Philosophical Terminology in Arabic and Persian* [Leiden, 1964], p. 120 ff.; and see A.M. Goichon, *Lexique de la Langue Philosophique D'Ibn Sīnā* [Paris, 1938], p. 411 f.). It is used apparently as a synonym for *annīyah*, as below, 120. 17. Cf. also above, n. to 113. 1.

119.17 "as has been explained": كما قد اتضح . Cf. above, 117. 14 ff.

119.18 "concomitant of the body": اللازمة للجرم , that which adheres necessarily to, is inherent in, the body; cf. above, 11. 1 and 16. For duration as that which is counted by motion, cf. above, 117.5.

120.4 "due to its being": لأنيته , i.e., due to its basic nature. Cf. the text and nn. to 117.4 and 119.16 above, as well as 120.17 below. Al-Kindī has gone on for unnecessary length with this proof. The argument, beginning at 114.10, has long since established the impossibility of an infinite magnitude, from which the finiteness of all else follows (116.5ff.). Despite the emphasis on the dependence of time and motion upon body, the argument essentially reflects one of John Philoponus' arguments against the impossibility of eternal motion (cf. above, n. to 114. 11); and not his argument for the finite power of a finite body (as Davidson assumes, op. cit., p. 372).

120.5 "by means of another account": بقول آخر . This "other account" is taken ultimately from the set of John Philoponus' arguments for the finite power of a finite body. Such proofs were apparently contained originally in a separate treatise known to the Arabs and recorded separately by their bibliographers (cf. Davidson's summary of this treatise and sources, op. cit., pp. 358-365). Al-Kindī may well be aware of the peculiar nature of this argument, for it is missing entirely from *OE*, which, at pp. 196-197, paraphrases the previous and following proofs only. That it may well have been problematic for him may further be deduced from the fact, which Davidson has noted (ibid., p. 372), that al-Kindī transforms this proof into the same type of argument as the others.

120.6 "We therefore say": فنقول. Cf. again *UG*, AR I: 204.16-206.12, for comparison with our text from the following line to 122.4. *UG* continues in an apparently natural way from the equivalent of *FP* 117.12, progressing from a description of motion as a change of states (تبدل الأحوال) and an enumeration of the kinds of change, to an inclusion of composition and combination within motion. The impression is thus given in UG of only one proof.

120.7 "Composition and combination are part of change, for they . . . : إن ومن التبدل الائتلاف والتركيب ، لأن ذلك... (*UG* 204.16, من التبدل التركيب والائتلاف). Al-Kindī is using *i'tilāf* as a synonym for *tarkīb*, since he doesn't refer to *i'tilāf* again, and he refers to both in the singular *dhālika* (translated, though, as "they"). Both *tarkīb* and *i'tilāf*, however, are already subsumed in the categories of change mentioned above (cf. the preceding n.). Singling them out makes sense only if one wants to emphasize the finite nature of composite things for reasons not already given. Al-Kindī's reasoning, however, immediately becomes that which he has just used in the previous argument. Either his familiarity with the argument for finite power is hazy (as Davidson assumes, op. cit., p. 372), or he prefers to repeat essentially the same argument with minor, though for him probably significant, variations. It would not, it must be said, be out of character for al-Kindī if the latter were the case; this could, however, also imply that al-Kindī deliberately altered the nature of the argument.

Most of the proofs for creation from the finite power of the universe depend upon the composite nature of the heavens and of all substances, which, composed of unstable combinations of matter and form, do not remain in any given form permanently and are therefore not eternal as such; the power of such a contingent body is likewise, then, not self-sufficient or eternal (cf. Simplicius' commentary on the *Physics*, op. cit., pp. 1329-1331; and see Davidson's summary of Philoponus' proofs and illustrations of Saadya Gaon's use of them, op. cit., pp. 362-365). Now al-Kindī does not look upon the heavens as part of the sub-lunar world of generation and corruption; to him they are not composed of a form and matter which as a composite entity is corruptible (cf. above. n. to 113.5). Al-Kindī follows Aristotle rather in his description of the eternal nature of the heavens, and therefore it would be surprising to find him using John Philoponus' arguments for finite power which attack this view, were it not that he has qualified his identification with both Aristotle and Philoponus.

In addition, *Kalām* writers adopted the idea of composition as indicating contingency, and transformed the physical dichotomy of form and matter into one of accident and body, or atom (cf. Davidson, ibid., pp. 364, 365, 383-385). Al-Kindī, who again preferred Aristotle's scheme of things, in the sub-lunar sphère now, did not refrain from using an argument for creation the formulation of which could have identified him with the theologians, were it not for his explicit division of body into matter and form. His appreciation of the theoretical strength of this argument, moreover, is clear from his incorporation of it into the argument for the impossibility of an infinite magnitude above at 116.9; his partial use of it here; and his adaptation and extensive use of it in the following chapters.

120.8 "long, wide, deep substance, i.e., it possesses three dimensions": جوهر طويل عريض عميق ، أى ذو أبعاد ثلاثة . *UG* 204.17 reverses these clauses (giving the adjectives as nouns, طولا وعرضاً وعمقاً , "length, width and depth"), while the former clause is omitted from the definition of body in *On Definitions* AR I: 165, which simply says that "body is that which has three dimensions", الجرم ما له ثلاثة أبعاد (cf. *De Caelo* I: 1 268a 7 ff.; *Met.* V: 6 1016b 28). This tridimensionality is predicated of the heavens by Philoponus, op. cit., p. 1331.20 (and cf. Davidson, op. cit., p. 371).

120.9[1] "and of the long, wide and deep which is its specific difference": *UG* 205. 1, "and of the dimensions which are its specific differences", changing the *faṣluhu* of *FP* to *fuṣūluhu.*

120.9[2] "and it is that which is composed of matter and form": وهو المركب من هيولى وصورة . That the heavens are composed of matter and form is stressed by John Philoponus, op. cit., p. 1329.20 ff. (and cf. Davidson, op. cit., p. 363). He argues from this fact to their need of matter, hence their lack of self-sufficiency and infinite power. Al-Kindī, on the other hand, argues from the composition of body to its changeful nature; from change to motion, and from motion to time.

120.11[1] "state": الحالة ; *UG* 205.3, الاحوال .

120.11[2] "Composition... and if": والتركيب... فان ; *UG* 205.3, فالتركيب... وإن, showing the often arbitrary nature of *wa* and *fa* in our texts.

120.13 "body is, therefore, composite": *UG* 205.5 adds كما أوضحنا, "as we have explained".

120.14 "are not prior": لم يسبق ; *UG* 205.6, لا يسبق .

120.15[1] "movement is change": الحركة تبدل ; *UG* 205.7, الحركة تبدل ما, "movement is a kind of change".

120.15[2] "change is the number of the duration of that which changes, and motion is a counting of the duration of that which changes" : والتبدل عدد مدة المتبدل، فالحركة عادة مدة المتبدل . *UG* 205.7 والتبدل عاد مدة المتبدل, "change is a counting of the duration of that which changes", as at

204. 14. Judging by the close relationship of motion and change just mentioned, the *UG* variant and the coalescence of both predicates ("number of. . ." and "a counting of. . .") with change in 117.12 above, al-Kindī is apparently saying essentially the same thing for change and motion.

120.17 "and every body has duration, as we said previously, viz., that in which there is being, i.e., that in which there is that which it is": ولكل جرم مدة ، كما قدمنا ، أي ما هو فيه أنية ، أعني ما هو فيه هو ما (هو) (literally, ". . . i.e., that in which there is a certain that"), following AR's addition of a final *huwa* at 119.6 (though not, oddly, here), after which sentence ours is patterned and to which it refers. This parallelism highlights the synonymous usage as "being", in this context at least, of *huwīyah* and *annīyah*. *UG* 205.9 has ولكل جرم مدة هي الحال هو فيه أنية ، أعني الحال التي هو فيه, "and every body has duration which is a state in which there is being, by which I mean a state in which there is a that".

120.19[1] "nor is body": فالجرم لا; *UG* 205.10, والجرم لا .

120.19[2] "as we have explained": كما أوضحنا. Cf. above, 117.7.

120.20 "and they occur simultaneously in being": فهي معا في الأنية. *UG* 205.12, فهي معا , literally, "and they occur together". The remainder of this discussion to 121.5 is omitted from *UG*.

121.3 "in another way": بنوع آخر . The following proof, or rather proofs, of actual finiteness also belong to the genre of proofs for creation from the impossibility of an infinite magnitude first established by John Philoponus. As presented by al-Kindī, they incorporate a number of these proofs, using arguments some of which have been encountered already, but substituting time for magnitude.

121.5 "temporal segment": فصل من الزمان . Cf. n. to 116. 10 above, and see 121.15 below. *UG* 205.13 begins this section with a sentence not found in our text and which may be translated as follows: "Every change segments duration, and the segmented duration is time", فكل تبدل يفاصل (AR بفاصل) مدة، والمدة المفصولة هي الزمان .

121.6 "it cannot be": لا يمكن; *UG* 205.15, ولا يمكن .

121.8-9 "if it were possible. . . we would never reach a given time" : فان أمكن ذلك ... لا ننتهي إلى زمن مفروض أبدا (*UG* 205.17 partially corrupt, as AR notes there, n. 8), i.e., a distinct temporal period, viz., the present. I consider this sentence to be parenthetical. It is based upon the Aristotelian argument concerning the impossibility of traversing an infinite series (used by John Philoponus to prove the impossibility of an infinite number of actual transformations of things, *ibid.*, p. 1178, and cf. Davidson, op. cit., p. 365 f.). Al-Kindī reverts to this argument again at 121.15 f. below, and Davidson has apparently conflated the material in his translated excerpts, ibid., p. 371. The positive argument for the finite nature of time used here depends in fact upon the following sentence.

121.9 "for the duration from past infinity. . . regressing in times to infinity": لأن من لا نهاية في القدمة ... مصاعدا في الأزمنة إلى ما لا نهاية له. As al-Kindī attempts to elaborate, and as he reiterates at *OE* 197.5 f., equal intervals (or "durations") are those which have the same finite limits; which is also the case with equal bodies, as discussed above, 114.13 and 115.14 (part of the argument against infinite magnitudes based upon the finite nature of equal or unequal bodies due to addition or subtraction). Cf. the use of this argument in Saadya, *Kitāb al-Amānāt*, p. 36, Hebrew translation, p. 59, English translation, p. 45 (Altmann, p. 56); and see Davidson, op. cit., p. 366, comparison with al-Kindī, p. 373. As for "regressing", I read *muṣā^{c}idan* with the ms., which is probably a scribal error for *mutaṣā^{c}idan*, as given in the parallel passage of 197.8. *UG* 206.2 has *mutaḍā^{c}ifan*, which preserves the sixth form but is otherwise corrupt. Davidson, ibid., translates this term as "ascending back", noting that Saadya employs the same root form (*su^{c}ūd*).

121.15 "nor that before it until a time before it is reached"; *UG* 206.7, omitted.

121.15-
122.1 "Furthermore... a definite time". Time is here considered as a continuum capable by its nature of both infinite addition and division (cf. *Physics* IV: 11 219a 13 ff.,; 12 220a 31 ff.). The assumption again, here made explicit, is that it is impossible to traverse an infinite quantity (cf. above 11. 8-9 and note there). This assumption is likewise operative in the teaching of two early contemporaries of al-Kindī, the Mu^{c}tazilites al-Iskāfi (d. 854) and the already encountered al-Naẓẓām (cf. above, note to 114.18, and see below, note to 122.13-15); cf. their somewhat similar formulations of this argument, as reported by al-Khayyāṭ, *Kitāb al-Intiṣār*, op. cit., pp. 19, 31 and 33, French translation, pp. 12, 30, 32. Davidson, moreover, feels that some of their arguments refer, contrary to their appearance, to temporal and not spatial infinity (op. cit., pp. 375 and 379). This emphasis upon the traversal of an infinite calls to mind the argument attributed to Zeno (in which case a further parallel exists [with qualifications, for which cf. above, 116.13] between Saadya's and al-Kindī's presentation of the issue). It is therefore most interesting to note that al-Kindī does not even allude to Aristotle's solution of this dilemma, as given, e.g., in *Physics* VIII: 263a 4 ff. Al-Kindī simply dismisses the theory, arguing that since there *is* a definite time (the present), all time must be finite. This is tantamount to a rejection of the validity of Aristotle's distinction between actual and potential time (cf. *Physics* VIII: 263b 3 ff.); a rejection already indicated at 116.13 ff. above.

122.1 "its termination... exists": والإنتهاء ... موجود به ; *UG* موجود.

122.2 "segment": فصل ; *UG* 206.9, متصل, "continuity".

122.5[1] "It is (also) not possible": Here the parallel with *UG* stops, the latter text going on at 207.1 to argue from the impossibility of an eternal body for the necessity of a created world, and thus for a Creator.

The following lines are a variation of the argument presented at 121.9 above; whereas there equal intervals are seen to entail finiteness, here the same is true for unequal intervals. Cf. further, the second n. to 122.6 below.

122.5[2] "(the duration from) past time to a definite time": الزمان الماضي إلى زمن (!) محدود, literally, "the time which passed to a definite time" ("definite" time probably in the sense of present time ; as *mafrūḍ*, "given" time, above at 121.9).

122.6[1] "as we have said previously": كما قدمنا. Cf. above, 121.5 ff.

122.6[2] "and times are consecutive": والأزمنة متتالية. Cf. below, 1.10. As the given or present time is finite, so each similar segment added to it is likewise finite, the concept of an infinite segment having been rejected. We have, therefore, the addition of two finite intervals, for which (formulated in terms of bodies) cf. above, 114.16 ff.

122.10 "Time is a continuous quantity": والزمان من الكمية المتصلة. Cf. *Physics* IV: 11 220a 5 and VIII: 1 251b 20. This statement clarifies al-Kindī's use of "consecutive" above, l. 6, and his general treatment of time as if it were composed of a series of discrete segments (as Davidson so understands him, op. cit., p. 373). No more than Saadya (as Davidson has observed, ibid., pp. 366, 367) does al-Kindī distinguish between a series of segments and a continuous extension. While time is viewed as continuous in actuality, the impossibility of infinite time for al-Kindī allows him to treat time as though it were discrete. In other words, where time alone is concerned, it is regarded as continuous; where the beginning and end of all time is in question, however, time is handled as a series of discrete parts.

122.11 "the present": *al-ān*, "the now".

122.13-15 "If two definite times are continuous through one limit common to them both, then the remaining limit of each one of them is definite and knowable": فان اتصل زمانان محدودان بنهاية واحدة مشتركة لهما، فان نهاية كل واحد منهما البقية محدودة معلومة, since an infinite series is impossible. Overlooking the circular reasoning employed here by the term "definite times", it is clear that al-Kindī arrives at his conclusion by treating time as "continuous" within circumscribed limits; for which static and paradoxical view cf. above, note to 122.10. The argument that whatever has an end must have had a beginning and vice-versa (which is a fair paraphrase of our sentence), is not an uncommon one among Islamic and Jewish theologians and philosophers (cf. Davidson, ibid., p. 378, 379). It is mentioned first as being used (in a negative formulation) by Abū al-Hudhayl (d. 849) (cf. *Kitāb al-Intiṣār*, p. 18, French translation, p. 11; a passage partially alluded to by al-Ashʿarī, *Maqālāt al-Islāmīyīn*, op. cit., p. 358 f.). A variation of this argument, viz., the contention that whatever is finite in one direction must be so in all directions, is, moreover, attributed to al-Naẓẓām (*Kitāb al-Intiṣār*, p. 32, French translation, p. 31; and see Davidson, op. cit., p. 379).

122.15 "It has, however, been said": وقد كان قيل. Cf. above, 122.8, where the argument for an infinite sum is not really presented but only suggested, to be immediately refuted; our passage serving as further refutation.

CHAPTER III: NOTES

123.3 "An investigation whether it is or is not possible for a thing to be the cause of the generation of its essence, shall now follow the previous (discussion)": وقد يتلوما قدمنا البحث عن الشيء، هل يمكن أن يكون علة كون ذاته أم لا يمكن ذلك. As the previous chapter has argued for the finiteness of body, time and motion, al-Kindī now proceeds to reason that nothing of our acquaintance is fully self-sufficient or independent. Having denied the logical possibility of generation from nothing above, at 118.18 ff., al-Kindī now wishes to remove the possibility of something causing its own generation, i.e., being its own cause, or, as I have translated, being "the cause of the generation of its essence". While *dhāt* is used interchangeably by al-Kindī to denote "self" and "essence" (cf. below, 142.11 f.), it is the latter term which is clearly intended by our context, though the entire distinction between "a thing" and its "essence" is soon repudiated (124.3).

123.4 "We say that it is not possible for a thing to be the cause of the generation of its essence": فنقول إنه ليس ممكنا أن يكون الشيء علة كون ذاته. Al-Kindī's position, though not his terminology, may be traced to Aristotle's discussion of substance and essence in *Met.* VII: 3-6 (Asṭāt, for example, renders *Met.* VII: 6 1031a 15, "we should inquire whether each thing and its essence are the same or different [πρότερον δὲ ταὐτόν ἐστιν ἢ ἕτερον τὸ τί ἦν εἶναι καὶ ἕκαστον, σκεπτέον], as ولكن فلنفحص هل ما هو بالأنية والمفرد هو هو, [Bouyges, II: 821]; and generally translates τί ἦν εἶναι as ما هو بالأنية, reserving ذات for the pronoun of self, as at 1031b 5 and 13 [Bouyges, 822.15, 823.7, and see Afnan's list, (op. cit., p. 101) of other places in Aristotle in which *dhāt* has this meaning]; Avicenna, on the other hand, frequently uses *dhāt* in the sense of essence; cf. Goichon, op. cit., pp. 134, 135). Significantly, al-Kindī does not at all consider using *dhāt* in a more Platonic way, as the transcendental form or idea of things; there is no association here with the Neoplatonic hierarchy of universal beings and God as the ultimate essence from which individual beings derive their identity (cf. the "Sayings of the Greek Sage" [Plotinus, as discovered by Rosenthal] in Badawī's edition of *Plotinus apud Arabes*, p. 186 no. 6; translated by Lewis, op. cit., p. 474: 24). Such a terminological association, which would make essence "the cause of the generation of a thing", is obviously foreign to al-Kindī's thought here, though his ultimate theory of being requires some such emanationist relation (cf. *FP*, p. 161).

Al-Kindī's use of Aristotle here is, however, tempered structurally, though not conceptually, by the employment of a type of formal reasoning which is non-Aristotelian and is often associated with Stoic logic, viz., the conditional statement (cf. W. and M. Kneale, *The Development of Logic* [Oxford, 1964], pp. 98, 159 ff.). It is by the exercise of disjunctive and hypothetical propositions that al-Kindī formulates and "proves" his statement; assuming, by the law of the excluded middle upon which the Stoics placed great stress (ibid. p. 161), that the denial of one disjunct proves the affirmation of the other.

123.5[1] "its becoming a being": تهويه, the verbal form of *huwīyah*, being, apparently used uniquely as such by al-Kindī. Cf. Afnan, op. cit., p. 123.

123.5[a] "generation usually being predicated, in other places, of that which comes to be particularly from something." فانه قد يقال كون، فى مواضع اخر، الكائن من شيء خاصة . Cf. above, 113.11, which affirmed that an object does not perish completely; and 118.18 ff., which proved that the universe, and by implication any body, cannot (as we normally understand physical substance) be generated from nothing. As in the latter case, al-Kindī here entertains the possibility of generation from nothing only to show its logical impossibility, working within a strictly Aristotelian conceptual framework.

123.6-7 "existent...non-existent": أيس and ليس . Cf. al-Kindī's use of الأيس in 113.12 above (and see n. 113.11[a] there), as well as both terms together at 136.18, 137.3, 9, 16, etc., below. Elsewhere (AR I: 182) al-Kindī writes: إن الفعل الحقي الأول تأييس الايسات عن ليس , translated by Walzer ("New Studies on Al-Kindī", *Greek into Arabic*, p. 187) as "True primary action is to produce real things from nothing" (and with which may be compared al-Kindī's definition of *ibdāʿ*, AR I: 165, اظهار الشيء عن ليس , which Walzer renders [ibid.] as "*ibdāʿ* is to make a thing appear out of nothing"). As Walzer notes there, Asṭāt used الأيس to translate the τὸ ἔστι of *Met.* VIII: 2 1042b 25, Bouyges II: 1034.7 (as well as the τὸ τί ἔστι of 3 1043b 25, Bouyges II: 1062.12). Asṭāt also uses the terms انه ليس and ما ليس هو for the τὸ μὴ εἶναι and τὸ μὴ ὄν of *Met.* V. 7 1017a 31 and VI: 2 1026b 15 (Bouyges II: 555.10 and 716.1) respectively.

123.10 "for both cause and effect are predicated only of something which has existence of some sort" : لأن العلة والمعلول إنما هما مقولان على شيء له وجود ما . Cf. 101.3 and 12 above, in which al-Kindī describes the four Aristotelian causes and the substance with which each one is identified. In *On Definitions* (AR I: 169) he refers to the four causes as "the natural (or "physical") causes, العلل الطبيعية.

123.11 "However, it has been said that it is the cause of the generation of its essence": وقد قيل إنه علة كون ذاته . This explicit statement is missing in the ms., but, as it is the premise upon which the whole argument is constructed, it is possible that the original sentence read something like this (following the examples of pp. 124.8 and 124.14): "If a thing were non-existent and its essence were non-existent—and it were the cause of the generation of its essence—then...." It is so typical of al-Kindī's method to posit that which he wishes to disprove, and then proceed to show the internal contradictions which ensue, that it may be possible that he assumed the reader would have assumed the initial premise of the argument after l. 9 above.

123.16 "As however, it has been said previously...":وقد تقدم. See the preceding note.

124.3 "Though the essence of every thing is that thing": وكل شيء فذاته هي هو , literally "is it", is the thing itself, its being, and cf. *Met.* VII: 6 1031b 12, 19. AR's punctuation and division of paragraphs is here rejected , and the translation follows the parallel, and correctly punctuated, passage of 124.11.

124.17 "Inasmuch as this has been explained, we now say that every utterance must either be meaningful or not meaningful": وإذ قد تبين ذلك فنقول ان كل لفظ فلا يخلو من أن يكون ذا معنى او غير ذي معنى. From here to 126.14, al-Kindī reverts to the ultimately Alexandrian commentary on the *Isagoge* which he has utilized before (cf. above, 97.8 and 101.5 ff. and notes there). This passage bears particular resemblance to Elias' *Prolegomena*, 35. 18-36.30, beginning, as al-Kindī does, with the statement: ἡ φωνὴ ἢ σημαντική ἐστιν ἢ ἄσημος. Cf. for Ammonius' commentary, op. cit., 58.19-63.5.

124.20¹ "That which has meaning must be either a universal or particular thing": وما كان له معنى لا يخلو من أن يكون كلياً أو جزئيا. Cf. Elias, op. cit., 35.26: τῶν δὲ σημαντικῶν αἱ μὲν καθόλου, αἱ δὲ μερικαί.

124.20² "Philosophy does not inquire into particular things, for particular things are not limited, and that which cannot be limited, knowledge cannot comprehend": والفلسفة لا تطلب الأشياء الجزئية، لأن الجزئيات ليست بمتناهية، وما لم يكن متناهياً لم يحيط به علم. Cf. Ammonius, op. cit., 59. 18-60.1, beginning τὰ δὲ κατὰ μέρος ἄπειρα καὶ ἀπερίληπτα, and ending ἐπεὶ οὖν τὰ κατὰ μέρος πολλὰ ὄντα καὶ ἄπειρα ἐπιστήμην οὐ ποιοῦσιν. See too the more succinct variant given in the notes to 58.19, in which philosophers are said not to be concerned with individual substances, due to their unlimited number: αἱ μὲν καθ' ἑνὸς μόνου τῷ ἀριθμῷ λέγονται ... οἱ φιλόσοφοι διὰ τὸ ἄπειρα εἶναι οὐ καταγίνονται.

125.3 "Universal general things must be either essential or non-essential": والأشياء الكلية العامية لا تخلو من أن تكون ذاتية أو غير ذاتية. Cf. Elias, op. cit., 36.4, τῶν δὲ καθόλου αἱ μὲν οὐσιώδεις εἰσίν, αἱ δὲ ἐπεισοδιώδεις. Al-Kindī also offers immediately the same definition of the essential as follows in Elias, εἰκεῖνα δὲ λέγεται οὐσιώδη ὅσα καὶ παρόντα σώζουσι καὶ ἀπόντα φθείρουσιν.

125.5 "as life": كالحياة. For this, as well as for the other illustrations of the predicables which follow, cf. Porphyry as well as his commentators. See, for example, the *Isagoge*, op. cit., 2.20, Arabic (edited by Badawī, op. cit.), p. 1025. Al-Kindī may well have interspersed his use of the one source with the other. Elias, for example, uses "reason" as his example of an essential predicate (op. cit., 36.6).

125.7 "and the essential is that which is called substantial": والذاتي هو المسمى جوهريا. Cf. *Met.* VII: 6 1031a 18, "the essence is said to be the substance of each thing" (καὶ τὸ τί ἦν εἶναι λέγεται εἶναι ἡ ἑκάστου οὐσία), translated by Aṣṭāt (Bouyges II: 821.16) ويقال ما هو بالأنية أيضاً انه جوهر المفرد. Al-Kindī here takes the opportunity to clarify the nature of the "thing" with which essence is identified above, at 124.3.

125.8 "The substantial must be either a collective or distinct thing": والجوهري لا يخلو من أن يكون جامعاً أو مفرقاً. Cf. Elias, op. cit., 36.10: τὰ μὲν οὖν οὐσιώδη ἢ ὕπαρξιν δηλοῦσιν ἢ τρόπον ὑπάρξεως, "the essential is indicative either of a substance or of a mode of substance". Al-Kindī's preceding identification of essence with substance, and his phrasing of the subject of this sentence as "the substantial", الجوهري, may account for his complete divergence of terminology here, though his examples follow those of Elias.

125.13 "species": صورة, used for εἶδος by the early translators in logical as well as other contexts. Cf., e.g., *Met.* 1039a 26, τὸ εἶδος ἐκ τοῦ γένους ποιοῦσι καὶ τῶν διαφορῶν, rendered by Asṭāt (Bouyges II: 975) as ان الصورة من الجنس والفصول; and see Averroes' treatment there (ibid., p. 976) of *ṣurah* in terms of the more common term *nawᶜ*. Cf. also below, 159.8 and 12.

125.15 "animal": الحى, literally "living" or "living being", and as such translated above, 112.4 and 125.5. As synonymous with the latter, "animal" is the more conventional translation of the term in this context, representing the Greek τὸ ζῷον. Cf., for example, Isḥāq ibn Ḥunayn's translation of *Cat.* 5 2a 17, in Georr, op. cit., p. 322.

126.1 "Therefore that which is non-essential is in a substance which is its substrate and is not substantial": فهو إذن في الجوهر الموضوع [له] ، وليس بجوهري. For the relation of property and accident to the substance in which they inhere, belonging to it but not an essential part of it, cf. *Post. An.* I: 22 83b 19, *Topics* I: 5 102a 18 and 102b 4, and *Met* V: 30 1025a 22.

126.2 "On the contrary, it is an accident of the substance and is therefore called *accidens*": بل عارض الجوهر ، فسمى لذلك عرضا. *Accidens* is chosen to translate عرض here for its close etymological relation to "accident" as used below (ll. 7, 10) in the term "common accident", العرض العام (and see Goichon, op. cit., pp. 216 f.). Al-Kindī is thinking of "accident" in the broad sense of a concomitant or "coincident", a non-essential "attribute" (terms by which συμβεβηκός has been translated) of a subject; the ἐπεισοδιώδη or "adventitious" predicables of Elias (op. cit., p. 36.8, 16).

126.3 "That which is in a substance must be either in one thing...or it will be in many things": وهو الذي في الجوهر لا يخلو من أن يكون في شيء واحد .... أو يكون في أشياء كثيرة. Cf. Elias, op. cit., 36.16-18, τὰ δὲ ἐπεισοδιώδη ἢ μιᾷ μόνῃ φύσει ὑπάρχουσι καὶ λέγονται ἴδια . . . ἢ πολλαῖς καὶ λέγονται συμβεβηκότα. The "things" to which al-Kindī is referring are, as his examples indicate, species; a property being uniquely related to one species and therefore "convertible" (ἀντιστρέφει, انعكس) with its substance (ibid., 36.25, and see the *Isagoge*, op. cit., 12, 13, 21; Badawī, op. cit., pp. 1049f. ; cf. also *Topics* I : 5 102a 18). See further, below, 130.3 ff.

126.7 "common accident" : عرض عام translating the τὰ συμβεβηκότα κοινῶς of *Isagoge* 2.19, 3.6, 18 (العراض العامية in Badawī, op. cit., pp. 1025 ff.), and understanding the term in the sense of the "inseparable" accident (τὸ ἀχώριστον, غير المفارق) of *Isagoge* 12.25 (p. 1050 Badawī). Al-Kindī's distinction here between property and "common accident" is similar to the distinction between property and "inseparable accident" in *Isagoge* 22.5 (p. 1068 Badawī).

126.13 "and every utterance will be either universal or particular, and either collective or separate": (فكل ملفوظ) وإما كلا وإما جزءاً ، وإما مجتمعا وإما مفترقا, literally "either all or part, and either composite or separate". The slight variations upon the usages of 124.20 (كليا أو جزئيا) and 125.8 (جامعاً أو مفرقاً)

above do not require the introduction of new or modified concepts; for it is clear that, like Elias (op. cit. 36.20 ff.), al-Kindī is summarizing, in this paragraph, his preceding remarks.

126.14[1] "Let us now. . .speak of the number of ways 'one' is predicated": فلنقل على كم نوع يقال الواحد. Cf. *Met* V: 6 1015b 16 ff. and X 1 1052a 15 ff., for the variety of meanings Aristotle declares the term "one" possesses. The Aristotelian material is here integrated into the *Isagoge* classification of predicables, with the addition of the "individual" as a predicable (meaningful philosophically, as in 125.13 above, only in relation to species). It would appear likely that al-Kindī, and not an earlier commentator, is the author of the following section, since the emphasis upon the accidental nature of the unity found in all things is central to his position, and quite foreign to the distinction between accidental and essential unity mentioned here in the *Metaphysics*, and followed by the commentators.

126.14[2] "We say that one is predicated of every continuum, and also of that which does not receive multiplicity": فنقول: إن الواحد يقال على كل متصل، وعلى ما لم يقبل الكثرة أيضاً, these being the categories of things Aristotle calls "essentially one". Cf. *Met.* V: 6 1015b 36 ff.; X: 1 1052a 34-1052b 1.

126.18-127.1 "The individual will be either natural, as an animal or plant, and what is similar to them; or artificial, as a house and what is similar to it": والشخص إما أن يكون طبيعياً كالحيوان أو النبت وما أشبه ذلك وإما صناعياً كالبيت وما أشبه ذلك. Cf. *Met.* V: 6 1016a 4 for the juxtaposition of things continuous "by nature" and "by art", τὰ φύσει συνεχῆ ... τέχνῃ, rendered by Asṭāt as ما كانت متصلة بالطبيعة .. متصلة بالصناعة (Bouyges II: 527). The equivalent examples of man, plant and house are used by Aristotle in the *Met.* VII: 7 1032a 12 ff. discussion of things which are generated, the former two "by nature" (1. 18), the latter "by art" (1. 32, and 1032b 12). As this *Met. Z* chapter follows Aristotle's inquiry into the relation of a thing and its essence, which al-Kindī followed in the beginning of this chapter (cf. above, 123.3 ff., and see the note to 123.4), it appears that he was influenced by this chapter again in his choice of an illustration for the general remark of *Met. Delta*. See further below, 127.1[2].

127.1[1] "A house is continuous by nature": فان البيت متصل بالطبع. Cf. *Met.* V:6 1015b 36 ff., in which one of the examples of things called one by continuity in virtue of its own nature are pieces of wood made one by glue; which our text has apparently expanded into a house. The notion of the continuous is defined by al-Kindī in *On Definitions* (AR I: 176) as "the uniting of the extremities" (الاتصال هو اتحاد النهايات, and cf. *Physics* V: 3 227a 10).

127.1[2] "though its composition is continuous by accident, viz., through the (builder's) technique": وتركيبه متصل بعرض، أعني بالمهنة, i.e., the builder's "art". Cf. Asṭāt's translation of the τέχνη of *Met.* VII 7 1032a 12 and 28 (Bouyges II: 837, 838) as مهنة, which further attests to the probability of al-Kindī's use of the passage here. In *Met.* X 1 1052a 22 ff. Aristotle contrasts, among non-accidental unities, the form of a thing unified by glue with the form of a thing naturally one; the difference being that the latter has in itself the cause of its continuity. It is this distinction which is operative in al-Kindī's use of the term "accidental" in this and the following examples, going beyond Aristotle's preference for the naturally unified thing to establish causality (and particularly auto-causation) as the sole determinant of natural, non-accidental unity. In doing this, al-Kindī considers non-essential unity as equivalent to accidental unity, while to Aristotle both essential and non-essential unity are non-accidental, as long as they are in fact, and regardless of cause, unified.

127.7 "all is predicated of things having both similar and dissimilar parts": الكل يقال على المشتبه الأجزاء وعلى [الأشياء] اللاتي ليست بمشتبهة الأجزاء . Cf. al-Kindī's similar definition of "all" in *On Definitions* (AR I: 170): "(a substance) common to similar and dissimilar parts" (الكل — مشترك لمشتبه الأجزاء وغير المشتبه الأجزاء) . The particular illustrations al-Kindī chooses could have come to him from a number of sources. In *Met.* V: 3 1014a 30 ff. water is given as an example of something the parts of which are of the same kind, and, though the context is different, the elementary parts of body are also used as an illustration. In the *Rasā'il Ikhwān al-Ṣafā'* (Beirut, 1957) I: 430 we find the distinction between similar and dissimilar parts predicated of individual objects (الأشخاص), with body given as one of the examples of the latter category. The entire section which contains this distinction has been preserved in Latin as a separate treatise and is attributed in the translated manuscripts to a certain "*Mahometh discipulo Alquindi philosophi*" (for whose possible identity cf. H. Farmer, "Who was the Author of the 'Liber Introductorius in Artem Logicae Demonstrationis'?" *JRAS*, 1934, pp. 553-556); and Nagy has accordingly edited this material with the other al-Kindī Latin treatises (op. cit., pp. 41-64, and cf. pp. 42, 43 particularly for the above distinction).

According to the Arabic title of this *risālah* (في معنى أنولى طيقا الثانية),—the last of the first part of this encyclopedic work (which part is devoted to a syllabus which treats the subject matter of the *Quadrivium* plus geography, the *Isagoge* and *Organon*)—this section, purporting to discuss the *Posterior Analytics*, covers a wide variety of topics, including such issues as the relationships of cause and effect; the world, fullness and the void; and eternity vs. creation; themes which occupy al-Kindī in *FP* and elsewhere. Al-Kindī is known to have commented on the *Post. An.* (cf. above, n. 101.3[1]), and his use of these particular illustrations could well be inserted here from some commentary to the *Analytics* used both by him and the *Ikhwān al-Ṣafā'*. The attribution of the Latin version of this *risālah* to a disciple of al-Kindī, and thus indirectly to al-Kindī himself, may well, therefore, be closer to the truth than at first appears to be the case. Much of al-Kindī's writings, particularly his introductions to and surveys of Greek philosophy, mathematics and science, was probably well received by the *Ikhwān*, though as yet we cannot speak with any certainty of his influencing them.

127.11[1] "However...'whole' is not predicated of things having similar parts": فأما الجميع فلا يقال على المشتبهة الأجزاء. At *Met.* V: 26 1024a 1 ff., Aristotle distinguishes between "total" and "whole" quantities, in the former of which the position of the parts is seen as not making a difference. Water is then given as one of the examples of a 'total" quantity, for which properly speaking the phrase "the whole water" is deemed inappropriate. Al-Kindī is clearly following Aristotle here, understanding the position the parts of things have as due to their similarity or dissimilarity, and substituting this criterion for Aristotle's "position" of the parts.

Al-Kindī, interestingly, reverses here Asṭāt's translation of the πᾶν and ὅλος of this *Met.* passage as جميع and كل respectively (cf. Bouyges, II: 667); yet it may be (an earlier?) fidelity to Asṭāt's translation, and not a corrupt text, which has al-Kindī offer elsewhere a definition of جميع as "(a substance) particularly for similar parts", خاص للمشتبه الأجزاء (*On Definitions*, AR I: 170). While this is the opposite of his present use of جميع, it fits Asṭāt's use of it.

127.11[2] "for 'whole' is predicated equally of an aggregate heterogeneous by accident or in some sense unified though each diverse element is sustained by its own nature without the other, the name 'totality' referring to it": لأن الجميع أيضاً يقال على جمع مختلفات بعرض، أو أن تكون موحدة بمعنى ما وكل واحد منها قائم بطباعه غير الأخر ، فيقع عليها اسم المجموعة. Al-Kindī is following and expanding upon Asṭāt's translation of *Met.* V: 26 1024a 8, 9, accepting even Asṭāt's terminology, which he adjusts to fit his purposes. The *Metaphysics* passage reads πάντα δὲ λέγεται ἐφ' οἷς τὸ πᾶν ὡς ἐφ' ἑνί, ἐπὶ τούτοις τὸ πάντα ὡς ἐπὶ διῃρημένοις· πᾶς οὗτος ὁ ἀριθμός, πᾶσαι αὗται αἱ μονάδες ("To things, to which *qua* one the term 'total' is applied, the term 'all' is applied when they are treated as separate; 'this total number', 'all these units'", in W.D. Ross' translation); which Asṭāt renders (ibid., ويقال جميع التي قول الجميع عليها كقول المجموع على الواحد منها، كما يقال في المنفصلة مجموع (!)هذا العدد وجميع (!) هذه الآحاد). Al-Kindī is probably unaware that Aristotle's term for a quantity when its parts are taken together corresponds to his choice of كل and not جميع, and this inconsistency in his presentation of the subject is circumvented by a modification of the source and the omission of examples.

127.16 "In a similar way there is a distinction between 'part' and 'some'": وكذلك بين الجزء والبعض فرق. The following distinction is partially alluded to by al-Kindī in *On Definitions* (ibid.): الجزء – لما فيه الكل، البعض – لما فيه الجميع, " 'part' is that which is related to (literally 'in it is') the all, 'some' is that which is related to ('in it is') the whole"; omitting mention of "some" as also related to the all.

128.4 "predicables": المقولات, which is also the term usually translated as "categories". The context here, however, favors the use of "predicables" (cf. also Marmura and Rist, op. cit., p. 339 n. 5), even as that at 132.15 ff. below would seem to call for a translation of "predicate", referring to each member of every category of existence.

128.7 "As for the genus, it is in each one of its species": ولأن الجنس هو في كل

واحد من أنواعه . The relations between the predicables which al-Kindī mentions in the following paragraphs derive from the *Isagoge* or (more probably) *Isagoge* commentary al-Kindī has used before. Cf., for example, the relations between genus and species in the *Isagoge*, ed. Busse (op. cit.), pp. 2.10 ff., 4.2 ff. (Badawi, op. cit., pp. 1024, 1027).

128.8 "univocally": قولا متواطئا , i.e., the genus is the same in both name and definition for each of its species. Cf., for the definition of "univocal" (rendered as συνώνυμος in Greek, المتواطية in the Arabic, ed. Georr, op. cit., pp. 319, 325) *Cat.* 1: 1a 6, and see 5: 3a 33.

128.11 "The individual is one only by convention": والشخص إنما هو واحد من جهة الوضع , i.e., the parts into which the individual object is divisible form a unity, but not by any inherent or essential cause. Al-Kindī here posits a standard by which the unity of all things in any way divisible is considered, *a priori*, as not necessary. He thereby invokes a standard of "true unity" and "essential being" foreign to the Peripatetic tradition and closer to Platonic and Neoplatonic thought.

128.15 "That which is not essential in the true nature of a thing is in it in an accidental manner, and that which occurs accidentally to a thing does so in virtue of something other than itself": وما لم يكن في الشيء لحقيقته ذاتيا ، فهوفيه بنوع عرضى ، والعارض للشيء من غيره ، (فالعارض أثر في المعروض فيه) . Cf. *Met.* V: 30 1025a 14-30, for this definition of "accidental", the sort which Aristotle says (l. 33) can never be eternal. See too the distinction Aristotle draws between essential and accidental attributes in *Post. An.* I: 4 73a 25 ff.

128.16 "An effect is a relative term, the effect coming from an agent": والأثر من المضاف ، والأثر من مؤثر ; literally أثر and مؤثر should be rendered as "impression" and "an impressing force" (and cf. Avicenna's use of the terms as outlined by Goichon, op. cit., pp. 2, 3). As relative terms (من المضاف) , مؤثر and أثر correspond to the relationship of "the active to the passive" (τὸ ποιητικὸν πρὸς τὸ παθητικόν, الفاعل إلى المنفعل) mentioned by Aristotle among his definitions of relative things (πρός τι, المضاف ; cf. *Met.* V: 15 1020b 26, 30, translated by Asṭāt [Bouyges, op. cit.,] at II: 608). In his treatise *On the True, First Perfect Agent*... (AR I: 183), al-Kindī also employs the terminology of مؤثر and أثر , as well as other nominal and verbal forms of the root. There, however, he gives as equivalents of these terms the more common فاعل and منفعل , which may also be translated as "agent" and "patient", or "affection", which latter term is equivalent in its usage to "effect". Viewed as either المؤثر or الفعال , God is there considered to be the only agent in the true, primary sense of the word, since He never is a recipient of action, always "influencing" (مؤثر) others, never "influenced" by others. As such He is also called there the "first (or rather, "primary") cause", العلة الأولى , both directly and indirectly responsible for the effects of all other "agents" so called, which are "really" the effects or "affections" of His action (though see the introduction, p. 30). Al-Kindī's choice here in *FP* of مؤثر and أثر instead of فاعل and منفعل or علة and معلول may thus be explained in terms of the allusions to God's role in nature which the terms would be thought to convey; and to the intimation, by the use of terms not necessarily associated with matter, of a view of causality that is ultimately free of physical determination.

129.1 "That which is a species through its essence is multiple": فالنوع بالذات كثير. This contradicts Aristotle's view of the species of things which have a common genus as being considered one; cf. *Met.* V: 6 1016a 24, b 31. While Aristotle clearly views the species and genus as possessing unity, it is the kind of unity—indivisible in thought *qua* genus or species—which al-Kindī disqualifies as non-essential since it is composite in fact. Thus al-Kindī limits the applicability of the term "one" severely. He may, however, have felt he was in agreement with Aristotle's view as expressed in *Met.* X: 1 1052a 32, in which the indivisible in kind (i.e., formal unity, that of the species and genus) is considered as indivisible in intelligibility and in knowledge; and *its* cause is considered one in the primary sense (εἴδει δὲ τὸ τῷ γνωστῷ καὶ τῇ ἐπιστήμῃ (ἀδιαίρετον) ὥσθ'ἕν ἂν εἴη πρῶτον τὸ ταῖς οὐσίαις αἴτιον τοῦ ἑνός, translated by Asṭāt (Bouyges, op. cit., III: 1237 واما الواحد بالصورة فالذي لا قسمة له بالمعرفة وبالفكرة فاذا الواحد الأول هو الذي هو للجواهر علة الواحد). As given by Asṭāt, al-Kindī could have thought Aristotle to mean that true formal unity should in no conceivable way be divisible.

129.6 "The genus. . . indicates the essence of the thing. . .": والجنس. . .منبىء عن مائية الشيء. Cf. above, 101.8 and see n. 101.8-10.

129.7 "each one of its species being. . . an independent substance": وكل نوع من أنواعه فهو هو هو, understanding هو هو as the equivalent of هوية, "being" or "substance". The repetition of هو, if not a scribal error, may be meant to emphasize the individual nature of each species.

129.12 "The specific difference . . . indicates the quality of a thing. . .": والفصل . . . منبىء عن أيية الشيء. Cf. above, 101.9 and see n. 101.8-10.

130.3 "The property . . . indicates the existence of a thing. . .": . . . والخاصة منبئة عن أنية الشيء. Cf. above 101.7 and n. there. See also *Topics* I: 5 102a 18: "A property is something which does not show the essence of a thing but belongs to it alone and is predicated convertibly of it", ἴδιον δ'ἐστὶν ὃ μὴ δηλοῖ μὲν τὸ τί ἦν εἶναι, μόνῳ δ'ὑπάρχει καὶ ἀντικατηγορεῖται τοῦ πράγματος; rendered by al-Dimashqī (ed. Badawī, *Manṭiq Arisṭū* II: 457) as والخاصة هي ما لم يدل على ماهية الشيء وكان موجودا للأمر وحده وراجعا عليه في الحمل. The translation of موجود for ὑπάρχει, understood literally, could allow one to say "the property indicates the existence of a thing"; and an earlier translation, such as that reported to have been written by Abū Nūḥ (fl. ca. 800, and cf. Peters, *Aristoteles Arabus*, p. 21), could have even used the terminology adopted by al-Kindī.

130.4 "It is not an (essential) part (of a thing)": وليس بجزء, i.e., not part of its essence, though it belongs to the thing, or "exists" along with it. Cf. preceding n.

130.5 "and because it has motion": ولأنها حركة, literally, "and because it is motion."

130.14 "The all... has portions": والكل . . . ذو أبعاض . *Ba^cḍ* has been translated as "some" above (cf. 127.5 ff.), in contrasting it with *juz*ᵓ, "part"; proper English usage here, however, requires the term to be rendered as "portions".

130.16 "and every genus has many species": فكل جنس ذات صور , as called for by the context of this sentence. The MS (followed by AR) actually reads فكل مقولة ذات صور , "and every predicable has many species".

131.4 "a substantial part will have either similar or dissimilar parts": والجوهري إما مشتبه الأجزاء وإما لا مشتبه الأجزاء . Cf. above, 127.7 and n. there. Al-Kindī expands here upon the examples of dissimilar parts of the body, perhaps from his own intimate acquaintance with the subject as a physician. The *Rasāᵓil Ikhwān al-Ṣafāᵓ* passage above mentioned (p. 431), however, also enumerates a number of the same parts.

131.7 "like the living body": فكبدن الحى , following the correction in the ms. written above الحيوان (as AR); and in conformity with the parallel constructions of ll. 9, 10 and 12 below.

131.15 "as a house": كالبيت . Cf. above, 127.1-3 and nn. there.

131.17 "and (other) parts of its structure": وأجزاء جرمه , literally "parts of its body (or 'mass')".

131.20[1] "as the mile": كالميل , another example of continuous things, corresponding to Aristotle's example of a line; cf. *Met.* V: 6 1016a 2, 1016b 26.

131.20[2] "it is an 'all' of (many) stadia as well as a part of a parasang": إذ هو كل للغلوات وجزء للفرسخ . The mile is considered as equivalent to 7 1/2 stadia, and 3 miles constitute a parasang. Cf. Rosenthal, "al-Kindī and Ptolemy", op. cit., pp. 450, 451 for other treatises in which al-Kindī refers to stadia and miles.

132.6[1] "and is an acquisition from a donating agent": فهو مستفاد من مفيد . These terms ordinarily belong to the terminology of emanationism, and as such foreshadow the conclusion of the treatise (cf. below, pp. 162.4, 13). As with أثر and مؤثر , al-Kindī again goes to a term not particularly associated with physical causality to explain natural phenomena.

132.6[2] "An effect comes from an agent, in that the effect and the agent are in a relation where one does not precede the other": والأثر من مؤثر ، لأن الأثر والمؤثر من المضاف الذي لا يسبق بعضه بعضا , i.e., logically, one term entailing the other; viewing agent and effect (مؤثر and أثر) as correlatives (cf. *Cat.* 7 7b 15).

132.8 "Furthermore, everything which is an accident in one thing is essential in another thing": وأيضا كل شىء كان في شيء آخر عرضا ، فهو في شىء آخر ذاتى . That which is an accident in a thing need not, by definition, have occured to it. It thus was a potential existent, while, as an essential existent, it would occur necessarily to a thing. The argument here is thus a reformulation of the one from possibility and necessity found above at 118.2-7, and see the notes there. The difference between these two arguments would seem to be that al-Kindī here clearly commits himself to the idea of the existence of an essential, i.e., necessary property in a particular substance, and not in the species only. Yet the existence of an essentially unified substance is necessary as a guarantor of accidental unity only on the assumption of an eternal universe in which it is possible to conceive of a given time in which all instances of accidental unity would not occur, and never, therefore, recur thereafter (cf. *Met.* IX: 8 1050b 8 ff.). In a temporally finite world, accidental unity could conceivably exist at all times without essential unity, and a time would never have to arrive when there would be no instances of such unity. Al-Kindī thus retains an argument for the existence of God based on a notion of eternity which he otherwise rejects.

The *muᶜtazilah* and *mutakallimūn* in general also have as a major tenet the accidental nature of the composition of all substances; they, however, did not adopt this particular argument, perhaps for the above reason as well in the realization that the "essentially one" here belongs to the same genus as the "accidentally one", and that this reasoning tends to make unity a "necessary" attribute of God. Among the philosophers, however, we find Avicenna, for example, using the same argument from accidental to essential existence in his proofs of the existence of various intellects; and as al-Kindī does, Avicenna also has recourse to a theory of emanation. (cf. Michael Marmura, "Avicenna's Psychological Proof of Prophecy", *JNES* 22 [1963]: 52-56).

132.15 "The nature of every predicate...must be either one or multiple, or one and multiple together, or some of these things one and not multiple at all, while others are multiple and not one at all": ... لا يخلو طباع كل مقول ... من أن يكون واحدا او كثيراً ، أو واحدا وكثيراً معا، أو بعض هذه الأشياء واحدا لا كثيرا بتة وبعضها كثيرا لا واحدا بتة. Al-Kindī here resorts to the type of reasoning to which he is partial (cf. above 115.1, 123.6, and see n. to 123.4), combining a curious mixture of logical and factual arguments in disjunctive and hypothetical propositions of an exhaustive and repetitious sort. The arguments in the remainder of this chapter have been well outlined by Marmura and Rist, op. cit., pp. 339-342, and they have supplied relevant Greek sources as well, pp. 347-348. Thus they point to the antinomies in Plato's *Parmenides* (noting differences as well as similarities) as a source for the argument which in the following posits the one and the many as mutually exclusive entities. One should not overlook, however, Aristotle's critique of this view, which sees the one and the many as absolute opposites; a critique which contains in brief the type of absurd conclusions al-Kindī enumerates at length (cf. *Met.* X: 6 1056b 3 ff., and see *Physics* I: 2 185b 5 ff.). We may, therefore, assume that in this section al-Kindī either drew upon some familiarity with the *Parmenides* which he possessed either "directly" or through excerpts in other Middle or Neoplatonic works; or/and that he used a (lost) commentary to the *Metaphysics* which in turn incorporated the Platonic material.

By "direct" familiarity with the *Parmenides,* I mean that al-Kindī might have had some paraphrase of the work, and not that he had access to a direct translation of it, the very existence of which is questionable (the *Fihrist*, op. cit., I: 246, mentions the *Parmenides* together with Galen's epitome of it; and see Peters, *Aristotle and the Arabs*, pp. 168-170, and Walzer, in *The Encyclopaedia of Islam*, new ed. s.v., "Aflāṭūn", I: 234-236).

133.2 "If the nature of every predicate were multiplicity only, then participation in one state or one concept would not occur" : فان كان طباع كل مقول الكثرة فقط ، فلا اتفاق اشتراك في حال واحدة أو معنى واحد, literally, "...there would be no occurence of participation..."; and so similarly at line 10 below. Some of the arguments for the existence of multiplicity (or "plurality") without unity are the opposites of those al-Kindī uses for positing the existence of unity without multiplicity. Many of the latter, in turn, are found in the *Parmenides*, references being given below in the latter set of examples. The argument here, for example, may be seen as the opposite of that below, 137.5, which states that if there were unity only, there would be no "differentiation"; i.e., "participation in one state or concept" *would* occur.

133.8 "in that the contrary of multiplicity is unity": لأن خلاف الكثرة الوحدة. Compare 136.14 below for a similar, opposite type of statement.

133.12 "then it would be dissimilar": فهى لا متشابهة. Compare the opposite type of argument concerning the need for no "exceptions", i.e., complete similarity, if there is unity only; given below at 136.19.

133.16 "they would be moving": كانت متحركة, and non-moving as well, as shown below, l. 20. We have here the first real set of antinomies of this series of arguments, since there results, from this premise of multiplicity without unity, the existence simultaneously of both motion and rest, and neither motion nor rest. Compare this with 138.16 below, in which al-Kindī argues that from unity alone there can be neither motion nor rest.

134.5 "individual members": ذات أشخاص. Compare the discussion of "parts" and "all" below at 139.13 f. In the ensuing argument here al-Kindī digresses to a brief discussion of the impossibility of an infinite quantity, applying a slight variation of the argument laid down in 115.1 ff. above, but discussing it from the viewpoint of the separated "section" of the infinite.

135.6 "multiplicity would not be subject to number": لم تقبل الكثرة العدد. Al-Kindī develops the relation of number and the one in chapter 4, 146.18 ff. below, from which chapter this and the following argument may be derived. Cf., however, *Parmenides* 144a 4 ff., which establishes that if the one is, number must also be, and if number, then multiplicity.

135.14 "Knowledge impresses the description of that which is known into the soul of the knower as one state" : المعرفة ترسم رسم المعروف في نفس العارف, بحال واحدة, i.e., in its universal, intelligible form. Cf. chap. 4 below, 155.1 and 5.

136.8 "It is, however, multiplicity": وهو كثرة, rejecting Abū Riḍah's suggested emendation, "it is however (not multiplicity and) multiplicity", (فهو ليس كثرة) وهو كثرة, as not absolutely necessary.

136.12 "Similarly, we shall now explain that it is not possible for unity to occur without multiplicity": كذلك نبين أنه لا يمكن أن تكون وحدة بلا كثرة.

The following arguments, to 140.15, are elaborations and repetitions of the arguments found in the *Parmenides*, mostly at 137c-139b. The difference between Plato's and al-Kindī's reasoning is that Plato constructs strictly logical antinomies, while al-Kindī's arguments have the appearance of antinomies, but are mostly straightforward and rather simply reasoned refutations of the initial premise of his syllogisms.

136.14 "contrariety would not exist": لم تكن مضادة . Cf. above, 133.8 ff., and see *Parmenides* 139b 4 ff. for a discussion of the relation of the "one" and the "other".

136.19 "then there would be no exception": فلا استثناء . Cf. above, 133.12 and n. there.

137.7 "then there would be no differentiation": لم يكن تباين . Cf. above, 133.2 and n. there.

137.11 "neither agreement nor disagreement, conjunction nor separation": فلا اتفاق ولا اختلاف ، ولا اتصال ولا افتراق . These states may be subsumed under the preceding argument from "differentiation".

137.13 "neither agreement nor disagreement": لم يكن اتفاق ولا اختلاف , literally, "neither agreement nor disagreement nor agreement" (ولا اتفاق), the last two words being obviously superfluous, as AR surmises in 137, n. 5, though he includes them in the text. The original passage may well have been, as it should be, "neither agreement nor disagreement, and neither conjunction nor separation."

137.18 "neither beginning, middle nor end": فلا ابتداء ولا توسط ولا آخر . Cf. *Parmenides* 137d 4 f.

138.6 "then there would be no figure": فلا شكل . Ibid., 137d 8 ff. Plato's examples, however, being the round and the straight.

138.16 "neither move nor rest": لا متحركة ولا ساكنة . Cf. above, 133.16 and n. there , and see *Parmenides* 138b 7 ff.

139.3 "not dwindling": لا مضمحل, which for some reason al-Kindī prefers to "not decreasing", لا ناقص , which one would have expected from 139.1.

139.13 "there would be neither part nor all" : لم يكن جزء ولا كل . Cf. above, 134.5 ff., and see *Parmenides* 137c 5 ff. "Part" is here related to "all" in a general sense, broader than that given above, 128.1.

140.10-12 "Thus it is clear from all these investigations...while it is clear from some of these investigations...": فقد تبين من جميع هذه الأبحاث ... ومن ... بعضها . By contrasting جميع (in the general sense of "all"; literally "whole", following the remarks of 127.6 ff. above) with بعض *vis-a-vis* investigations of multiplicity and unity respectively, al-Kindī is declaring that he has not exhausted (or disproved) all the possibilities of predicating unity of things; the theme, in fact, of the following chapter.

140.16 "the nature of things has unity and multiplicity": طباع الأشياء وحدة , وكثرة, literally, "is unity and multiplicity"; this being the abbreviated way al-Kindī regularly expresses himself in this section, but not intending thereby to imply that beings have no nature other than unity or multiplicity (which could be construed from the literal translation).

141.4 "is in every sensible object...": في كل محسوس . By emphasizing "sensible objects" and their concomitants as having been thoroughly discussed, al-Kindī is apparently showing awareness that he has not yet covered the multiplicity of such non-sensible abstractions as number and ideas (or the intellects), though he has shown their unity (cf. above, 135.6 ff.).

141.7 "If the association were through chance, then there would be a separation...": فان كانت بالبخت فقد كانت متباينة, i.e., things associated by chance are essentially separate.

141.22 "As by itself the cause precedes the effect, as we have explained in our writing concerning the separation (between cause and effect)": ولأن العلة قبل المعلول بالذات كما بينا في كتابنا على المباينة. Cf., among al-Kindī's other writings on causality (also referred to below, 142.12), AR I: 183, 217 ff, which treatises assume rather than state this proposition directly. See too 101.1 above. Al-Kindī may here be basing himself on such Aristotelian passages as *Cat.* 12 14b 12 and *Met.* V: 11 1019a 2.

142.9 "It has, however, been explained that it is impossible for there to be an actual infinite thing": وقد تبين أنه لا يمكن أن يكون شيء بالفعل بلا نهاية. Cf., regarding arguments for the impossibility of there being an infinite series of causes, given primarily in relation to temporal segments, 121.5 ff. above; and see nn. to 121.8, 9 and 121.15-122.1 there. See too *Met.* II: 2 994a 1 ff.

142.14 "If this were the case, however": فان كانت كذلك, viz., auto-causation.

142.16 "Furthermore, (the cause of the association of multiplicity and unity) is not in that which is generic to them": وأيضا ليست بمجانسة لهما. The examples of house, man (and dog) as belonging to a common genus and as such called "one", are given in *Met.* V. 6 1016a 24 ff.; and al-Kindī has rejected this sense of unity above, 129.6. In now rejecting the possibility that the ultimate cause of multiplicity and unity can be a generically similar thing, he is in effect—and probably intentionally—rejecting Aristotle's first cause, the unmoved mover; which, for all its special characteristics, is understood within the conceptual, generic framework of substantial being (cf. *Met.* XII: 7 1072a 21 ff.). Though not prior in time, this substance is first in actuality and causality of being.

142.20 "It is not with them in (having) one likeness": فليست معهما في شبه واحد. As the preceding paragraph appears to be a discreet refutation of Aristotle's first principle of being, so this paragraph may well be directed against Plato's theory of ideal forms, in the likeness of which substances here are created; cf. *Phaedo* 100b-101c, *Republic* 596b, and *Timaeus* 30c-31b (Plato himself criticizing the notion of participation in the ideas, inherent in the concept of likeness, in *Parmenides* 132c-133a).

143.4 "if it were multiple, then it would contain unity": فان كانت كثيرة ففيها الوحدة. Al-Kindī has just established that there can be no resemblance or likeness between the association of multiplicity and unity and its cause. Yet here he uses a concept of multiplicity that is the familiar one, associated with unity, and as such obviously inadequate. However, he next proceeds to assert that the only possible cause of this association is a unity, though he has rejected the concept of unity as an existent separate from multiplicity above, at 140.18. Obviously al-Kindī is thinking of unity in a unique sense, though he insists on arriving at the concept by using conventional terms; employing in the process, however, a double standard of logic which allows "unity" to be used in a way not allowed "multiplicity".

CHAPTER IV: NOTES

143.14-15 "Let us now speak of the way in which unity exists in the categories, of that which is truly one, and of that which is one metaphorically and not truly" : فلنقل الآن بأى نوع توجد الوحدة في المقولات ، وما الواحد بالحق ، وما الواحد بالمجاز لا بالحقيقة. This introductory statement is practically identical with the closing remark of the previous chapter, the sort of repetition that a speaker would indulge in if an interval has passed between his lectures. Much in this last chapter repeats and is derived from that which has preceded, again conveying the impression that this material was originally presented as a lecture in which the speaker could permit himself this indulgence (and cf. p. 11 of the introduction).

Al-Kindī's distinction between the "true" and the "metaphorical" one is reminiscent of the same distinction as applied to the term "agent" in his treatise entitled "On the True, First, Perfect Agent and the Deficient Agent which is (called agent) Metaphorically" (AR I: 182). As there, so here, his use of the term "metaphorical" is not meant to convey worthlessness, but only an inferior status. In the total context of the argument it is of course the unity applied to the "True One" which is used metaphorically, since it is beyond our comprehension of the term; except that for reasons of piety and fidelity to the Neoplatonic tradition, al-Kindī could not, and probably did not even conceive of so putting it.

143.17 "The large and small, long and short, much and little are never predicated absolutely of anything, but, rather, relatively": إن العظيم والصغير، والطويل والقصير ، والكثير والقليل، لا يقال شيء منها على شيء قولا مرسلا ، بل بالاضافة. Cf. *Cat.* 6 5b 14 ff., with the addition of a third pair of relatives, for which cf. below, 146.7. The use of the following relatives allows al-Kindī to introduce a mathematical discussion in which possible ways of finding the absolute, essential one in a quantity or number are eliminated.

143.19 "misfortune": هناة, possibly a scribal error for هنات, "little, trifling things"; which would be the equivalent of Aristotle's "grain" in the similar examples of *Cat.* 6 5b 18 (κέγχρος in the Greek, rendered by Isḥāq ibn Ḥunayn [ed. Georr, op. cit., p. 330] as السمسمة; and cf. AR, n. 6).

144.3 "If the large—as, similarly, the small—were predicated absolutely...": ولو كان يقال العظيم مرسلا (على ما يقال عليه العظيم) وكذلك الصغير. Al-Kindī diverges here from Aristotle's bare statement (ibid., l. 20) that we simply can't use such terms as "small" and "large" in an absolute sense, to expand upon the themes which he has mentioned in the preceding chapters.

144.14 "and multiplying a quantity by two exists, in actuality or in potentiality...and therefore the absolute large has a double": وتضعيف الشيء) . تثنية كيته) ، وتثنية كيته موجودة بالفعل أو بالقوة ... فاذا للعظيم المرسل ضعف . Al-Kindī here takes the potential doubling of an object as tantamount to its actual doubling, assuming that necessary correlation between the two which he has rejected above at 116.13-117.1, the last time he specifically dealt with this issue in terms of arithmetical relationships (and cf. the n. to 116.13-16 above). The difference may be explained by the fact that in the earlier passage of this treatise potential existence is seen as a threat to the doctrine of a finite universe, and therefore its significance for actual existence is discounted; while here potential existence is enlisted, as an aid to actuality, in the doctrine of the relativity of all existents, and can therefore be accepted.

145.7 "Similarly...the all would be smaller than the part, and this is even more absurd and ugly": وكذلك يعرض...أن يكون الكل أصغر من الجزء ، وهذا أشد إحالة وشناعة, contradicting as it does one of the "first premises" al-Kindī has enumerated above, 114.18, and see note there.

146.8 "the long and short are predicated of all quantitative things which are continuous": الطويل والقصير فيقالان على كل كمية متصلة. With this remark and that concerning "the little" and "the much" as predicates of discrete quantity (1. 12 below), al-Kindī assigns quantitative properties to the two types of unity Aristotle mentions in *Cat.* 6 4b 20. Among the discrete quantities there mentioned (1. 23) is number, concerning which al-Kindī next elaborates.

146.15 "if the first number is two... two is then the least of the numbers": إن كان أول العدد اثنين ... فان الإثنين أقل الأعداد. The following analysis essentially investigates the possibility of positing "one" as the basic number, the "absolute little", and the senses in which this is and is not deemed permissible. Notions of equality and inequality, odd and even as related to one are particularly examined, and similarities with the number two are brought out. Two is ultimately considered as the first, smallest number, though not an absolute unity. Many of the ideas al-Kindī mentions can be found separately in Aristotle, Plotinus, and Nichomachus of Gerasa, among others (see above, p. 19 of the introduction, and cf. also Marmura and Rist, op. cit., p. 349). The Hellenistic commentators on Aristotle and the *Isagoge* used Nichmachus' writings on arithmetic, as is evident, for example, from David's discussion of the subject in the introduction to philosophy which precedes his commentary to the *Isagoge* (ed. Busse, op. cit., pp. 49-52). David there acknowledges one to be the principle of number, a principle being different from that of which it is said to be the principle; one is thus not number, which is further shown by its failure to pass tests of multiplication and addition (whereas al-Kindī applies tests of division). According to the standard by which the sum and product of adding and multiplying a thing by itself should yield different results, two is also considered not a regular number (and cf. Nichomachus' *Introduction to Arithmetic*, ed. D'Ooge, p. 117), though David argues the case back and forth in a manner similar to al-Kindi's deliberations with the one; finally accepting the number three as the first number in the fullest sense of the word.

We have seen al-Kindī previously make use of an *Isagoge* commentary, or some paraphrase of one (cf. above, 101.5 ff., 105.3 ff. and 124. 17 ff.); and it is highly likely that such is again his immediate major source here, though he would have been familiar with the views of the other above-mentioned authors as well (and cf. the introduction, p. 20 above). Al-Kindi's Aristotelian bias emerges in that he does not follow the Neo-Pythagorean conclusions regarding the number three of a David, but chooses, with Aristotle (and cf. Heath, op. cit., I: 73), to regard the number two as prime, if in a qualified way.

146.21 "and if one were a quantity... it would be equal and non-equal": وإن كان الواحد كية ... أنه مساو ولا مساو, i.e., equality and inequality would be predicated of it, as of all quantity; and cf. *Cat.* 6 6a 26 ff. Al-Kindī takes this statement at first to mean that the one itself would have to possess equal and unequal units, i.e., equality and inequality would be within itself; and he thus speaks in 147.2 ff. below of the "smaller" and "larger" units of the one. At 147.16, however, he rejects this use of equality and inequality, and at 148.5 offers the proper application of these terms.

147.2 "for the 'smaller one' would be inferior to the 'larger one' or inferior to a portion of it": لأن الواحد الأصغر بعد الواحد الأكبر أو بعد بعضه. This is one of the "true first premises" mentioned above, at 114.18.

147.14 " 'One', then, would not be a number naturally, but homonymously": فاذا الواحد ليس بعدد بالطبع ، بل باشتباه الاسم. The homonymous use of the term "one", while ostensibly rejected in all areas, is actually al-Kindi's solution when applied to God; though he inists that the unity of the One God is the primary reference of the term (cf. p. 19 f. of the introduction).

148.6 " 'two' would not be a number, since no number is smaller than it, but only larger": فالاثنان ... لا عدد، إذ ليس عدد أقل منه. Assuming one is not a number since no number is smaller than it, two is then similarly not a number, being deprived of one. Cf. the similar argument of David, op. cit., 50.12, 51. 1; this line of reasoning being capable of infinite extension for all numbers (ibid., 52.14 ff.).

148.13 "then either even or odd": فاما أن يكون زوجا وإما فردا. This distinction of number goes back to the Pythagoreans, as Aristotle says in *Met.* I. 5 986a 17 (and see Heath, op. cit., I: 70 f.).

149.5 "since the odd number does not have to be divided necessarily": إذ ليس يوجب أنه منقسم اضطرارا, i.e., the potential divisibility of one, with its logically impossible consequents, need never be actualized. Al-Kindī here again employs that un-Aristotelian view of potentiality which he has resorted to before; though elsewhere, and just recently, he has used the concept in its regular Aristotelian sense (cf. 144.14 above, and see n. there).

149.7 "The element of something...is not the thing (itself)": إن ركن الشيء....

ليس هو الشيء. The equivalent of the following passage may be found, in Aristotle for example, in *Met.* X: 1 1052b 1 ff.; and see too *Met.* XIV: 1 1088a 6 (and cf. Heath, op. cit., I: 69).

149.8 "the articulated letters": الحروف الصوتية. Cf. *Met.* X : 1 1053a 13, "and in speech the letter" (is the starting point and measure), καὶ ἐν φωνῇ στοιχεῖον, rendered by Asṭāt (ed. Bouyges, op. cit., III : 1255) as وفي الصوت الحرف. The "letters" are clearly understood by Aristotle in vocal and not written terms, as shown also by the synonymous use of φωναί in 1053a 17 and as qualified in *Cat.* 6 4b 34. Al-Kindī is also probably influenced in his formulation of this passage by the Muslim grammarians, who emphasized the articulation of the letters in their analysis of the alphabet (cf. H. Fleisch in *The Encyclopaedia of Islam*, new ed., s.v. *Ḥurūf al-Hidjā*ʾ, III: 596-600).

149.12 "Then the one would be number": فيكون الواحد عددا, i.e., since it is not an element (to itself, being the element of numbers other than itself), one might be regarded as a number. This ignores the fact that the numerical one is initially understood in this paragraph only in relation to and distinct from numbers, of which it is the element; having no nature "by itself" which could be seen as a "number" in some absolute sense of the term. Al-Kindī does not even bother to refute this obvious bit of sophistry, which leads him, however, to formulate additional possibilities of considering one as number.

150.4 "it has been said that substance is three-fold": قد قيل إن الجوهر ثلاثة. Cf. *De Anima* II: 1 412a 6 ff., 2 414a 14 ff.

150.10 "and the body . . . happens to be a substance" : فعرض للجسم . . . أن يكون جواهر, literally, "substances", as again at l. 17 below.

150.16 "it is a unit": فهو آحاد, literally "units".

151.2 "Two is, then, the first number": فاذا الإثنان أول العدد. Cf. *Met.* XIV: 1 1088a 6, and see too *Physics* IV: 12 220a 27; though al-Kindī's reasoning in the following lines is the opposite of that in the *Physics* passage.

151.9 "each one of them is related to another only in the same genus": وإنما يضاف كل واحد منهما إلى آخر من جنسه. This could be a variation and elaboration of *Met.* V: 6 1016b 25 or/and X: 1 1053a 24 ff.

152.9 "Time too belongs to continuous quantity": والزمان ايضاً من الكمية المتصلة. Cf. above, 122.10 and n. there.

152.13 "Thus, one says 'a long number', i.e., (one which occurs) in a long time": فانه يقال عدد طويل – أى في زمان طويل. Compare *Cat.* 6 5b 2.

153.1 "The True One": الواحد بالحقيقة (literally, "the one in truth"), i.e., the absolute, unique one, a term used in contrast to the "metaphorical one", الواحد بالمجاز (cf. above, 143.15), which we now see includes all the predicables and properties of being, all shown as containing multiplicity in one form or another, and thus only relatively and accidentally one.

153.3 "We have already stated that what has a genus is not eternal, and that the eternal has no genus": وقد قدمنا أن ما له جنس فليس بأزلي وان الأزلى لا جنس له. Cf. 113.5 above, and see too 143.1.

153.4 "and the One should not be spoken of in relation to something other than itself": ولا يقال واحد بالاضافة إلى غيره. Al-Kindī here sounds the theme of the conclusion of this treatise, returning to it with greater emphasis below, 160.6 ff.

153.13-16 "motion... is multiple": والحركة ... متكثرة, using motion as a synonym of "change". Cf. above, 117.7 (and see note 117.8[1]), of which passage this and the following two paragraphs constitute an expanded version.

154.7 "since unity is predicated of the undetermined whole": إذ الوحدة يقال على الكل المطلق, i.e., whole as a general, unqualified concept. Cf. Goichon, op. cit., p. 206 for this sense of مطلق (usually rendered as "absolute") as used by Avicenna.

154.10 "As every thing perceived through the sense or intellect either exists, in itself or in our thought, as a natural existence...": وإذ كل مدرك بالحس أو بالعقل إما أن يكون موجودا في عينه أو في فكرنا وجوداً طبيعياً, it being "natural" for sensations and ideas, wherever their primary base may be, to exist in the soul of man, a "rational animal"; whereas speaking and writing, al-Kindī next implies, must be learned, and as such are "accidental". As between sensory and intellectual perceptions, the former has been described as "nearer" to man, the latter "nearer" to nature (cf. above, 106.5 ff., 107.2 ff.); as such it is the sensible which exists "in our thought" as a natural existent, while it is the intelligible which exists "in itself" as a natural existent.

154.12 "various dispositions and passions which accompany the soul": اخلاق لازمة للنفس شتى وآلام. Al-Kindī makes a passing reference here to non-intellectual faculties of the soul, to which he has also referred above at 104.1, and see the n. there. The "thoughts" or *fikar* which are next mentioned stand, if not as a general synonym for perceptions of all kinds, for the material of the imaginative faculty (and compare the definition of *fikr* given by Isaac Israeli [op. cit., p. 55], rendered as "cogitation" by Stern there, who also mentions Wolfson's analyses of the various interpretations given this term by later Arabic philosophers).

154.16 "The end result of thoughts ... is (directed) toward the intellect": نهاية الفكر ... إلى العقل, i.e., apprehension of ideas proceeds from the (rational) imagination to the intellect. Cf. 106. 12, 13 and 107.2 ff., and see the notes there. The following section, from 154.17-155.9, has received a "tentative" translation from Richard J. McCarthy, "Al-Kindī's Treatise On the Intellect", op. cit., pp. 143-144.

154.17 "Intellect is the species of things ... as well as that which is above them": وهو أنواع الأشياء ... وما فوقها, viz., the genus as well as the species. Cf. 107.4 ff. for this and the following sentence, and see too al-Kindī's *On the Intellect* (AR I: 354), in which immaterial form, which "falls under the intellect", is said to be نوعية الأشياء وما فوقها, "the specificality (after Stern, *Isaac Israeli*, pp. 37, 38; McCarthy, op. cit., p. 126, "kind-ness") of things and that which is above it". The same treatise (AR, p. 356) refers to the "first intellect" (and not the "acquired intellect", as McCarthy [ibid.] and Abū Rīdah [n. 4] assume) as "the specificality of things which are [or: is] always in actuality", نوعية الشىء

التي هى بالفعل أبدا (following Stern, op. cit., p. 37, and cf. Atiyeh's translation, op. cit., p. 213). The *On Definitions* manuscript preserved in the British Museum attributes the phrase "specificality of things" to the "universal intellect" (العقل الكلى, as quoted by Stern in "Notes on Al-Kindī's Treatise On Definitions", op. cit., p. 34, and in *Isaac Israeli*, p. 38), an entity apparently equal to the "first intellect" of *On the Intellect.* This definition of the British Museum ms. also divides the "universal intellect" into "universal" and "particular" universal intellects, an oddity which Stern attempts to resolve ("Notes", loc. cit., n. 1), and which may also possibly be understood as referring to both the universal "first" or agent intellect, and to the particular "acquired" intellect, for which cf. below, 155.17 and n.

155.1 "When, however, they are united with the soul" : فاذا اتحدت بالنفس, viz., as species, which McCarthy understands (op. cit., p. 143) as the subject of the sentence. Besides turning the preceding sentence into a digression, such a translation overlooks the fact that al-Kindī tends to speak (loosely) of the individual as an intelligible object. Cf. particularly 126.16 above (and see n. 126.14[1] there), and the expressions "species of individuals" and "individuals of species" in 107.4 and 5, which indicate al-Kindī's awareness of an ontological relationship between the particular and the universal; even as his remarks in 108.5 ff. describe his particular view of the relation of a sensory to an intellectual perception. In his treatise *On Sleep and Vision* (AR I: 302), al-Kindī distinguishes between these perceptions in a manner similar to our present passage, concluding that "the genera, species and individuals comprise all the intelligibles", والأجناس والأنواع والأشخاص هى جميع المعقولات ; retained partially in the Latin as *et species quidem et individua sunt omnia nota* (ed. Nagy, op. cit., p. 19, and see McCarthy's translation, op. cit., p. 146).

155.1-2 "intelligence in actuality . . . intelligence in potentiality": عاقلة بالفعل . . . عاقلة بالقوة, rendered by McCarthy (ibid., p. 143) as "intellect-ing in act" and "intellect-ing in potency". Al-Kindī here begins to refer briefly to his views on the nature of intellection and the intellect, which he mentions at greater length in his treatise *On the Intellect* (AR I: 353-358, edited and translated also by McCarthy, op. cit., pp. 122-128, and translated too by Atiyeh, op. cit., pp. 210-215; Atiyeh also summarizes [ibid., pp. 113-122] the various interpretations which may be given al-Kindī's doctrine of the intellect, and Stern briefly describes it as well, *Isaac Israeli*, p. 38).

155.6-7 "universal things . . . are the acquired intellect of the soul which the soul had in potentiality": فكليات الأشياء . . . هي عقل النفس المستفاد الذي كان لها بالقوة . Cf. *On the Intellect* (AR I: 356, فهذه الصورة التي لا هيولي لها ولا فنطاسيا هي العقل المستفاد للنفس من العقل الأول , "this form, then, which has neither matter nor phantasm, is the intellect acquired, for the soul, from the first intellect" (following McCarthy's translation, op. cit., p. 126); the preceding sentence there stating that the intelligibles existed in potentiality in the soul before being in actuality.

155.8 "and they are the intellect in actuality which has brought the soul from potentiality to actuality": فهي العقل الذي بالفعل الذي أخرج النفس من القوة إلى الفعل . The "first intellect", which we saw defined in both *On the Intellect* and (as "universal intellect") *On Definitions* as the "specificality of things" (cf. the n. to 154.16 above), is said in the former treatise (AR 356.5) to be in actuality and مفيد, a source of emanation upon the soul, bringing about the acquired intellect, العقل المستفاد (and see the preceding n.). This parallel thus suggests that the "intellect in actuality" of our text is this "first" or "universal" intellect, and that the acquired intellect is related to and in part identical with it. Al-Kindī thus alludes here to the existence of a (first, universal) intellect which is in actuality always, and, in man, an acquired intellect which passes from the state of a potential intellect to that of an actual intellect.

155.9 "and consequently the intellect is multiple": فالعقل متكثر, since it is composed of a multiplicity of universals and because the intellect, as has been stated, is neither simple nor ultimately one; though the various stages of man's intellect are related to each other and to the universal intellect.

In asserting the subdivision of the active and passive states of Aristotle's intellect (cf. *De Anima* III. 5 430a 15f.) into three (or four) intellects, al-Kindī is following some exposition of the writings of Alexander of Aphrodisias on the subject (cf., e.g., his *De Anima,* edited by I. Bruns, *Alexander Aphrodisiensis Praeter Commentaria Scripta Minora CAG* Supp. 2. 1 [Berlin, 1887], pp. 84-86, and see O. Hamelin, *La Théorie De L'Intellect D'Après Aristote Et Ses Commentateurs* [Paris, 1953], pp. 31-37, for an analysis of Alexander's views). Yet in emphasizing the multiplicity of the intellect and in explicitly separating it from the ultimate First Principle, the Divine Intelligence (viewed in terms of the True One), al-Kindī modifies the doctrine along Neoplatonic lines (cf. e.g., *Enn.* V. 3, 11 and 12, equivalent to that translated from the *Epistola De Scientia Divina* by Lewis in Henry-Schwyzer, op. cit., II: 321; and cf. Marmura and Rist, op. cit., p. 351).

Incidentally, the division into *four* intellects mentioned in al-Kindī's *On the Intellect,* in which the actual intellect in man is divided into an acquired but relatively passive, latent state of actuality, and an active, "apparent" (ظاهر) state (cf. AR, pp. 353, 354 and 358; McCarthy, op. cit., nos. 2 and 10, pp. 122, 123 Arabic, 125-127 English; Stern, *loc. cit.*; and Atiyeh, op. cit., pp. 211, 214-215 and 121, n. 24), reflects an interpretation of Alexander's remarks on the human intellect when viewed *in habitu* and *in actu,* as given in his *De Anima* (ibid., and cf. too his περὶ νοῦ, ed. Bruns, op. cit., pp. 106-113, the relations of which text to al-Kindī's having been discussed by Étienne Gilson, "Les sources gréco-arabes de l'Augustinisme Avicennisant", *Archives d'Histoire Doctrinale et Littéraire du Moyen Age* 4 [1929]: 22-27; cf., however, Fazlur Rahman's qualification of some of Gilson's thesis, *Prophecy in Islam* [London, 1958], p. 22, n. 6, and see Atiyeh's summary of past scholarly viewpoints on this subject, op. cit., p. 121, n. 25).

Al-Kindī thus anticipates, in these all too brief remarks on the intellect, doctrines which later philosophers, notably al-Fārābī and Avicenna, were to develop (cf. Rahman, op. cit., pp. 11-29). Like them (and particularly like Avicenna; ibid., pp. 14, 15), al-Kindī views the intellect in man as acquired from a universal active intelligence (which, however, he does not—in contrast to his successors—relate to any scheme of emanated intelligences), partially uniting with it by thinking the universal ideas (cf. *On the Intellect*, AR pp. 356, 357; no. 8, 9 in McCarthy, pp. 123 Arabic, 127 English; Atiyeh, op. cit., pp. 213, 214). Man's intellect thus belongs essentially to a universal entity, though al-Kindī does not develop this view explicitly. The implications of this doctrine for the status of a personal soul and for personal immortality are left unresolved, which is in keeping with al-Kindī's other *philosophical* remarks concerning the soul, in such treatise as his *On Grief* (ed. Walzer and Ritter, *Studi* II, op. cit., no. 4, pp. 35 Arabic, 51 Italian); *On the Soul* (AR I: 274-276, and cf. above, n. 104.2); and in his *Abbreviated, Short, Statement... On the Soul* (AR I: 281-2, translated by Stern, op. cit., p. 43).

155.12 "synonymous names" : الأسماء المترادفة. Cf. Aristotle's discussion of homonyms and synonyms in *Cat.* 1 1 la ff.

155.17 "and the star which is called dog": والكوكب المسمى كلبا, viz., the constellation *Canis Major* (or *Canis Minor*).

155.21[1] "the actual quiddity": العين القائمة, that which exists in actuality. العين can mean both substance and essence, as well as the thing itself. Cf. also below, 156.1, and elsewhere, AR I: 217.1.

155.21[2] "for the writing, which is a substance": فان الخط الذي هو جوهر, i.e. the writing represents a substance, is symbolic of the "actual quiddity".

156.8 "forms": المثل, literally, "patterns" or "shapes"; *al-mithāl* is used as a synonym for *al-ṣurah* here (as suggested by AR, n. 4) and in the following lines, as well as at 158.1 below.

156.10 "through the first matter, i.e., through possibility" : بالعنصر الاول ، اعنى بالامكان. Cf. above, 113.11 and n. 2 there.

156.13 "since corruption of that which undergoes corruption is generation for another (substance): إذ فساد الفاسد كون لآخر. Al-Kindī here speaks of natural change in a continuous and apparently autonomous way, applying a kind of conservation-of-matter principle which has no need, ostensibly, for an external Creator. In effect, however, he holds to both views, as we have seen.

157.12 "and each one of them is continually subject to division and multiplication into its own species" : وكل واحد منها قابل للتفصيل والتكثير قبولا دائماً إلى نوعه, continually but not to infinity; cf. above, 116.5 ff. Al-Kindī again seems to forget himself in discussing the natural properties of things.

158.3 "separability": تفصيل, used synonymously with انقسام, "divisibility", as at line 8 below, and thus translated interchangeably, as in the preceding note.

158.7 "neither a position nor a common (factor)": ولا وضع له ولا مشترك. Cf. *Met.* V. 6 1016b 25.

158.9 "for it is the numerically one which is the measure of all things":

[وهذا هو الواحد العددي مكيال كل [الأشياء ; i.e., as related to things the numerically one, in spite of its differences from the things (as the measure is different from that which is measured), is considered multiple. Cf. above, 151.1 ff.

158.10 "articulated letters": حروف الأصوات, literally, "the letters of voices." Cf. 149.8 above and see the n. there.

158.15 "the point": العلامة. Cf. *Met* V: 6 1016b 25.

158.16 "It is multiple, however, in its subjects": وهي متكثرة بحاملاتها. Cf. above, 122.10 ff. The text has here jumped from discussing the point of a line to speaking of the instant of time, with which the point is compared above, 157.16. The probably identical sentence, "it is multiple, however, in its subjects", with which both arguments (regarding the point and the line) must have ended, probably led a copyist to skip a line or two in his transcription.

158.18 "That which is indivisible by virtue of its whole is (also) said to be one": ويقال واحد أيضاً الذي لا ينقسم من جهة الكلية. Cf. *Met* X: 1 1052a 22, the circle being given as the primary kind of an extended whole in l. 28 there.

158.19 "*raṭl*": A pound weight, or one of several variously defined measures.

159.8 "Its first division may occur either through continuity... form... name ... or ... genus": وينقسم قسمة أولى إما بالاتصال ... بالصورة ... بالاسم ... وإما بالجنس. Cf., for this and the following two paragraphs, *Met.* V: 6 1016b 31 ff.

160.6 "The True One is not one of the intelligible things": الواحد الحق ليس هو شيء من المعقولات. The list of negations which follows places al-Kindī firmly in the tradition of those who describe God with negative attributes; a tradition which goes back to Albinus in the second century A.D. (cf. H. Wolfson, "Albinus and Plotinus on Divine Attributes", *HTR* 45 [1952]: 115-130) and which is represented by Plotinus, Pseudo-Dionysius, John of Damascus and others before Islam (cf. Wolfson, "Philosophical Implications of the Problem of Divine Attributes in the Kalam", *JAOS* 79 [1959]: 74, and see also Marmura and Rist., op. cit., pp. 348, 349). This tradition was continued in various ways by the first generation of *mutakallimun* and their successors, in the 8th and 9th centuries (cf. Wolfson, ibid., pp. 74-78). Among the *muᶜtazilah* who give a negative interpretation of the predicates we find al-Naẓẓām and Abū al-Hudhayl, whom we have met before as writers who expressed arguments similar to those used by al-Kindī (cf. p. 25 f. of the introduction). For all the similarity, however, al-Kindī's philosophical approach to this issue is different from that of his contemporaries, and he proceeds to allude to a relation of the One to the world via emanation, a view which the *muᶜtazilah* did not accept.

160.16 "pure": محض, the term describing The One which is found in the title of the Arabic paraphrase of Proclus' *Element of Theology*, *Kitāb ... al-Khayr al-Maḥḍ;* which work contains similar views to those expressed here by al-Kindī. Cf. p. 40 of the introduction.

161.7 "It is impossible for things to be infinite in actually": وليس يمكن أن يكون الأشياء بلا نهاية بالفعل. Cf. above, 142.13 f.

161.11 "Every caused unity simply passes from its unity (that of the True One) to that which is other than its being, i.e., the True One is not multiple with respect to its existence": فكل واحد من المعلولات للوحدة إنما يذهب من وحدته إلى غير هويته، أعني أنه لا يتكثر من حيث يوجد. Al-Kindī here draws a distinction between the being and existence (mostly used interchangeably) of the One and that of other unified existents (a distinction which may be contrasted with the Plotinian passage mentioned in p. 16 of the introduction); though immediately proceeding, at 162.2, to build a bridge, however unstructured, between the One and the world.

162.2 "and consequently, the emanation of unity from the True One, the First, is the coming to be of every sensible object and what is attached to the sensible object; and (The True One) causes every one of them to exist when it causes them to be through its being": فاذا فيض الوحدة عن الواحد الحق الأول هو تهوى كل محسوس وما يلحق المحسوس ، فيوجد كل واحد منها إذا يهوى بهويته إياها . That unity which we saw as completely separate, in the preceding note, is now regarded as somehow endowing all creation with its being. Clearly al-Kindī has in mind some mediating hypostasis (or hypostases) which bring the diametrically opposed Creator and creation into this relationship, something in addition to the universal intellect which we have seen he acknowledges elsewhere (cf. the n. to 154.17 above); but he nowhere states his views on this issue in detail.

162.7 "so the cause of creation is the True One, the First": فعلة الابداع هو الواحد الحق الأول. Creation, or rather "creation from nothing" (literally, "innovation"), is asserted by al-Kindī elsewhere as the most characteristic and greatest of all God's acts (cf. AR I: 183, and see the note to 123.6, 7 above; cf. too Stern's translation of al-Kindī's treatise which discusses this issue, and his tracing of the concept of creation from nothing to earlier and later Neoplatonic circles, in *Isaac Israeli*, pp. 68-74).

162.13 "Inasmuch as that which we wanted to clarify . . . ": فاذ قد تبين ما أردنا إيضاحه . . . Much of this closing remark is found, with similar terminology and expressions, in al-Kindī's paraphrase of the *Almagest* (cf. Rosenthal, "Al-Kindī and Ptolemy", op. cit., p. 437); that work also promises to be continued, and Rosenthal entertains a small doubt if al-Kindī is doing more in saying so there than copying his source. It is, nevertheless, possible that *On First Philosophy* did have a second part, and we may look forward to the day when more of this or other treatises of al-Kindī's will come to light.

List of Abreviations

FP "On First Philosophy"

AR M. ʿA.H. Abū Rīdah's edition of *FP* and other treatises, in the *Rasā'il al-Kindī al-Falsafīyah*

AH A. al-Ahwānī's edition of *FP*

UG "On the Unity of God and the Finiteness of the Body of the World"

EF "An Explanation of the Finiteness of the Body of the World"

OE "On the Essence of That Which Cannot Be Infinite and That of Which Infinity Can Be Predicated"

Bibliography

Afnan, Soheil Muhsin. *Philosophical Terminology in Arabic and Persian.* Leiden: E.J. Brill, 1964.

Alexander of Aphrodisias. *De Anima.* Edited by I. Bruns in "Alexander Aphrodisiensis Praeter Commentaria Scripta Minora." In *Commentaria in Aristotelem Graeca,* supp. 2, pt. 1, 1887.

Altmann, A., and Stern, S.M. *Isaac Israeli.* Oxford, 1958.

Ammonius, Alexandrinus. *In Porphyrii Isagogen sive V Voces.* Edited by A. Busse. In *Commentaria in Aristotelem Graeca,* vol. 5, no. 3, 1891.

Andalūsī, Sā᾽id al-. *Kitāb Ṭabaqāt al-Umam.* Edited by Louis Cheikho. Beirut, 1912.

———*Kitāb Ṭabaqāt al-Umam.* Translated (into French) by Regis Blachère. Paris, 1935.

Arberry, Arthur John. *The Koran Interpreted.* 2 vols. New York: Macmillan Co., 1955.

Aristotle. *Categoriae et Liber De Interpretatione.* Edited by L. Minio-Paluello. Oxford, 1961.

———*Categoriae et Liber De Interpretatione.* Translated by E.M. Edghill. In *The Basic Works of Aristotle,* ed. by Richard P. McKeon. New York: Random House, 1941.

———*Aristotle's Categories and De Interpretatione.* Translated by J.L. Ackrill. Oxford: Oxford University Press, 1963.

———*Les Catégories D'Aristote Dans Leurs Versions Syro-Arabes.* Edited by K. Georr. Beirut, 1948.

———*Aristotle's Prior and Posterior Analytics.* Edited by Sir David Ross. Oxford, 1949.

———*Aristotle's Prior and Posterior Analytics.* Translated by J. Warrington. London, 1964.

———*Aristotelis Organon Graece*. Edited by T. Waitz. Leipzig, 1846. Vol. 2, *The Topics*.

———*Organon: V, Les Topiques*. Translated by J. Tricot. Paris, 1939.

———*Manṭiq Arisṭū* [Aristotle's "Organon"]. Translated (into Arabic) and edited by ᶜAbd al-Raḥmān Badawī. 3 vols. Cairo, 1948-52.

———*Aristotle's Physics*. Edited by W.D. Ross. Oxford, 1960.

———*Aristotle's Physics*. Translated by R.P. Hardie and R.K. Gaye. In *The Basic Works of Aristotle*, op. cit.

———*Al-Ṭabīᶜah* [The Physics]. Translated (into Arabic) by ᶜAbd al-Raḥmān Badawī. 2 pts. Cairo, 1964-65.

———*De Caelo*. Edited by C. Prantl. Leipzig, 1881.

———*Aristotle on Coming-to-be and Passing Away* (*De Generatione et Corruptione*). Translated by Harold H. Joachim. In *The Works of Aristotle*, vol. 2. Oxford: Clarendon Press, 1922.

———*De Coelo*. Translated (into Arabic) by ᶜAbd al-Raḥmān Badawī. Cairo, 1961.

———*De Anima*. Edited by Sir David Ross. Oxford, 1961.

———*De Anima*. Translated and edited by R.D. Hicks. Cambridge, 1907.

———*Aristotle's Metaphysics*. Edited by W.D. Ross. 2 vols. Oxford, 1958.

———*Aristotle's Metaphysics*. Translated by W.D. Ross. In *The Basic Works of Aristotle*, op. cit.

———*Aristotle's Metaphysics*. Edited by Maurice Bouyges. In Averroes, *Tafsīr mā baᶜd aṭ-ṭabīᶜat*. Beirut: Imprimerie Catholique, 1938-52.

———*Aristotelis Dialogorum Fragmenta*. Edited by Richard Walzer. Florence, 1934.

———*Select Fragments*. Translated and edited by Sir David Ross. In *The Works of Aristotle*, vol. 12. Oxford, 1952.

Ashᶜarī, al- *Kitāb al-Lumaᶜ* [The Theology of al-Ashᶜarī]. Edited by Richard J. McCarthy. Beirut, 1952.

———*Maqālāt al-Islāmiyīn*. Edited by Hellmut Ritter. 2d. ed. Wiesbaden, 1963.

Atiyeh, George N. *Al-Kindī: The Philosopher of the Arabs*. Rawalpindi: Islamic Research Institute, 1966.

Averroes. *Rasā'il Ibn Rushd.* Hyderabad: Osmania, 1947.

———*Tafsīr mā ba[c]d aṭ-ṭabī[c]at.* Edited by Maurice Bouyges. Notice and 3 vols. Beirut: Imprimerie Catholique, 1938-52.

———*Averroes' Tahafut al-Tahafut.* Edited by S. Van den Bergh. London, 1954.

Breton, S. *Philosophie et Mathématique chez Proclus.* Paris, 1969.

Corbin, Henry. *Histoire de la Philosophie islamique.* Vol. 1, *Des Origines jusqu'à la Mort d'Averroës* (1198). Paris: Editions Gallimard, 1964.

David. *Prolegomena et in Porphyrii Isagogen Commentarium.* Edited by A. Busse. In *Commentaria Aristotelem Graeca,* vol. 18, no. 2, 1904.

Dionysius the Areopagite [pseud.]. *Mystical Theology.* Translated by A.B. Sharpe. In *Mysticism: Its True Nature and Value.* London, 1910.

Elias. *Eliae in Porphyrii Isagogen et Aristotelis Categorias Commentaria.* Edited by A. Busse. In *Commentaria Aristotelem Graeca,* vol. 18, no. 1, 1900.

Eutychius of Alexandria. *The Book of the Demonstration.* Edited by Pierre Cachia. Louvain, 1960.

———*The Book of the Demonstration.* Translated by W. Montgomery Watt. Louvain, 1961.

Fakhry, Majid. *Islamic Occasionalism and Its Critique by Averroes and Aquinas.* London: Allen & Unwin, 1958.

Finkel, J. *Three Essays of Abū Othman [c]Amr Ibn Bahr al-Jaḥiẓ.* Cairo, 1926.

Flügel, Gustave. "Al-Kindī, genannt 'der Philosoph der Araber.' " *Abhandlungen für die Kunde des Morgenlandes,* I, fasc. II. Leipzig, 1857.

Frank, Richard. *The Metaphysics of Created Being According to Abū l-Hudhayl al-'Allāf.* Istanbul, 1966.

Gardet, L., and Anawatī, M.M. *Introduction à la Théologie musulmane: Essai de théologie comparée.* Paris: J. Vrin, 1948.

Gibb, Hamilton A.R. *Studies on the Civilization of Islam.* Boston: Beacon Press, 1962.

Goichon, A.M. *Lexique de la langue Philosophique d'Ibn Sīnā.* Paris: Desclée, 1938.

Goldziher, Ignác. *Vorlesungen über den Islam.* 3d ed. Heidelberg, 1925.

———*Die Richtungen der Islamischen Koranauslegung.* Leiden, 1920.

Hamelin, O. *La Théorie de l'Intellect d'après Aristote et ses Commentateurs*. Paris, 1953.

Hammond, W. *Aristotle's Psychology*. London, 1902.

Heath, T. *A History of Greek Mathematics*. Oxford, 1921.

Ibn ᶜAbd Rabbih. *Kitāb al-ᶜIqd al-Farīd*. Edited by A. Amin *et al*. Vols. 1-3. Cairo, 1940.

Ibn Abī Usaybiᶜah. *Kitāb ᶜUyūn al-Anbāʾ fī Ṭabaqāt al-Aṭibbāʾ*. Edited by A. Müller. Königsberg, 1884.

Ibn al-Nadīm. *Kitāb al-Fihrist*. Edited by Gustave Flügel. Leipzig, 1871.

Ibn al-Qiftī. *Taʾrīkh al-Ḥukamāʾ*. Edited by J. Lippert, Leipzig, 1903.

Ibn Juljul al-Andalūsī. *Kitāb Ṭabaqāt al-Aṭibbāʾ wa l-Ḥukamāʾ*. Edited by F. Sayyid. Cairo, 1955.

Ikhwān al-Ṣafāʾ. *Rasāʾil Ikhwān al-Ṣafāʾ*. Beirut, 1957.

Jāḥiẓ, ᶜAmr Ibn Baḥr al-. *Kitāb al-Bukhalāʾ*. Beirut, 1952.

———*Le Livre des Avares*. Translated by C. Pellat. Paris, 1951.

Job of Edessa. *Book of Treasures*. Edited by A. Mingana. Cambridge, 1935.

John of Damascus. *Saint John of Damascus: Writings*. The Fathers of the Church, vol. 37. New York, 1958.

Khayyāṭ, Abū l-Ḥusain al-. *Kitāb al-Intiṣār*. Edited and translated by Albert Nader. Beirut, 1957.

Kindī, Yaᶜqūb ibn Isḥāq al-. *Kitāb al-Kindī ilā al-Muᶜtaṣim Billāh fī al-Falsafah al-Ūlā*. Edited by Aḥmad Fuʾād al-Ahwānī. Cairo, 1948.

———*Rasāʾil al-Kindī al-Falsafīyah*. Edited by M. ᶜA. H. Abū Rīdah. 2 vols. Cairo, 1950-53.

Kirk, G.S., and Raven, J.E. *The Pre-Socratic Philosophers*. Cambridge, 1966.

Kneale, M., and Kneale, W. *The Development of Logic*. Oxford, 1964.

Lane, W.E. *Arabic-English Lexicon*. London, 1863-93.

Laoust, Henri. *Les Schismes dans l'Islam*. Paris, 1965.

McCarthy, Richard J. *Al-Taṣānīf al-Manṣūbah ilā Faylasūf al-ᶜArab*. Baghdad, 1962.

Maimonides. *Dalālat al-Ḥāʾirīn*. Edited by S. Munk. 3 vols. Paris, 1856-66. Reprint. Jerusalem, 1929.

———*S. Moreh Nebukhim*. New York, 1946.

———*The Guide of the Perplexed*. Translated by Shlomo Pines. Chicago: University of Chicago Press, 1963.

Nagy, A. "Die philosophischen Abhandlungen des Jaᶜqūb ben Isḥāq Al-Kindī," *Beiträge zur Geschichte der Philosophie des Mittelalters*, II, fasc. 5 (1897), xxiv, 1-84.

Nasr, Seyyed Hossein. *An Introduction to Islamic Cosmological Doctrines: Conceptions of Nature, and Methods Used for Its Study by the Ikhwān al-Ṣafāʾ, al-Bīrūnī, and Ibn Sīnā*. Cambridge: Harvard University Press, 1964.

Nichomachus of Gerasa. *Introductionis Arithmeticae Libri II*. Edited by R. Hoche. Leipzig, 1866.

———*T̲abit b. Qurra's arabische Übersetzung der* ʾΑριθμητικὴ Εἰσαγωγή *des Nikomachus von Gerasa*. Edited by W. Kutsch. Beirut, 1959.

———*Nichomachus of Gerasa: Introduction to Arithmetic*. Translated by Martin L. D'Ooge. New York, 1926.

———*Nichomachus' Theologomena Arithmeticae*. Edited by F. Ast. Leipzig, 1817.

Patton, W. *Aḥmed ibn Hanbal and the Miḥna*. Leiden, 1897.

Perier, A. *Petits Traités apologétiques de Yaḥyā ben ᶜAdī*. Paris, 1920.

Peters, Francis E. *Aristotle and the Arabs: The Aristotelian Tradition in Islam*. Studies in Near Eastern Civilization, no. 1. New York: New York University Press, 1968.

———*Aristoteles Arabus*. Leiden, 1968.

Pines, Shlomo. *Beiträge zur Islamischen Atomenlehre*. Berlin, 1936.

Plato. *Platonis Opera*. Edited by John Burnett. Vol. I: *Plato's Phaedo*. Vol. II: *Parmenides*. Vol. IV: *Republic, Timaeus*. Oxford, 1962.

———*The Dialogues of Plato*. Translated by B. Jowett. 2 vols. New York, 1937.

Plotinus. *Plotini Opera*. Edited by P. Henry and H.R. Schwyzer. Translation by G. Lewis. Paris-Brussels, 1959.

———*Plotinus apud Arabes*. Edited by ᶜAbd al-Rahman Badawī. Cairo, 1955.

Porphyry. *Porphyrii Isagoge et In Aristotelis Categorias Commentarium*. Edited by A. Busse. In *Commentaria in Aristotelem Graeca*, vol. 4, no. 1, 1887.

———*Manṭiq Arisṭū*, pt. 3. Edited by Abd al-Raḥmān Badawī. Cairo, 1952.

Proclus. *The Elements of Theology*. Edited by E.R. Dodds. Oxford, 1963.

———*Kitāb al-iḍāḥ fī al-Khayr al-Maḥḍ*. Edited by ʿAbd al-Raḥman Badawī, *Neoplatonici apud Arabes*. Cairo, 1955. pp. 1-33.

Ptolemy, Claudius. *Opera quae Existant Omnia*. Vol. 1, *Syntaxis Mathematica*. Edited by J.L. Heiberg. Leipzig, 1898.

———*Ptolemy: Syntaxis Mathematica*. Great Books of the Western World. Translated by B.C. Taliaferro. Chicago, 1938.

Rahman, Fazlur. *Prophecy in Islam*. London: Luzac & Co.; New York: Macmillan & Co., 1958.

Rescher, Nicholas. *Al-Kindī: An Annotated Bibliography*. Pittsburgh: University of Pittsburgh Press, 1964.

———*Studies in Arabic Philosophy*. Pittsburgh, 1967.

Rosenthal, Franz. *Aḥmād b. aṭ-Ṭayyib as-Saraḫsī*. New Haven, 1943.

———A History of Muslim Historiography. Leiden, 1952.

Saadya Gaon. *Kitāb al-Amānāt wa-l-Iʿtiqādāt*. Edited by S. Landauer. Leiden, 1880.

———*Sefer ha-Emunot we-ha-Deʾot*. Josefov, 1885.

———*The Book of Beliefs and Opinions*. Translated by S. Rosenblatt. New Haven, 1948.

———*Saadya Gaon: The Book of Doctrines and Beliefs*. Abridged and translated by A. Altmann. Oxford, 1946.

Sambursky, S. *The Physical World of Late Antiquity*. New York: Basic Books, 1962.

Schacht, Joseph. *The Origins of Muhammadan Jurisprudence*. Oxford, 1950.

Sharif, M.M., ed. *A History of Muslim Philosophy*. 2 vols. Wiesbaden, 1963-66. Vol. 1.

Simplicius. *Simplicii in Aristotelis Physicorum Libros . . . Commentaria* (Part 2). Edited by H. Diels. *CAG* vol. 10. Berlin, 1895.

Steinschneider, Moritz. *Die Hebraeischen Übersetzungen des Mittelalters und die Juden als Dolmetscher*. Berlin, 1893.

Theon. *Commentary on the Almagest*. Edited by A. Rome. Studi e Testi, 72. Citta del Vaticano, 1936.

Van Ess, Josef. *Die Erkenntnislehre des ʿAdudaddin Al-Ici*. Wiesbaden, 1966.

Walzer, Richard. *Greek into Arabic*. Oxford, 1962.

Watt, W. Montgomery. *Islamic Philosophy and Theology*. Islamic Surveys, no. 1. Edinburgh: Edinburgh University Press, 1962.

———*Muhammad At Mecca.* Oxford, 1960.

Wolfson, H. *Crescas' Critique of Aristotle.* Cambridge, Mass., 1929.

ARTICLES

D'Alverny, M.T. "Anniya-Anitas." *Mélanges offerts à Étienne Gilson,* 1959: 59-91.

Davidson, H. "Arguments from the Concept of Particularization in Arabic Philosophy." *Philosophy East and West* 17 (1968): 299-314.

———"John Philoponus as a Source of Medieval Islamic and Jewish Proofs of Creation." *Journal of the American Oriental Society* 89 (1969): 357-391.

Dunlop, D.M. "Biographical Material from the *Ṣiwān al-Ḥikmah.*" *Journal of the Royal Asiatic Society,* 1957-58: 82-89.

The Encyclopaedia of Islam. Edited by M. Th. Houtsma, *et al.* 4 vols. Leiden-London, 1913-34. New ed. edited by H.A.R. Gibb, *et al.* 5 vols. Leidon-London, 1960-.

Fackenheim, E. "The Possibility of the Universe in Al-Farabi, Ibn Sina and Maimonides." *Proceedings of the American Academy for Jewish Research* 16 (1946-47): 39-70.

Farmer, H. "Who was the Author of the 'Liber Introductionis in Artem Logicae Demonstrationis'?" *Journal of the Royal Asiatic Society,* 1934: 553-556.

Finkel, J. "A Risāla of al-Jaḥiẓ." *Journal of the American Oriental Society* 47 (1927): 311-334.

Frank, Richard. "The Origin of the Arabic Philosophical Term انية." *Cahiers de Byrsa* (1956): 181-201.

———"Some Fragments of Isḥāq's Translation of the De Anima." *Cahiers de Byrsa* 8 (1958-59): 231-251.

Gardet, Louis. "Le Problème de la 'Philosophie Musulmane.' " *Mélanges offerts à Étienne Gilson,* 1959: 261-284.

Gilson, Étienne. "Les Sources gréco-arabes de l'Augustinisme avicennisant." *Archives d'Histoire Doctrinale et Litteraire du Moyen Âge* 4 (1930): 5-158.

Goldstein, B. "A Treatise on Number Theory from a Tenth Century Arabic Source." *Centaurus* 10 (1964): 129-160.

Guidi, Michelangelo, and Walzer, Richard. "Studi su al-Kindī I: Uno scritto introduttivo allo studio di Aristotele." *Atti della Reale Accademia Nazionale dei Lincei* (Classe di scienze morali, storiche e filologiche), ser. 6, vol. 6, fasc. 6 (1940): 375-419.

Hirschfeld, H. "The Arabic Portion of the Cairo Genizah at Cambridge." *Jewish Quarterly Review* 15 (1903): 677-697.

Kraus, Paul. "Plotin chez les Arabes: Remarques sur un nouveau Fragment de la Paraphrase arabe des Enneades." *Bulletin de l'Institut d'Egypte* 23 (1941): 263-295.

Lewin, B. "La Notion de Muḥdat dans le Kalām et dans la Philosophie." *Orientalia Suecana* 3, fasc. 2.4 (1954): 84-93.

Mahdi, Muhsin. "Alfarabi Against Philoponus." *Journal of Near Eastern Studies* 26 (1967): 233-260.

Malter, H. "Al-Kindī: 'The Philosopher of the Arabs.'" *Hebrew Union College Annual* (1904): 55-71.

Margoliouth, D.S. "Abū Bishr Mattā and Abū Saᶜid al-Sīrāfī." *Journal of the Royal Asiatic Society* (1905): 79-129.

Marmura, Michael E. "Avicenna's Psychological Proof of Prophecy." *Journal of Near Eastern Studies* 22 (1963): 49-56.

Marmura, Michael E., and Rist, John M. "Al-Kindī's Discussion of Divine Existence and Oneness." *Mediaeval Studies* 25 (1963): 338-354.

McCarthy, Richard J. "Al-Kindī's Treatise on the Intellect." *Islamic Studies* 3 (1964): 119-149.

Meyerhof, Max. "New Light on Hunain ibn Isḥāq and His Period." *Isis* 8 (1926): 685-724.

———"Von Alexandrien nach Bagdad." *Sitzungsberichte der Preussischen Akademie der Wissenschaften*, phil.-hist. Klasse, 33 (1930): 389-429.

Moosa, M. "Al-Kindī's Role in the Transmission of Greek Knowledge to the Arabs." *Journal of the Pakistan Historical Society*, vol. 15, fasc. 1 (1967): 1-18.

Pauly-Wissowa. *Real-Encyclopädie der Classischen Altertumswissenschaft*, Zweite Reihe 6. Stuttgart, 1937.

Perier, A. "Un Traité de Yaḥyā Ben Adī: Défense du Dogme de la Trinité contre les Objections d'Al-Kindī." *Revue de L'Orient Chrétien*, 3rd ser., vol. 2 (1920): 2-31.

Pines, Shlomo. "Une Version Arabe de Trois Propositions de la ΣΤΟΙΧΕΙΏΣΙΣ ΘΕΟΛΟΓΙΚΉ de Proclus." *Oriens*, vol. 8, no. 2 (1955): 195-203.

Ritter, Hellmut, and Plessner, Martin. "Schriften Ja[c] qūb Ibn Isḥāq Al-Kindī's In Stambuler Bibliotheken." *Archiv Orientální* 4 (1932): 363-372.

Ritter, Hellmut, and Walzer, Richard. "Studi su al-Kindī II: Uno scritto Morale inedito di al-Kindī." *Memorie della Reale Accademia Nazionale dei Lincei* (Classe di scienze morali, storiche e filologiche), ser. 6, vol. 8, fasc. 1 (1938): 5-63.

Rosenthal, Franz. "Al-Kindī and Ptolemy." *Studi Orientalistici In Onore Di Giorgio Levi Della Vida* 2 (1956): 436-456.

———"From Arabic Books and Manuscripts VI: Istanbul Materials for al-Kindī and as-Saraḫsī." *Journal of the American Oriental Society* 76 (1956): 27-31.

———"Al-Kindī als Literat." *Orientalia*, n.s., 11 (1942): 262-288.

Steinschneider, Moritz. "Miscellena 26." *Monatschrift für Geschichte und Wissenschaft des Judentums* (1893): 68-77.

Stern, S. "Ibn al-Tayyīb's Commentary on the *Isagoge*." *Bulletin of the School of Oriental and African Studies*, vol. XIX, no. 3 (1957): 419-425.

———"Notes on Al-Kindī's Treatise on Definitions." *Journal of the Royal Asiatic Society* (1959): 32-43.

Walzer, Richard. "The Rise of Islamic Philosophy." *Oriens* 3 (1950): 1-19.

Watt, W. Montgomery. "The Logical Basis of Early Kalām." *The Islamic Quarterly* 6 (1962): 3-10, and 7 (1963): 31-39.

———"Political Attitudes of the Mu[c]tazila." *Journal of the Royal Asiatic Society* (1963): 38-57.

Wolfson, H. "Albinus and Plotinus on Divine Attributes." *Harvard Theological Review* 45 (1952): 115-130.

———"The Internal Senses in Latin, Arabic, and Hebrew Philosophic Texts." *Harvard Theological Review* 28 (1935): 69-133.

———"Isaac Israeli on the Internal Senses." *Jewish Studies in Memory of George A. Kohut* (edited by S. Baron and A. Marx) (1935): 583-598.

———"The Kalām Arguments for Creation in Saadia, Averroes, Maimonides and St. Thomas." *Saadia Anniversary Volume* (1943): 197-245.

———"Muᶜammar's Theory of Maᶜnā." *Arabic and Islamic Studies in Honor of H. A. R. Gibb* (1965): 673-688.

———"Philosophical Implications of the Problem of Divine Attributes in the Kalām." *Journal of the American Oriental Society* 79 (1959): 73-80.

Index

This index refers to authors and places (and not, generally, to editors or translators) mentioned in the Introduction and Commentary of this work. For references to particular terms and themes of FP, *cf. the résumé of the text given in ch. 2 of the Introduction, p. 8 ff.*

Index of Aristotelian Sources

(An asterisk indicates comparison of the Greek of Aristotle with the Arabic of the translators)